Gworge Jones Varney

A Brief History of Maine

Gworge Jones Varney

A Brief History of Maine

ISBN/EAN: 9783743349759

Manufactured in Europe, USA, Canada, Australia, Japa

Cover: Foto ©ninafisch / pixelio.de

Manufactured and distributed by brebook publishing software (www.brebook.com)

Gworge Jones Varney

A Brief History of Maine

FIGHT BETWEEN THE ENTERPRISE AND BOXER, SEPT. 5, 1813.

A BRIEF HISTORY OF MAINE

BY

GEORGE J. VARNEY

MEMBER OF MAINE HISTORICAL SOCIETY

SECOND EDITION

PORTLAND, ME.
McLELLAN, MOSHER & CO.
1890

TO THE

YOUNG PEOPLE OF MAINE

THIS STORY OF THE STATE

IS DEDICATED

PREFACE.

THIS BOOK includes the author's earlier **"Young People's History,"** and six entirely new chapters. The former work ended at the settlement of the State boundaries in 1842,— a date so remote that the book was less useful and entertaining than the *entire story of the State,* now for the first time presented to the people of Maine.

Dealing exclusively with the formative period of the State, all mention in detail of the Temperance movement, then just beginning, was necessarily excluded. Whatever may be the ultimate outcome of our legislation on the subject, there can be no gainsaying the good accomplished by our laws relating to this subject, both directly and even more powerfully in the wide-spread indirect influence over public opinion that has resulted therefrom. In the "Maine Law" a new phrase has been given to the political vocabulary — a phrase which has become known throughout the civilized world.

The story of Maine in the Rebellion,— that noble record of brave men who helped save the Union,— and the later development of our natural resources, including the extension of railways and the building up of industries of all kinds, which, since the war, have gone on with very little hindrance, were also left untold.

These things imperatively demanded a hearing, and in

this edition they are given in as exhaustive a manner as due regard to limits for general reading would allow. In thus extending our survey, it also seemed needful to give a new title to the work — one that would not convey the idea of incompleteness so noticeable in the former title-page. The new frontispiece will commend itself as more appropriate than the State House, bringing to mind a stirring event of a critical time, while an index now appended is an increased convenience to every student.

Finally, that the history of a State should be familiar to its children, whether old or young, would seem to require no elaborate argument. Within the past year this view has had practical recognition in the issue of various historical series designed to this end. We have therefore undertaken in the following pages to present, in a compact and pleasing manner, our own State history; believing that there is not a word of it that any of Maine's sons and daughters could wish were otherwise,— but that her name and fame are an heritage of honor to all ages.

CONTENTS.

CHAPTER		PAGE
I	The Coast Explored	13
II	The First Colony of New England	20
III	Early Events on the Coast of Maine	27
IV	Colonies and Colonists	33
V	Politics, Property and Civil Affairs	40
VI	Counties, Customs and Characters	45
VII	Wars and Rumors of Wars	52
VIII	The Indians of Maine	57
IX	The First Indian War	68
X	The First Indian War, continued	77
XI	The First French and Indian War	90
XII	The First French and Indian War, continued	98
XIII	Witchcraft, Piracies and an Indian Treaty	111
XIV	Queen Anne's War	115
XV	The Beginning of Lovewell's War	123
XVI	The Destruction of Norridgewock	131
XVII	Lovewell's Fight	136
XVIII	Manners and Customs of the English Settlers	144
XIX	King George's War	155

CONTENTS.

CHAPTER		PAGE
XX	King George's War, continued	162
XXI	The Sixth and Last Indian War	167
XXII	The Dawn of the Revolution	177
XXIII	Early Events of the Revolution	184
XXIV	Arnold's Expedition, and the War in the East	191
XXV	Events of the Revolution on Sea and Land	199
XXVI	After the Revolution	209
XXVII	The Malta War	216
XXVIII	The War of 1812	223
XXIX	The British on the Penobscot	231
XXX	The Separation and Attendant Events	238
XXXI	Men and Affairs after the Separation	247
XXXII	Aroostook War, and Settlement of Boundaries	252
XXXIII	Temperence Movement and Political Parties	258
XXXIV	Maine in the Rebellion	272
XXXV	From Williamsburg to Gettysburg	281
XXXVI	From Gettysburg to the Close of the War	289
XXXVII	State Development, 1865–1888	299
XXXVIII	The same — concluded	313
	Supplementary Notes	325
	Index	329

LIST OF ILLUSTRATIONS.

The Enterprize and Boxer	FRONTISPIECE
Old Apple Tree Planted at York in 1629	44
Ancient Indian Inscription at Machiasport	66
Garrison House at York, built about 1645	103
Monument of Ralle, Norridgewock	135
View of Lovewell's Battle-ground	142
Sir William Pepperell	158
Last Block House of Fort Halifax	160
Governor Thomas Pownal	178
General Henry Knox	217
Governor William King	242

A BRIEF HISTORY OF MAINE.

CHAPTER I.

1. My young friends will remember that Christopher Columbus made his famous voyage of discovery in 1492. On this voyage he discovered islands only, and did not reach the great western continent until his third voyage, in 1498.

2. But John Cabot and his son, Sebastian, were before him here; for they had sailed along the coast from Newfoundland to Albermarle Sound the year previous. They took possession of the country in the name of the English sovereign; but England soon became so busy with affairs at home that she made no attempt to settle the new country for nearly a hundred years.

3. Yet I should here speak of other visits made long before this time. Certain marks found on the rocks of Monhegan Island and at one or two points on the mainland, are thought by some to show that the Norwegians, who peopled Iceland and Greenland, also visited the coast of Maine about the year 990, and later. It is also said that our coast was seen by Verrazzani, a French navigator, in 1524; by Gomez, a Spaniard, in 1525; and by an Englishman named Rut, in 1527. Again, in 1556, a Catholic priest named Andre Thevet sailed in a French ship along the whole coast; spending several days in Penobscot Bay, where he held conferences with the natives. Yet all these belong to the ancient period, and nothing came of any of them.

4. It was in 1602, the last year of the reign of the "Good Queen Bess," that Bartholemew Gosnold sailed along the coast of Maine; and, though he did not give any exact account of his voyage, we know that he touched at the Isles of Shoals, and at other points northward. He came at last to a long, bending arm of land stretching out to sea, where he caught many codfish, and therefore called it Cape Cod. The next year, just a few days after the death of Queen Elizabeth, Martin Pring started from England with two vessels, bound on a trading voyage to America. One of his vessels was named "Speedwell," and carried thirty men and boys; the other was the "Discoverer," carrying only thirteen men and one boy. Early in June they sailed into a bay which contained many islands; and beyond it was "a high country full of great woods." It was Penobscot Bay. They found here good anchorage and plenty of fish. Some of the company went ashore at the islands, seeing on one of them some silver-gray foxes; so they gave this group the name of Fox Islands, which it bears to this day. Captain Pring had brought a stock of bright colored clothing, with hatchets, knives, kettles, brass and silver bracelets, rings, and other cheap and showy ornaments, such as savages like, in order to trade with the natives. Not meeting with any of these about the Penobscot, he sailed southward, passing through Casco Bay, and ascending Saco river six miles. The companies were delighted with the many fine groves and strange animals they saw, but found no Indians until they came to Narragansett Bay. Here they exchanged their merchandise for furs and sassafras, and went back to England with a valuable cargo.

5. Then King James sent out Captain George Weymouth in the ship Archangel; who, in May, 1605, anchored his vessel on the north side of an island, now known to be Monhegan. The long boat was lowered, and Captain Weymouth went on shore and took pos-

session in the name of his sovereign. He named the island St. George; also setting up a cross in token that he meant to establish there the Christian religion. They found ashes and coals, showing where a fire had been only a short time before; and they knew by this there were human beings near. Close by the fire, too, were the shells of eggs — bigger than those of a goose; and they saw many sea fowl about the place — some of them large enough to have laid the eggs. They also caught from the vessel thirty large cod and haddock. A number of small mountains were in view from here, while away to the west were the grand White Mountains of New Hampshire, which these voyagers called the "Crystal Hills." Then, sailing toward these hills, they quickly came to a fine haven in the mainland, which Captain Weymouth named Pentecost Harbor, because they entered it on that day of the Christian year. This is supposed by some to be Townsend Harbor in Boothbay, though others believe it to have been George's Island Harbor, which is a little to the east. Here they staid for several days, resting themselves from their long voyage. Some planted a garden, and sowed barley and pease; while others explored the rivers, harbors and islands. In sixteen days from the planting of their garden some of the vegetables had grown to eight inches in height. These were the first fruits of English culture on the shores of New England.

6. Though Captain Pring found no Indians here, Captain Weymouth met with a great number; and they brought many furs to exchange with him for trinkets. There was no hair on the face of these Indians, and that on their heads was black, coarse and straight. It was cut short over the forehead, and the remainder tied up in a single mass, which hung over their backs. Their skin was of a dark copper color, where it was not painted; and the only clothing they wore was a short coat about the waist. At one time several

women and two boys came down the shore to look at the white strangers and their ship. The boys were only two or three years old—fat, lively little fellows; but all naked except that they wore leathern buskins laced nearly to the knees, and held in place by strings running up to a belt about their waists; and this belt was hung full of little round pieces of copper.

7. One day the natives met the English, as they came ashore, with more than usual politeness, and led them to some fires around which many others of the Indians sat laughing and talking, while puffs of smoke rose from their mouths. Probably these sailors had never before seen any one smoke, for tobacco was an American plant, then but little known in Europe. The English were seated on deer-skins; and the pipe, made of a lobster's claw, was passed to them; and they sucked the smoke into their mouths just as the dirty natives did. Doubtless it made them feel quite sick, but they pretended that it was good. They called this operation "drinking tobacco."

8. Not long after, the English and Indians grew suspicious of each other; and both parties were quite cautious in their intercourse. When Captain Weymouth was nearly ready to leave the place, two canoes came to the ship, with three Indians in each. Two of them from one of the canoes climbed on board, and they were immediately thrust below deck. The one who had been left in the canoe pretty soon put ashore, having heard, probably, the outcries of his imprisoned companions. Those in the other canoe did not come on board, and a dish of pease was given them where they were. They went ashore to eat them; and when these were finished they sent a brisk young fellow back with the bowl. So the sailors caught *him;* and then seven or eight of them went in a boat which they called the "light horseman," to capture the other savages, taking with them another dish of pease,—an article of which the natives were very fond. They

went to the fire the savages had kindled; but the one who had been frightened ashore ran away into the woods. The other two remained; and when well occupied with the viands, they were seized and forced down to the shore. It was as much as the eight men could do to get them into the boat; for their clothing was not sufficient to hold them, and they had to be dragged on board by their topknots. This act of Captain Weymouth was no doubt wrong; but it must be remembered that the ideas of personal rights in that day were not as clear as ours; besides, he intended to have them instructed in his language and religion, which, certainly, would be a benefit to them and their brethren, as well as to the English merchants and colonists.

9. As Captain Weymouth was preparing to sail, two other canoes with seven savages came to the ship. These were very stylishly fixed up with paint, furs, feathers and jewels. Some of their faces were painted black, with white eyebrows; other faces were red, with a stripe of blue across the nose, upper lip and chin. They had jewels in their ears, and bracelets of round bits of bone on their arms. One had a coronet of fine stuff like stiff hair colored red, while others wore on their heads the skins of birds with the feathers on. This was a royal embassy which had come to invite the strangers to the court of the Bashaba, or King of the Indians. I do not know what Weymouth said to them, but he did not want to go; for, you know, he had at that very moment five of the Bashaba's subjects shut up in the hold of his vessel. When the embassadors left, Captain Weymouth sailed away as soon as he could. When he got to England he gave three of the Indians to Sir Ferdinando Gorges,—of whom we shall presently learn more.

10. The French, also, were growing more active on the northern coast; and this, probably, was one reason why Weymouth had been sent there. A year before

his voyage a company had left France to found a colony somewhere in the north. It was led by Sieur de Monts, a Huguenot, or French Protestant; while his seventy followers were both Huguenots and Catholics. Their pilot was Samuel Champlain, who had already explored the St. Lawrence River in the service of France. De Monts explored the Bay of Fundy, and discovered the St. John's River; but they chose for the place of settlement an island at the mouth of the St. Croix River, since called St. Croix or Neutral Island. Here they built a fort, and within it several cabins and a chapel. So much wood was used in building, that little remained on the island; and they were obliged to go to the mainland on the west for both water and fuel. They suffered dreadfully with the scurvy, and before spring half their number died. As soon as warm weather came, all that remained of the colony went again on board the vessel, and sailed away westward in search of a more suitable place for a plantation. They first visited Penobscot Bay, having before heard of the region under its Indian name, *Norumbegua*. Continuing their voyage, they went unconsciously past Pentecost Harbor, where, probably, Weymouth's vessel then lay at anchor. At Kennebec, De Monts set up a cross and claimed the country in the name of the king of France. But this was of no effect, as Weymouth had already taken possession for the English king; and according to the usage of the Christian world, any new country belonged to the nation which first took possession in due form. Next, Casco Bay spread its smooth waters and picturesque islands before the roving Frenchmen; but still they sailed on, past rocky headlands, sparkling rivers and verdant hills, until the sandy curves of Cape Cod hemmed them in. At this point they encountered savages, with whom they had a skirmish. They went no farther, but turned back to their starting place; finding at St. John's another vessel with forty more colonists. Both ships now went across the bay, where they founded a town which they called Port Royal. It was on the site of the present town of Annapolis. Here, for nearly three years, they lived an easy, rollicking life. They carried on a profitable trade with the natives about them, obtaining abundance of corn, venison and furs. But the vessels of the Dutch merchants now came along the coast and interfered with their trade, and, worse still, the king revoked their charter; so, in the spring of 1608, they abandoned the country.

In what year was the continent of America discovered? In what year did Gosnold visit the coast of Maine? What islands were named by Pring? What river did he ascend? Who took possession of the territory of Maine in the name of the English king? What name did he give to the White Mountains of New Hampshire? What was his object in carrying away Indians? What Frenchman was on the coast of Maine at the same time with Weymouth? Where did De Mont's colony pass the previous winter?

CHAPTER II.

1. You have now learned of four famous voyages to this coast, and that none of them formed any settlement which was sustained. But when the ships returned, their companies showed the many curious things they had brought, and told such wonderful stories about what they had seen, that a great many people became interested in the far off country beneath the sunset. So in 1606 a number of noblemen, gentlemen and merchants belonging about London and Plymouth in England, joined themselves together for the purpose of sending out colonies, and of making Christians of the heathen natives. This association was called the "North and South Virginia Company;" and King James granted to it all the territory between the thirty-fourth and forty-fifth degrees of north latitude. The London men chose for their portion the division south of the Hudson River, while those of Plymouth took the part north of the mouth of that river.

2. In August of the same year the Plymouth company sent out two ships under Thomas Hanham, one of the company, to make a settlement at Sagadahoc; but one of the vessels was captured by the Spaniards, and the other, after a short stay on the coast, returned to England. In December the London company sent out three ships with planters; and these became the founders of Jamestown in Virginia. In June of the next year the Plymouth company again sent out two vessels with an hundred and twenty colonists. The leader of the expedition was Captain George Popham, brother to Lord John Popham, chief justice of England. His ship was named the "Gift of God"; and the other, the "Mary and John," was commanded by

Captain Raleigh Gilbert. On the sixteenth of August they landed on an island; finding a cross, by which they knew it to be the one Captain Weymouth had visited, afterward called Monhegan.

3. On board of the "Mary and John" was Skidwarroes, one of the savages who had been carried away by Weymouth two years before. When the poor fellow found himself once more so near his home he became much excited, and wished to go at once to his native place near by on the mainland. Near midnight Captain Gilbert manned his boat; and, guided by the eager savage, ere dawn they were at Pemaquid, now the town of Bristol. They landed in the early light of the morning, and approached a village of the natives. There was a sudden cry of alarm; and the warriors ran with hastily snatched weapons to drive the white men back. At the head of his braves was the chief of the village, Nahanada,—who was also one of those carried away by Weymouth, but returned the year before by Hanham. As soon as Nahanada and Skidwarroes perceived each other, they ran together and embraced. Then the brethren and family of the restored savage came forward and joined in the hearty greetings. Two hours soon passed, when Gilbert's party returned to the vessel, taking Skidwarroes with them.

4. The next day was Sunday; and the companies of both ships went ashore on Monhegan; and here, beside the cross which Weymouth had planted, was preached the first sermon of New England. On Monday Captains Popham and Gilbert, with fifty men, went again to Pemaquid. Skidwarroes was with them, but Nahanada and his braves appeared distrustful. The sight of so many armed men made them fear that the treachery of Weymouth was to be repeated. Suddenly the savages withdrew into the wood, and Skidwarroes with them; where, from behind the trees, they menaced the white men with their

arrows. It was the desire of the English to avoid bloodshed; so they retired to the boats and rowed across to the other side of the harbor, where they spent the night. The ships next sailed westward in search of the river Sagadahoc, or Kennebec. They passed Seguin (which they called *Sutquin*) without recognizing it, and examined the islands on the northern shore of Casco Bay. Then a storm arose and drove them away to the eastward. When the storm was over they again turned westward; and just at night the "Gift of God" got into the mouth of the river Sagadahoc; and in the morning she sent her boat and helped in the "Mary and John."

5. They now searched about for a good site for their town, and finally chose the peninsula of Sabino, so called from Sebenoa, the sagamore of the region. This peninsula is part of the present town of Phipsburg. It lies on the western side of the Kennebec at its mouth, and contains, perhaps, one or two hundred acres. It is almost an island, having the Kennebec on the east, the sea on the south, Atkin's Bay on the north and west, while a narrow neck on the southwest alone connects it with the mainland. Fort Popham, a fine fortification of stone, now stands on the northeastern extremity, commanding the river; on the northern shore are a few small houses; and on the east of the steep woody hill that runs across the peninsula from north to south, stands a fine old house with a flag staff in front. A little southward of this house, at the foot of a grassy slope, is a beautiful little sheet of fresh water; while, only a few rods away on the other side of a bank of sand scantily covered with vegetation, beat the surges of old ocean; and the waves have been known in time of storms to dash quite over the narrow bound into the quiet little pond.

6. On Wednesday, the 29th day of August, 1607, the colonists went on shore and engaged in a religious service, led by Richard Seymour, their chaplain. The

Plymouth company had given them a sealed package containing the laws and a list of officers for the government of the colony; and after the service this was opened and read. They found that Captain George Popham was their president, and Captain Raleigh Gilbert admiral. Then they **went to** work building a fort, storehouse and dwellings, **and even** a vessel. Digby, a ship carpenter from London, was **the** master builder. **She was** called "Virginia," and her size **was thirty tons.** Her first voyage was made the next **spring to Virginia, and thence to** England. Therefore **the Kennebec river, which has since sent out so many vessels, has the honor of** producing **the first vessel built** by English **hands** in America.

7. While the **colonists** were erecting their dwellings, Captain Gilbert and his crew explored the coast, going through Casco Bay quite to Cape Elizabeth. He next ascended the river on which the settlement was made, where he saw **many** natives, and visited one **of** their villages. **He offered** them **tobacco in** exchange **for their** skins, **but those** they **brought** were **so poor that he would not** purchase them. **This made the Indians angry,** and **the** English **barely got away without a serious fight.**

8. By and by some of the **Wawennock tribe from the eastward visited the plantation,** representing **that the** Bashaba, **their king,** expected all strangers coming **into his dominions to** pay their respects at his court. The president sent a deputation to visit him, but it was driven back by a storm. When the Bashaba learned of this misfortune he sent his son with a retinue **to** visit the president at Sabino. **After** such treatment as these **people had received** from Weymouth, **this action was a mark of a generous nature.**

9. The Indians were for some time after this quite intimate with the colonists. At one time forty **men, women and children, being on a** visit to the planta**tion,** sat down to meat with **the** English. They

attended worship, also, behaving with great reverence. Indeed, they were so much impressed with the government and religion of the English, that they would say, "King James is a good king, and his God is a good God; but our god, Tanto, is a naughty god."

10. The colonists were industrious; and by the time the winter came on with its sleet and snow, they had finished a storehouse, one large dwelling, and a number of small cottages. They had also completed their fort, which they named St. George, in honor of their president. But with the winter came trouble. Quarrels arose between them and the natives; and tradition tells us of two fatal affrays. Once the planters got the Indians to assist in moving one of the cannon in the fort; and while they were pulling on a long rope directly in range of the gun, it was discharged. Though the gun was loaded with powder only, some were killed, others knocked over and injured, and the remainder badly frightened.

11. The men, probably, had not intended to do them any harm, but to impress them with a wholesome dread of their weapons; yet this action only tended to produce the very hostility they feared. In a quarrel which happened a little later, one of the English was killed and the others driven out of the fort, leaving the Indians in possession. In ransacking the storehouse, which was within the fort, the Indians came upon a cask of powder; not being able to make out what it was, they scattered it about very freely. Pretty soon it caught fire, and then there was an explosion. I do not know how many of the Indians were killed, but all the others were quite overcome with terror. They thought the God of the English had done it because he was angry with them for killing the white stranger; and they besought the planters to forgive them and be their friends. But their penitence did not last long, and they were soon more hostile than ever.

THE FIRST COLONY OF NEW ENGLAND.

12. The explosion had set the storehouse on fire, and all the provisions of the colonists and the furs they had bought were burned up; and for the remainder of the winter they were obliged to live on fish, a little lean game, and even dog meat. The season, too, was a terribly cold one; and their weak, little cabins could not keep out the doleful winds and biting frosts. With all these privations and misfortunes, it is no wonder that the men grew low-spirited, and longed to be in their native England again. Many became sickly; but the only one who died was their good president, George Popham. "I die content," said he; "for my name will be always associated with the first planting of the English race in the new world. My remains will not be neglected away from the home of my fathers and my kindred." You see that he did not suppose the plantation would be given up; and the belief that he had been useful to his country was a consolation to the last hours of this aged pioneer. Yet the spot of his burial remains unknown to this day.

13. The "Mary and John," and probably, the "Gift of God," had returned to England in the autumn; but in the spring a ship came with supplies. It brought the news of the death of chief justice Popham, and of Sir John, brother of Captain Gilbert. The death of the president had left Gilbert the chief in command; but, being his brother's heir, he determined to go back to England. In these men the colonists believed they had lost their best friends, and were altogether discouraged; so some returned to England with Captain Gilbert, while others went in the little vessel they had built to Jamestown in Virginia.

What company sent the first English colonies to America? Where was the first colony sent? In what year was the settlement made in Virginia? In what year was the first colony planted in Maine? Who was the leader of this colony? On what peninsula did they settle? Where is Sabino? What did they name their fort? What name did they give to the vessel they built? Where was the first voyage of this vessel made? What explorations did Captain Gilbert make? What Indians often visited the colonists? What happened to their storehouse during the winter? What one of their number died during the winter? What ill news did they hear in the spring? What effect did these misfortunes have upon the colonists?

CHAPTER III.

1. The next colony settled at Mt. Desert Island, which was then called St. Saviour. It was sent out in 1613 by the French Catholics, and consisted of twenty-five colonists, together with the Jesuits, Biard and Massé, who had come to the coast a few years before.

2. The Virginia magistrates soon heard of this settlement, and decided to remove the intruders at once; for Mt. Desert was within the limits of the charter which the English king had granted to the North and South Virginia Company. Eleven fishing vessels with fourteen pieces of cannon and sixty soldiers, under the command of Captain Samuel Argal, were sent against them. The French had two vessels in the harbor and a small fortification on shore; but this attack took them by surprise, and the place was easily captured.

3. Several were wounded in this conflict, but the only one killed was a Jesuit named Gilbert Du Thet, who fell by a musket ball while in the act of aiming a ship's gun against the English. Argal treated his prisoners with kindness, giving them the choice to return to France by such vessels as they could find, or to go with him to Virginia. He also visited and captured Port Royal, where the French had again planted a small colony.

4. All who have read the history of the United States will remember about Captain John Smith and Pocahontas. The same Captain Smith came in 1614 to the coast of Maine. He had two ships and forty-five men, and meant on this or a later voyage to form a settlement. They touched at Monhegan first, then went to Sagadahoc. In this vicinity he built seven boats. Some of these were used by his men in fishing, while

with others he explored the coast and rivers. The men spent the best part of the fishing season in catching whales, and in search of **gold** and copper mines. They found no mines, **and the whales were not** such as yield much **oil; thus a great deal of time was** wasted. They had one **skirmish with the savages, in which they** killed **several, but came off themselves without loss.**

5. **Late in the summer** Smith returned to **England** with **a valuable** cargo of fish and furs; but the **other vessel staid** behind. Her master was Thomas Hunt. Smith indignantly says of him, "**He** purposely tarried **behind to** prevent me from making a plantation, and to **steal savages."** Hunt prowled along the **coast** as far as **Cape Cod,** capturing natives **at several places.** Finally he sailed away with twenty-seven **of them;** and going to Malaga, he sold them to the Spaniards for **slaves.**

6. The next **year** Smith started **again** for the **shores** of Maine; but on the way he **was** captured **by** the French, and his colonizing schemes broken **up.** He always made good use of his time, however; **and soon** after his liberation he published **a map** and **a short** history of the northeastern **coast. It was in** this **work** that the portion of our country called **New** England first received its name. Smith had explored the coast from Sagadahoc to Cape Cod, finding twenty-five harbors and several large rivers, and visiting forty villages of the natives.

7. **How the** rough islands, jagged capes, and the **many bays and** snug little havens **must have surprised him, as** he paddled industriously among **them; and how** pleasing the numerous rivers, **with** their **woody hills and grassy intervales!** Yet he **did** not see **the** lakes and the myriad ponds that held back the **water** from the sea, or the cataracts that throw it down; where, in after years, the ringing saws should cut up the forest for house and ship, or larger mills spin and weave **the** wool and the cotton into cloth for the comfort of **man.**

8. The natives of Maine were at this time united in a confederation under a chief sachem, or king, called the Bashaba. They were divided into three nations; the Sokokis, who lived about the Saco river; the Abnakis, on the Androscoggin, Kennebec, and several smaller rivers eastward; and the Etechemins, who occupied the country from the Penobscot river to the St. John's, in Nova Scotia. The Bashaba belonged to the Wawennocks, a powerful tribe of the Abnakis, who dwelt upon the small rivers on the coast between the Kennebec and Penobscot.

9. Shortly after Captain Smith's visit, the Tarratines, or Penobscot Indians, who had become very numerous, rebelled against the Bashaba. They defeated the warriors sent to subdue them; and, invading the Wawennock territory, killed the monarch, burned his villages, and nearly destroyed the tribe. Then other quarrels happened among them, and many more were killed. After the war came a pestilence; and the Indians died in great numbers—even whole villages being swept away. The disease was so rapid and fatal that in some places none were left to bury the dead; and their white bones were long after seen bleaching on the ground. The plague was the worst in the winter of 1616 and 1617; and a company of Englishmen spent this very season at the mouth of the Saco river.

10. They visited the sick, and spent many nights with them in their cabins; yet not one of the English had even so much as a headache. The leader of this company was Richard Vines, who had been educated a physician; and probably it was the cleanly and wholesome habits which he enforced among his men, that saved them from the disease. Vines was in the employ of Sir Ferdinando Gorges, and spent the winter on this shore by his request, to try if the climate was too severe for English folk to endure. The place was named Winter Harbor; and Vines must have been much pleased with it, for he soon after made the Saco river his permanent residence.

11. **Gorges** now persuaded the Plymouth company to make another attempt at settlement; therefore in 1618 they sent out a vessel under Edward Rocroft. He was to find Captain **Thomas Dermer**, then at Newfoundland, and proceed with him to form a plantation. He did not meet Dermer, but kept on to Monhegan. There he captured a French trading vessel and a large quantity of furs; sending the Frenchmen to England in his own vessel, which was smallest. His crew soon after formed a plot to murder him for the sake of the cargo. But he discovered the plot; and, running into **Winter** Harbor, set the conspirators ashore. Then he **sailed away to** Virginia, where he was killed in a quarrel with a planter. Probably Vines and his company had gone from Winter Harbor, or would not allow the conspirators to stay with them; for they made their way to Monhegan, and spent the winter there.

12. Next came **Captain** Dermer, looking for Rocroft. He found the Indians very hostile, on account of the wickedness of **Hunt and** others in stealing away their people for slaves. Dermer **had** brought back two of Hunt's captives, **Samoset** and **Squanto**; and these gave him a great deal of assistance in pacifying the angry savages. **Near** Cape Cod he found and redeemed a Frenchman, the sole survivor of the crew of a French ship which had been wrecked on the coast a few years before. The crew had escaped to the shore, where the savages prowled about them until they killed all but three or four. They made prisoners of these, sending them about from one tribe to another to be tortured for their sport. When the poor men reproached them for their babarity, and warned them that the wrath of God would come upon them, the savages laughed, and said scornfully that they were "too many for God." In less than two years after, great numbers of them died of the plague.

13. Among other places, Captain Dermer visited **Martha's** Vineyard; but the natives here, instead of lis-

tening to terms of peace, made a murderous assault upon a boat's crew which went ashore. They were nearly all killed; and an Indian had Captain Dermer down, and would have cut his head off had not the rescued Frenchman come to his aid. Dermer remained on the coast until midsummer of 1620; and in December the Pilgrims came and founded their famous town. Though he had made peace with the natives to the northward, those about Cape Cod remained hostile, waylaying and killing the settlers whenever they could.

14. Just at the close of that first gloomy winter at Plymouth, the afflicted pilgrims were one day startled by the sight of a stately savage walking from the woods toward their cabins. But instead of the war-whoop, they heard from his lips, "Welcome, Englishmen! welcome, Englishmen!" Yet they looked fearfully about, lest some stealthy followers might fall upon them unawares. Bow and arrows were in his hands, but he offered no one any harm. It was Samoset, native lord of Pemaquid. His captivity had saved him from war and pestilence; and he had been restored to his native shores to find his country desolate and his kindred perished.

15. The pilgrims entertained the chieftain with food and lodging. In return he told them about the plague which had carried away the people, and gave them much needful information in regard to the country. He went away the next morning, but returned a few days after, bringing other natives to visit them, among whom was the famous Massasoit.

16. When Captain Levett, in 1623, sailed along the coast in search of a place to settle, he met Samoset near Pemaquid, and received from him the same generous welcome. He aided Levett in obtaining furs, and introduced his squaw. Levett says, "The next day I sailed for Quack, or York, with the king,* queen and prince, bow and arrows, dog and kitten, in my vessel; his noble attendants rowing by us in their canoes."

<small>* See close of chapter.</small>

17. Soon after this, Samoset sold to one John Brown a tract of land at Pemaquid, comprising the present towns of Bristol and Damariscotta. The deed of the sale was made in 1625, and is the first ever given by a native of America.

18. The noble sachem lived for many years after at Pemaquid, always remaining the good friend of the English. He was remarkable for his love of truth and justice, and his generous confidence in others.

*The person taken on board his vessel, and spoken of by Levett as a king, was Cogawesco, sagamore of "Quack," who had his lodge on Stroudwater river, in old Falmouth.

Who drove the Jesuits from Mt. Desert Island? In what year did Capt. Smith visit the coast of Maine? How did his men waste much time? How many harbors did Smith explore? How many villages of the natives did he visit? What name did he give the northern country in his history? Who stole natives of Maine for slaves? What three nations of Indians occupied Maine at this time? What happened among the Indians soon after? In what years did Richard Vines spend a winter at Saco? Who made peace with the Indians on the coast soon after? What noted chieftain of Maine met the pilgrims with words of welcome? What was the character of Samoset?

CHAPTER IV.

1. Early in the year 1620 the Plymouth, or Northern branch of the North and South Virginia Company gave up its charter. A new company was then formed, consisting of forty noblemen, knights, and gentlemen. It was described as "The Council established at Plymouth in the County of Devon, for planting, ruling and governing New England in America;" but it was usually called the New England Company. The king granted to it the territory from a little south of the Hudson River to the Bay of Chaleur on the north, and from "sea to sea." Sir Ferdinando Gorges, who had been president of the old company, was made chief agent of the new one.

2. This gentleman was born in the year 1573, in the county of Somerset, in England. Before he was thirty years old he had won great honor in the war with Spain; and the king, to reward his services, made him governor of the fortified town of Plymouth, in the south-western part of England. Among his friends were Sir Walter Raleigh and Sir Humphrey Gilbert; and from these he, no doubt, imbibed that enthusiasm for America which made him through a long life the constant friend of the colonies.

3. The French, who had two or more colonies on the St. Lawrence river, were now attempting settlements further southward within the limits of the New England Company's patent. It was plain that this northern boundary was likely to cause trouble. Gorges, to relieve himself of the difficulty, procured for Sir William Alexander, Secretary of State for Scotland, a grant of all the territory east of the St. Croix, and

northward on the line of this river to the St. Lawrence. All this region was at that time known as Canada, but the new proprietor named it *Nova Scotia*, or New Scotland. It was his intention to settle it with Scotch, who, it was thought, would prove an effectual barrier against the French.

4. Gorges was constantly on the watch for persons desirous of a home in the new world; and thus he came to learn of a number of English families who had removed to Leyden in Holland that they might be at liberty to worship God in the way which they believed to be right. They at first chose the Hudson as the place for their plantation; but, landing on the shores of Massachusetts, they concluded to make that their residence; and Gorges obtained for them a grant of the place where they had settled. Thus were introduced to the world the famous Pilgrims of New Plymouth.

5. In its political action the English government always regarded Popham's colony as the initial settlement of New England; though it was not permanently maintained. It is, however, quite certain that some points in Maine — as Monhegan, Pemaquid and Saco, had been occupied for several years previous to the settlement of Plymouth; but the inhabitants were fishermen, and probably few of them remained at any of these places throughout the year. I think, therefore, that the pilgrims of the Mayflower must, in a social sense, be considered the first settlers of New England; for in this colony were found man, woman and child — the triple parts of the integer of human life.

In 1622 the New England Company granted to Gorges and Captain John Mason the whole territory between the Merrimac river and the Kennebec. The proprietors named this country *Laconia*. It was described as the paradise of the North, having a salubrious climate, fine scenery, bays and rivers swarming with fish, and forests full of game.

6. These gorgeous reports brought many good people to our shores; but there had come, also, many lawless adventurers. Complaints soon reached the proprietors that persons without right or license were carrying away timber, burning the forests, destroying the game and catching the fish. The Indians, too, were becoming enraged by these acts, and because the traders cheated them and made them drunken; and frequent bloody quarrels happened between them and the English. So in 1623 the New England Company sent out Robert Gorges, a son of Sir Ferdinando, as governor. They also sent an admiral to regulate trade and fishery about the coasts, and a minister to oversee religious affairs. These three were to appoint civil officers, and to sit as judges on all cases which should arise in the province. But Parliament opposed the privileges of the company, and the governor was recalled; the minister found his office unwelcome; while the fishermen were so stubborn that the admiral could do nothing with them;—so in a year or two all had returned to England.

7. Meantime many people who were oppressed at home sought refuge in this country; and the settlements increased all along the coast. The little band of pilgrims had been joined by others of their brethren, and were profitably engaged in fishing and in trade with the Indians; having a trading house on the Penobscot, and another at Sagadahoc near the site of Popham's fort. In order to favor this persevering colony and to aid in spreading christianity among the natives, the New England Company gave them a tract of land on the Kennebec, reaching from near Swan Island northward fifteen miles from each shore to the great bend of the river. In this territory they had exclusive rights of trade and fishery, and the legal power necessary for the protection of their property. Here they erected other trading houses,—one in the present town of Richmond, and another at Cushnoc, now Augusta.

8. These houses were stocked with blankets, coats, shoes, iron implements, hard bread, and various sorts of ornaments and trinkets suited to the fancy of the savages. They had also *wampum*, which served the Indians for both ornament and money. This was a kind of bead made by the Indians west of Narragansett Bay from the inner part of the shells of the whelk and quahog. It was of two kinds,—the purple and the white; white being valued at a farthing each and the purple at two farthings; but later the value changed.

In 1627 some Puritans in England received from the New England Company a grant of the land embraced between New Plymouth and the Merrimac river. These became the Massachusetts Bay Colony; and the king gave them a charter of their territory with the right of government within its limits. In 1629 a division of Laconia was made between Gorges and Mason. The latter took the part south of the Piscataqua, which he named New Hampshire; and thus was fixed the south-western boundary of the State of Maine.

9. The next notable patent was that of Lygonia, issued in 1630, and sometimes called the "Plough Patent," from the name of the vessel which brought over the colonists. The vessel bore this name because the company intended to plough the land and raise crops as their principal business, instead of trading with the natives and fishing, like the other plantations. Their territory extended from the Kennebunk to Royal's river; and they settled near Casco Bay. This colony was laughed at a great deal, because it broke up within a year; its members scattering among other plantations southward.

10. The same year the territory lying between Muscongus Bay and Medomac River at the east was granted to some persons who had trading houses there. This was called the "Muscongus Patent;" but nearly a hundred years later it passed into the possession of the Waldo family, and was afterward known as the "Waldo

Patent." The "Pemaquid Patent" was the last grant made by the New England Company within the limits of our State. It was issued in 1631, and comprised the territory between the Medomac and Damariscotta rivers. West of this was the Sheepscot plantation, called the "Garden of the East," for its fruitfulness; while the settlement at Cape Newagen was, probably, the most ancient of all. There was no patent issued for the region between the Damariscotta and Kennebec before the grant to the Duke of York; and the settlers held their lands by Indian deeds. Among other purchases made of the natives was that of the present town of Woolwich, of the sachem Robin Hood, for a hogshead of corn and thirty pumpkins.

11. In 1625 King Charles, the new English sovereign, was betrothed to the Princess Henrietta Maria, daughter of the French king; and in the marriage treaty he ceded to France the whole of **New** Scotland. This territory, you remember, had been given by the New England Company to **Sir William Alexander, who** undertook to people it with Scotch. He did not succeed in bringing in many settlers, and was now in constant fear that his province would soon be seized by France; therefore he gladly sold the whole for a small sum to M. La Tour, a Huguenot, or French Protestant, who wished to plant a colony there. A condition of the sale was that La Tour should hold the country subject to the Scottish crown; but he quickly proved his dishonesty by secretly procuring from the French king a patent of a large tract of the same territory, to be held by him as a subject of France.

12. Thus the whole country eastward of the Penobscot became disputed territory; for Parliament denied the king's right to give away territory without its consent. But France took possession, naming the country *Acadie;* and the French thought themselves safe in plundering all the trading houses and vessels of the English which they could find within their limits. A

French fishing vessel came to the trading station of the New Plymouth colony on the Penobscot, pretending that they had put into harbor in distress, and begged permission to repair leaks and refresh themselves. They were kindly received, and allowed to go about on shore as they liked. The villainous crew quickly learned that most of the men belonging to the station were absent; and they immediately seized the swords and muskets in the fort, and ordered the keepers to surrender on pain of instant death. Then they forced them at the point of the sword to carry the merchandise of the fort on board their vessel. But the spirited Puritans were not easily dismayed, and they soon after stocked their trading house anew, and the very next spring opened another at Machias. A year later La Tour himself attacked this one, killing two of the men, and carrying the remainder away prisoners to Port Royal.

13. Some English vessels, also, still ventured to trade with the Indians along the coast, as before; and a few of them were caught. One belonged to a man named Dixy Bull. As the French had taken his cargo but left him his vessel, he decided to turn pirate. At this time many low, vagabond fellows were prowling about the coast, sometimes hunting and sometimes fishing for a subsistence; and from these Bull soon made up a numerous crew of desperadoes. He then proceeded to rob his own countrymen, taking their furs, provisions, arms and ammunition, and sinking their vessels. In 1632 he stole into the harbor of Pemaquid and surprised the village. The villagers were at work in the fields and woods, and off on the water fishing; and before they could rally for defense, the pirates had laden their boats with plunder from warehouse and dwelling. But the people made an attack upon them as they were embarking, and killed one of the leaders. At last the settlements at the westward were aroused; and a force was fitted out at Piscataqua to capture the

freebooters. The little squadron consisted of four vessels, and carried fifty men. It cruised three weeks in search of the pirates; but they had become frightened, and fled. They left behind them a message for the authorities, which read in this way: "We now proceed southward,—never shall hurt any more of your countrymen,—rather be sunk than taken. *Fortune le Garde.*"

14. Bull seems to have been more prudent than most of his class, for he never allowed his crew to become drunken. At the hour when good captains had evening prayer he would say to his men, "Now we'll have a story and a song." But he met with his deserts at last. Having gained some riches, he returned to England, where his crimes were found out, and he was tried and executed.

Soon after New Scotland became the property of France, that government sent over General Razilla as governor; and his deputy over the region between St. Croix and the Penobscot was M. D'Aulney. This gentleman made his residence at Biguyduce, (now Castine) where he had a fort, mill, and a fine farm. When Razilla died D'Aulney claimed to be his successor against M. La Tour, who was the owner of a large part of what is now New Brunswick. D'Aulney was a Catholic, and La Tour was a Huguenot; therefore D'Aulney received the support of French ecclesiastics, while La Tour obtained private aid from the English. Consequently D'Aulney manifested all the hostility toward the English that was consistent with his safety. At last he captured La Tour's fort at St. John's; carrying Madame La Tour away to his own fort, where he kept her a close prisoner until she died. Soon after D'Aulney died also; and his enemy, La Tour, married his widow, and succeeded to his possessions.

What territory did the king grant to the New England Company? To whom did the New England Company grant New Scotland? What points in Maine were inhabited before 1820? What name was given to the territory **of Gorges and Mason?** In what year was the first governor sent over? Where did the Plymouth colony establish **trading houses?** In what year was the division of Laconia made? What boundary did this division fix? What were some of the most notable patents? When was New Scotland ceded to France? What did France call the country?

CHAPTER V.

1. In 1635 **the New England Company was** dissolved. Its territory was **divided into** twelve provinces, of which four were within **the** present limits of Maine. The first embraced the region between the St. Croix and Penobscot rivers, and was named the County of Canada, and assigned to Sir William Alexander; **the** second, lying between the Penobscot and Kennebec, was given to the Duke of Yor**k; the third** embraced **the** land between the Kennebec and **the** Androscoggin; **while** the fourth extended to **the Piscataqua. Both the last were** given **to** Sir Ferdinando Gorges, **and by him named** New Somersetshire; and in 1636 he sent over his nephew, William Gorges, as governor of this province. **This gentleman** chose for assistants Richard Bonython, **of Saco, Thomas** Cammock and Henry Joscelyn, **of Black Point in** Scarborough, Thomas Purchas, of Pejepscot (Brunswick), Edward Godfrey and Thomas Lewis, of the Piscataqua river settlements.

2. The first session of court was held at the house of Richard Bonython **in Saco. An action** was tried concerning a cornfield, **and** another **of debt.** Among the **laws they** made, was one **relating to** "mischievous In-

dians," and others in regard to drunkenness, and the sale of intoxicating liquors. The last prohibited the sale of any strong drink except a small quantity just after dinner. The settlers, it is said, had fallen into the habit of drinking too much; and this first government of Gorges was wise enough to restrain a practice so dangerous to the prosperity of the young State.

The new country was now found to afford secure homes and a comfortable support; and so many English were emigrating that King Charles began to be alarmed. At one time he detained some emigrant vessels in port for several weeks, to the great distress of the passengers. He next ordered that no subject should leave the realm without taking the oaths of allegiance and religious supremacy. As he wished to secure to himself some profit from these New England subjects, he ordained that no colonist should entertain a stranger or admit any person as a household tenant without a license from the crown.

3. The colonists, especially the Puritans, were represented as being rebellious, and unworthy of confidence; therefore the king instituted a general government for New England, and appointed Sir Ferdinando Gorges as governor. A ship was nearly ready to bring him over, when, as the builders were at work upon her side, she turned bottom upward. This misfortune delayed the voyage; and other difficulties succeeded, so that Gorges never visited the country for whose settlement he had labored so long.

His nephew, the governor of New Somersetshire, soon returned to England; and Gorges offered the management of his province to the Puritans, but it was declined. In 1639 he procured a charter from the king making him proprietary lord of the province, with full power of government therein. This grant extended from the Piscataqua river eastward to the Kennebec, thence north and west to Dead river and Umbagog lake. The name of the territory under the new charter was changed to **"Maine,"** in honor of the Queen, whose patrimonial estate as **Princess of France,** was the French **province** of *Mayne.*

4. By **this** charter **no person had** a right to trade, **hold property, or reside within the** province, except by **permission of the** proprietor; and he was entitled to a **quitrent from the** settlers of sixpence **an acre yearly.** For the government of his province he chose a deputy **governor, chancellor,** marshal, **treasurer, admiral, master of ordnance,** and secretary. These sat each month **as a court** of justice; and, joined with eight deputies **elected by** the people, they formed a legislative assembly, which levied the taxes **and made** laws.

The first general court for the province of Maine was held at Saco in June, 1640. George Burdet, the chief man of the Agamenticus plantation, was fined forty-five pounds **for lewdness, breaking** the peace, and slanderous speaking; John Lander was fined two shillings for "swearing **two** oaths;" Ivory Puddington was fined for being drunk at Mrs. Tyms; **and** John Smith for running away from his master, **was sentenced to be whipped and sent back.** Perhaps **Smith** was an apprentice learning a trade, **or he might have** been sold for a certain time to pay a **debt—possibly to pay his passage** across the seas; **for** they **had such a custom in those** old days.

5. Yet most of those who now came to Maine brought money with them, as well as their furniture and the implements of their trade. Many came to till the land, and had their stock to buy; so the domestic animals raised by the older settlers brought them a handsome price—a good yoke of oxen often selling for fifty pounds sterling. Money was scarce, **too; and** all kinds of grain, **with** sheep, goats and pigs, **were considered** as good, **if** not legal, tender. The people had **to pay in** money **or furs** for clothes, which were then **mostly** brought from **England; so** after a while it was **found best** to raise flax **and wool, from** which, with the

great hand looms, they wove the strong cloth for bedding and wearing apparel. Until about this time, too, all the meal and flour used were brought from England, or ground in the mills at Boston or at Sheepscot; so there was a great demand for more mills for grain, as well as for cutting lumber. This demand was further increased by the opening of a trade in lumber with the West Indies; while the settlers could now have molasses, sugar, coffee, spices, and other tropical products, which they had before done mostly without.

6. All these advantages tended to a rapid increase of the settlements; and Gorges was rejoiced at the prospect of a rich reward for his years of labor. With the eye of hope he saw in his province of Maine a noble inheritance for his children and children's children. He selected the plantation of Agamenticus for his capital; and, in 1642, he made it a city, naming it for himself, Gorgeana. It comprised twenty-one square miles on the north side of the York river and on the sea. The city had a mayor, aldermen, and councilmen, together with sargeants, (policemen) whose badge was a white rod. Yet Gorgeana never had even three hundred inhabitants; and, ten years later, it was changed to the town of York.

7. But reverses now began to overtake Gorges. Emigration fell off, so there were few to take up land or to buy cattle of the settlers; and business became very dull. Then the Lygonia, or "Plough Patent," was revived, though it really had become void. After the failure of the colony it fell into the hands of Sir Alexander Rigby, who set up his own government in the territory. Gorges held his province by the king's charter; but Rigby was favored by Parliament, which was now bitterly opposed to the king; and though Rigby was finally obliged to abandon the claim, he obtained the profits of the territory for several years. Thus was Gorges robbed of more than half his seacoast.

3

OLD APPLE TREE AT YORK, PLANTED 1629.

On the Piscataqua, at the other side of his province, the settlers entered into a compact that they would not be subject to his government; for, being Puritans, they were unwilling to live under a charter which required them to be subject to the church of England. Yet Gorges never insisted that his people should worship in the English form, but allowed freedom of conscience to all; and the Puritans, with the Baptist and the Quaker, whom they persecuted, alike found refuge from royalty and from each other in the province of Maine.

8. A civil war now broke out in England; and Gorges, who had received many favors from his sovereign, took his part against Cromwell's party. King Charles lost his cause, and Gorges was thrown into prison. He was now over seventy years old; and,

worn out by misfortune and hardship, he died in **1647,** soon after his release.

He had ever been the earnest advocate **of** settlements in America, and the constant friend of the colonists; and for these reasons he is very properly called the "Father of American Colonization." For more than forty years he had fostered the settlements on our coasts, his chief motives being in his **own** simple but noble words,—"The enlargement of the christian **faith, the** support of justice, and the **love** of peace."

Into how many provinces was Maine divided in 1635? Which of these were given to Gorges? What was Gorges' province called? Where was the first court held? Who was now appointed governor of New England? **Did he** ever come to this country? What was his province called under the king's charter? Where did the settlers obtain clothes, meal and flour? What did they export to the West Indies? What city did Gorges found for his capital? To what was it afterward changed? What title has sometimes been applied **to Gorges?**

CHAPTER **VI.**

1. At **the** death of Gorges in 1647 the present territory of Maine was under six governments, all entirely independent of each other. The whole country east of the Penobscot was held by the French; while west of that river was, first, the Muscongus Patent, then the Pemaquid, next the Kennebec, then the Lygonia, or "Plough Patent,"—and, lastly, the remnant of Gorges' **Province of Maine.** So many governments, each jealous of the **other, caused much** disorder in the country; for evil doers **in** one province or patent took refuge in another, and thus, too often, escaped **the** punishment due to their offenses.

2. Once a magistrate of Plymouth, named John Alden, was arrested in the streets of Boston on the charge of murdering a man on the Kennebec River. John was a Pilgrim boy, one of the company who came over in the Mayflower — and the first person, it is said, to spring ashore when they landed. He is the same John Alden of whom Longfellow tells us in the "Courtship of Miles Standish." Perhaps you will remember that Standish, the Puritan warrior, sent his friend John Alden to court the fair Priscilla for him. John was then young and ruddy; and it is no wonder that when he plead the cause of the doughty widower, the blushing maiden should exclaim, "Why don't you speak for yourself, John?" And no doubt all will remember that after a while John did speak for himself; and that Priscilla became his wife, and rode home after the wedding on a white bull, which John led by a rope.

3. The Plymouth colony, you know, had the exclusive right of trade on this river;* and when in 1634 a vessel from New Hampshire came there to trade, this John Alden, who was then in charge of the colony affairs in the region, ordered it away. Instead of obeying, the captain (whose name was Haskins) brought his vessel still farther up the river; therefore Alden sent some men to cut the ropes by which she was moored. They had severed one, when Haskins, seizing a musket, swore that if a man of them touched the other he would shoot him. The boatmen had too much courage to neglect their duty for a mere threat; and one raised his axe to strike, but before it could fall the angry captain had shot him dead. A moment later Captain Haskins fell in his turn, pierced by a bullet from a comrade of the man he had killed. The Plymouth folk advocated Alden's cause; and finally the Bay magistrates pronounced the act "justifiable homicide." So there was no one punished.

* The Kennebec.

4. Thomas Purchas, who lived at the head of New Meadow River in Brunswick, (then Pejepscot) owned an extensive tract of land on both sides of the Androscoggin River. He had opened a trading house at this point about the year 1625; but becoming fearful of the Indians around him, he, in **1639**, put his territory under the government of Massachusetts for protection.

5. Indeed, this government was so often called upon for arbitration and protection, that its chief men began to contrive how they might obtain more complete control of the eastern settlements. On examining their charter the magistrates thought that its words would allow them to take the *source* of the Merrimac river as the northern extremity of their territory, instead of the *mouth* of that river, which had before been considered the limit. So their surveyors presently found the new boundary to be a direct line from the northern part of Winnipesaukee Lake to the mouth of the Presumpscot river; and, behold, Gorges' province of Maine, the Lygonia Patent and Mason's grant of New Hampshire were under the Puritan charter!

6. In 1652 the commissioners appointed by Massachusetts came into the province of Maine to set up their government. A meeting was called in Gorgeana to consider the change. The authorities of the province were there, headed by Governor Godfrey; and on the other hand sat the commissioners. The governor harrangued the people against submission; the commissioners replied, promising that there should be no interference with religious worship nor with the estates of the settlers. When the question was referred to the people, to the great astonishment of the governor, every vote beside his own was in favor of Massachusetts.

7. Thus all went smoothly with the Bay colony's project in the western part of the province of Maine; but

when it came to the collection of taxes, there was trouble in Lygonia. The foremost to resist the collecting officers was **John Bonython of Saco.** He furthermore wrote a **defiant letter** to the **General Court**, denying the right of Massachusetts within the **Lygonia Patent.** He seems in this action only to have stood up for the rights of the proprietor of the patent; yet he was declared an **outlaw** by the **Massachusetts magistrates**, and a price set upon his body. But no doubt he was a bold, perhaps an unscrupulous **man**; for when he died some person wrote this couplet on his tombstone for an epitaph:—

"Here lies Bonython, sagamore of Saco;
He lived a rogue and died a knave, and went to Hobomoko."

8. The province of **Maine was now** made a county of Massachusetts under the name of Yorkshire, and sent two delegates to the **General Court, as the** legislature of Massachusetts was called. A court was held in the county twice a **year,** alternately at Kittery and **York.** A part of the magistrates were chosen by the **General Court,** and others by **the people of the county;** and besides **trying civil and** criminal **cases,** these were authorized to appoint three commissioners **in each** town to decide petty cases.

9. **A militia was** organized the same as in Massachusetts. The smallest division was the "trainband," which consisted of not fewer than fifty-four **men nor more than two hundred. Its officers were a captain, lieutenant and ensign, and a sergeant for the pikemen.** The sergeant **was armed with a halberd,—a** weapon formed by the combination of an axe **and spear,** and set on a long handle. The other officers wore swords and pistols; and **the chief officers** carried "partisans," which are colored **rods,** indicating leadership. The soldiers were armed **with pikes** and muskets. The pike, **or spear,** was a **staff about** ten feet in length **with a sharp point of** metal; but sometimes, instead

of a proper spear head, they tied on a stout knife or a piece of scythe. Men of large stature were always chosen for pikemen; and there were twice as many musketeers as pikemen in a trainband. Some muskets had matchlocks, but most had the flintlock. Each musketeer, at trainings, carried a crotched stick called a rest, on which the gun was laid in taking aim.

10. In fighting Indians the soldiers must be good marksmen; for generally these foes scattered widely apart, or hid behind stumps, stones and trees. Massachusetts had already been through one Indian war, when her forces destroyed the Pequots; and she knew now how to meet savages. Each soldier wore about him a bandoleer, containing little leather boxes for powder and bullets. Some of them wore corselets of iron, which covered the breast and stomach; while others had their coats thickly padded with cotton to protect them from arrows. They must have been queer looking soldiers, plated with iron and stuffed with cotton,—no two being dressed alike; yet they were men of courage, daring to face the scalping savage in his forest ambush. But when it really came to fighting savages, the pikes, breastplates and stuffing were all abandoned; nothing but guns, hatchets and knives or swords were of any service. At first there was company training every Saturday, but after a few months they were less frequent. All males, from stout men of forty-five down to beardless boys of sixteen, were enrolled in the militia; and I have no doubt that the boy soldiers enjoyed "training-day" greatly. Yet they had for a long time no music but a drum; neither had they bright colored uniforms, nor shining arms to relieve the sombre appearance of the ranks.

11. On training as on other days our brave forefathers had regard to the Great Being who presides over all the affairs of men; and prayer was offered at the opening of the day's drill and at the close. But

on training days there was also an unusual draft on the barrels and butts of West India rum and Holland gin, which were kept in almost every shop; for the law against dealers was not then strictly enforced; but if any became drunken and quarrelsome, they were set in the stocks, where the fit might wear itself harmlessly out.

12. These instruments were usually ready, and nigh at hand. For there were four or five things which the good people of those days placed as near the center of their settlements as possible; and these were the church, the graveyard, the school-house and the stocks. Usually, also, there were a whipping post, a pillory and a ducking stool. The last was quite an amusing instrument. It consisted of a long plank suspended near the middle, and having a chair fastened on the end overhanging a pool of water. When the offender was tied in place the light end of the plank was let go, and the chair with its occupant splashed in the water.

13. The penalty for a great number of crimes was death; for lesser ones there were whipping, cropping the ears, and branding with a hot iron. There was not much imprisonment in those times, for the very good reason that criminals did not choose to stay in the weak jails. But the people of Maine were not the makers of these laws, and they were not here carried to such extremes as in Massachusetts.

14. The people of Maine, too, were allowed to vote without becoming members of the Puritan church; yet the promise made to them at their union with Massachusetts that there should be entire freedom of worship, was not fully carried out. The Rev. Robert Jordon, at this time the only Episcopal minister in the province, was persecuted for baptizing children and performing other duties belonging to his pastorate; while the Baptists and Friends were fined and whipped. Cromwell favored the Puritans; but when Charles II. came to the throne he at once ordered

Massachusetts to cease interfering in **religious matters.** Then all societies again had freedom **to observe the christian** ordinances **in the manner which their consciences approved.**

15. But I must not close the present **chapter without telling you something about the Rev. John Brock,** a noted Puritan minister of **this period. The Isles of Shoals, then a part of Maine, were the scene of his labors for many** years**; and his influence over the islanders and the fishermen who frequented their shores was very** excellent. **He had a happy talent in conversation, his sermons were animated, and his faith was very remarkable. A fisherman of his** parish had been wont generously **to use his** boat in helping the inhabitants of other islands in the group to the one on **which public** worship was held; **but one day in a violent** storm the **boat broke away** from its fastenings and was lost. While the **poor** man was lamenting it, Mr. Brock **said to him, "Go home** contented, **good** sir; I'll **mention the matter to the Lord ;—to-morrow you** may **expect to find your boat." This boat had** been of **such service to the poor that the good minister** felt that **its recovery might properly be made the** subject **of prayer ; and, sure enough, the next day the boat was brought up on** the **flukes of an anchor. Many other quite** interesting things **were done by him** during **his ministry at** this and other places, **some of** which are told us **by** Rev. Cotton Mather in **his** "Magnalia."

How many separate governments existed **in Maine in** 1647? What incident happened **on** the **Kennebec?** What government tried this case? What proprietor in Maine put himself **under the protection of Massachusetts? By what** means **did Massachusetts extend her jurisdiction over Maine? Where did the Massachu**setts officers meet **with difficulty? What** troublesome **person led the opposition? Into what** county **was the** province of Maine now made? What arms did the militia bear? What was done with those who became drunken? What objects were usually to be found near the center of a **Puritan settlement?**

CHAPTER VII.

1. The principal reason why the inhabitants of Maine submitted to become a part of Massachusetts, was that every one feared a war with the Indians, and thought if they yielded readily to the wishes of their powerful neighbor they would receive the more assistance from her.

England was at this time at war with Holland; and it was believed that the Dutch were inciting the Indians to rise against the English colonies. The Massachusetts magistrates wrote to the Dutch governor at Manhattan about the matter, and he wrote back indignantly denying the charge, and regretting that they should put any confidence in the statements of the natives. Yet the magistrates were not satisfied, and applied to the British government for aid to drive the Dutch away. After several months the ships came; and five hundred men were enlisted in the colonies to operate with them against Manhattan. Before the expedition set out England and Holland had made peace with each other; and Cromwell, the Lord Protector, ordered the forces to take possession of Acadia. This was really the point of greatest danger from the Indians; for the French had been selling them guns and hatchets, and inciting them to hatred towards the English. The enterprise was therefore very pleasing to the people of Maine.

2. The first point of attack was Biguyduce, on Penobscot Bay; but the place was not defended, and they proceeded to La Tour's settlement on the site of the present city of St. John, in New Brunswick. He appeared quite willing to change masters, if only his property might be secure. The governor, Le Borgne,

made some resistance; but in August Acadia, or New Scotland, was again in possession of the English. The leaders of this expedition were Major Robert Sedgwick and Captain John Leverett; and Captain Leverett was left in charge of the province until Sir Thomas Temple was appointed governor. Sir Thomas brought in many settlers, and carried on a large business in fish, furs and lumber. It has been said of him that he was "as true a gentleman as ever set foot in America." He was noted for his humane and generous disposition. When Massachusetts was hanging Quakers or Friends, who came into her borders preaching their doctrines, he told the magistrates that if they really, as they said, desired "the Quaker's lives absent rather than their deaths present," he would carry them away and provide for them at his own expense.

3. In the year 1664 the king granted to his brother, the Duke of York, the country about Hudson River, and the territory between the Kennebec and St. Croix rivers. The duke was also made viceroy of New England, and sent Colonel Nichols over as his governor. Gorges' son soon after sent an agent with a letter from the king to the Puritan authorities, ordering them to restore the province of Maine to its owner. But Massachusetts was unwilling to give up her control; and she kept possession until the next year. At that time three commissioners, who had been sent by the king to aid Colonel Nichols, came into the county of Yorkshire, and, organizing a court and legislative body, revived the old province of Gorges. Thus the people of Maine had the hard fate of being subject to two conflicting governments, and were liable to be punished by each for obeying the other.

When they had settled affairs in the province of Maine, the commisioners went eastward to attend to the Duke of York's possession. They called the region between the Kennebec and Penobscot the "county of Cornwall," of which the Sheepscot plantation was made the shire town, and named New Dartmouth. They made Pemaquid (Bristol) their capital, where one of them remained until **1665**, regulating the affairs of the colonies.

4. **Soon after his departure,** a war broke out between **England and France; and the colonies began to** look **for a conflict with the French and Indians. This afforded a** good opportunity for Massachusetts **to re-establish** her authority in Yorkshire; and commissioners **were** accordingly appointed for that purpose. When Governor Nichols heard of this at New York, he wrote **to** the Massachusetts magistrates, warning them not to meddle with the province of Maine, and intimating bloodshed if they **persisted.** He soon after returned to England, and Governor Lovelace succeeded **him.** The Puritans **were** not much alarmed by the warnings of **the** retiring **governor,** and her commissioners soon after set about their task of changing a province into a county. They entered Maine with a small company of horsemen and footmen in brilliant array, and issued **their orders for an** election **of deputies** to the general court. A **county court was held by** them in a meeting house at **York.** The morning session over, they went to their dinner. **After** dinner, **as they walked** unsuspectingly back, **the** province **marshal marched** through the streets proclaiming with **as much** authority as if he had an army behind him, "**Observe ye and** obey **the** commands of **his** majesty's justices." **When the commissioners came to the meeting-house, behold, it was full of people, and the justices** of the province were preparing **to hold a court of their own!**

5. "Give place to the commissioners;" cried their marshal, as he went before them to the benches **where** the justices sat.

"You are the authors of an **affront** we little expected," said the commissioners **to the** justices, "but your **course will avail you nothing; you** might have called

your meeting elsewhere, **and at another time.**
Depend upon *this,* we shall **not be deterred from exe-
cuting any part** of the delegated trust **to which we are
commissioned."**

Then the people fell to disputing among themselves,
and for a while confusion reigned **supreme ; but** the
province justices at length were able to **read the King's**
letter ordering Massachusetts to restore **the province
government** to **Gorges.** To meet this, **the commissioners** could **only urge the new** charter **boundary**
under **which** they **had at first set up their claim. But
the justices and** their **adherents had a prudent regard
for that troop of "horse and foot", and** they finally
gave way. And thus was **effected** what has been hu-
morously termed the "Conquest of **Maine,"** which
ended the "Commissioners' War."

A few years later Rigby's claim **to Lygonia was**
abandoned, **and Gorges'** right **was** purchased by **Massachusetts; so that the** whole **region from** the Piscataqua **to the Kennebec became rightfully subject to the**
Puritan **government, and was all included in the county of Yorkshire.**

6. **By an article tacked on to the treaty of Breda in
1668, the French were again in possession of Acadia,
with its boundary at the Penobscot, or, possibly, farther
west. The inhabitants did not relish the** prospect **of
becoming** French **subjects; so** they turned **for** aid to
the only government **that could** protect them — which
was that of Massachusetts. Under these circumstances
what could the Bay colony **do but** examine again her
very elastic charter, and order **a new** survey **to** correct
the errors of the first ? **This was** precisely **what she
did; and by it her boundaries were made to include
the chiefest part of the county of Cornwall.**

In 1773 **the Dutch re-captured New York, and Governor Lovelace went home. There were** now none of
the Duke of York's officers in the way ; **and the next
year Cornwall was made a part of** Massachusetts, **and**
received the **name of the county of** Devonshire.

7. Now for a short **time**, the settlements flourished, so that in the beginning **of** the year 1675 there **were** thirteen towns and plantations within the present limits of Maine, while the inhabitants numbered between five and **six** thousand **souls.** The vessels of the villagers bore **away ample freights of lumber from the** mills, **furs from the trading houses on the rivers, or loaded themselves with fish from** the sea **; the fields yielded abundantly, and thriving** herds **of cattle were in the woody** pastures.

8. Then came the Indian wars; **and the scene was changed.** Several years previous to this time there had been war between the eastern **Indians and the** Mohawks, **who lived about the** Hudson **river, in the State of New York. A** decisive battle **was fought in** the year **1669, in** which **the Eastern** Indians were **beaten.** The victorious Mohawks pursued their assailants into **Maine,** destroying the **villages of the Tarratines, and** penetrating nearly to **the St. Croix ;** and **many** generations after the Indians pointed **out on** the shores of **one of the Passamaquoddy ponds** the scene of the final **battle. But in a** few years **the** tribes had greatly **recovered from their** losses; **and,** encouraged **by their new friends, the** French, **they** were **eager for war** with their **new foes,** the English settlers **of Maine.**

What was the chief reason that Maine **so** readily submitted to **Massachusetts?** Who were found to be inciting the Indians against **the English? What** English ruler ordered the colonial forces to **take possession of Acadia? To whom was the territory between the Kennebec and St.** Croix granted? **What** did the King's com**missioners form in the** Duke of **York's territory ?** When the commissioners were gone what did **Massachusetts do ?** What has this tour of the commissioners been humorously called? **By** what means did Massachusetts obtain the right of control in the province of Maine? By what treaty did France again obtain possession of **Acadia?** How did Massachusetts obtain control of the Duke of **York's settlements ?** What county did she make of this new pos**session ?**

CHAPTER VIII.

1. Before I tell about the wars with the **Indians,** some further account of these people will, I think, be interesting to my readers. The natives of Maine are generally called Abnakis, though the name has been more especially applied by American writers to those dwelling on the Androscoggin and Kennebec rivers. This name comes from *Awahbenahghi,* the name applied to the Maine Indians by those living west of the Hudson river. It signifies *our fathers at the sun rise.* According to their own account, the Indians of Maine are all descended from a common stock. The Sokokis, who dwelt on the Saco river, were oldest; and the Anasagunticooks or Androscoggins, Canibas or Kennebecks, Wawennocks and Etechemins followed in order. The last nation was composed of the Tarratines, or Penobscots, the Openangoes, or "Quoddy" Indians, who dwelt on the ponds and rivers emptying into Passamaquoddy Bay, and the Marechites, who occupied the region of the St. John's river. The peninsula of Nova Scotia was inhabited by the Micmacs, who were of a separate origin, and differed widely in language and customs.

2. The word "Etechemins," in English, is *canoe men,* and was probably given them because they made such long journeys at sea. "Openangoes" means *little sables,* and signifies that they were a very cunning people. The Wawennocks were a very brave people, and that is what the name means. At the time of Captain Smith's visit to the coast, this was the superior tribe in Maine; and their sachem, called the Bashaba, was ruler over the tribes from the St. John's river to the Merrimac. The region between

the Penobscot and Kennebec, occupied by them, was known as Mavooshen.

3. The mouths of the small rivers in this vicinity were specially noted for the abundance of oysters they produced. There are at this day on the banks of sheltered coves along our coasts long mounds composed almost wholly of the shells of oysters and clams. Those on the Damariscotta river are in some places fifteen feet deep and twenty rods in width. Layers of charcoal scattered through the mass show where the fires were made; and among the shells are found knives, gouges and spear-heads of stone and horn, and bits of pottery. Bones and whole skeletons of human beings have also been found, but no tradition tells us whence they came or why they are buried there. The Indians told Popham's colonists frightful stories of a nation of cannibals living to the northward, who were of great size and had teeth an inch long. The Jesuits of the early French missions upon the St. Lawrence river also relate that there was a tribe about the mouth of that river who devoured the bodies of their enemies. Uncas, chief of the Mohegans, was once seen by white men to eat the flesh of his foe; and English captives who escaped from the Indians have told of similar barbarities. These facts lead us to conclude that at the time of the discovery of this country, many of the native tribes sometimes fed on human flesh; and I fear that this must explain the presence of human bones in the shell heaps of Damariscotta. Before the breaking out of the war between the settlers and the Indians in Maine, the Wawennocks had ceased to exist as a tribe. A few had joined the Canibas, but the larger portion, influenced by the Jesuits, had removed to the River St. Francis, in Canada.

4. The natives of Maine were taller than the average of white men; and, if no stronger, were usually more agile. Their complexion was a copper brown, and their black, coarse hair usually hung in a long

mass over their backs, though the women's was sometimes braided, while the men's was more frequently cut short over the forehead and the remainder tied in a knot at the top or back of the head. They had broad, beardless faces, retreating foreheads, prominent cheek bones, small, glistening, black eyes, and large white teeth. Many of their women were of comely face and figure, and some of them would have been almost handsome, had they been cleanly. Yet both women and men were generally morose in countenance and manner.

5. In the summer the dress of men and women was rarely more than a girdle of leather having a short skirt or fringe below the waist, with the addition of moccasins, if they were hunting or traveling. In the winter the buskins, leggins and mantle of fur formed a warmer attire; but there were some families so poor that they were at times obliged to wear hard, furless skins, even in the cold weather. They had a way of tanning and dressing skins which made them very soft and pliable; one substance used in this process being an oil prepared from the brains of animals.

6. The household work and the cultivation of the soil were left almost wholly to the women and children. The only labor of this sort which the warriors undertook was the raising of their tobacco; and the boys were very impatient to become old enough for hunters and warriors, as they were then freed from the drudgery of the wigwams and cornfields. But sometimes to save the crop, the whole family took hold together, and made quick work with the cornfield. When not engaged in war or hunting, the men occupied themselves chiefly in making their bows, arrows, spears, knives and other implements. This was really a slow and laborious process, as flint and shells were their keenest tools.

7. On war and hunting trips, especially when these were short, the squaws were left behind, and the men

did their own cooking. Their wigwams at these times being only for temporary use, were of small size and of the simplest construction. They were generally formed of straight poles set on the ground in a large circle, but coming together at the top, and covered with broad strips of bark. The cabins in the villages were larger, with the top arched by bending the upper parts of the poles and binding the overlapping ends together. Others were in the form of a rectangle, with tall crotched posts along the middle and sides, supporting the ridge and eave poles. The largest wigwams of which we have any account in Maine were not over forty feet in length; and such were occupied by several families. Each family had its own fire, and there was sometimes a slight division of stakes and bark between. They obtained fire by rapidly twirling a dry stick with the end in a hollow in another, some light material being laid close about it to catch the first spark or tongue of flame. There was no fireplace except a hole in the ground or a few large stones to support the sticks. The smoke flowed and eddied to every part of the cabin before it found the opening at the top left for its escape. In this smoke along the highest part of the room were slender poles, where, in the hunting season, hung strips of flesh cut from the carcases of deer, bear and moose, being dried to preserve it for use in later moons.

8. Every winter the hunters went away to the streams and ponds at the heads of the rivers to hunt deer, moose and beaver; though smaller parties hunted game for food at all seasons and in all directions. Poor hunters would rarely kill moose or bear, and would secure few even of the smaller animals. But my readers will remember that the Indians had no guns or other weapons of metal, until the white men furnished them, so that, with their weak weapons, much skill and prowess was necessary. Sometimes a company of hunters would join for the capture of a herd

of deer. Having surrounded them with fire, they posted themselves near the open passages of the forest, then started the herd by frightful shouts; and large numbers of the beautiful animals would be killed as they tried to escape from the enclosure. At other times the hunter would encase himself in the skin of a moose or deer, and steal toward the herd, imitating their movements. They also made up large parties for duck hunting. The time was chosen in the month of August, when the old birds had shed their feathers, and the young were of good size, but yet unable to fly. The hunters, sweeping the pond in their canoes, drove the birds into the creeks and coves at the borders, where they were killed by thousands with clubs and paddles.

9. The ordinary canoe was very light, being formed of birch bark on a frame work of wood. They also made them of logs, which they burned hollow, then smoothed with their stone gouges. These log canoes were sometimes long enough to carry forty persons. They made fish hooks of bone and deer's horn, and with the same material they sometimes tipped their arrows and spears, though they generally used flint or jasper for this purpose. Their knives, axes and chisels were also made of some hard stone. They made thread, lines, and nets of the bark of trees, of strong grass, and of deer sinews. They built weirs of great stones and stakes in the ponds and rivers, in which the fish became entangled; but usually they caught them in nets, or with hooks, and speared them from their canoes by firelight.

10. When the sanup (husband) was lazy or a poor hunter the family depended mainly on the maize, beans and crookneck squashes which the squaw raised. She also gathered the fuel, dressed the game and cooked the food. This was first served to the sanup, and other grown up males; and when these had eaten, the squaw might satisfy her own hunger and that of the

children. When venison was plenty, and corn in the milk, the Indians fared sumptuously. The corn they roasted on the ear, or, boiling it with new beans, made the dish called *succotash*. The dry corn was parched and pounded into a coarse meal, which they called *nokehike*. Then there was *samp*, which was corn hulled in boiling lye; and *hominy*, which was corn broken and boiled. The season of berries afforded them a delicious relish, and they laid up great stores of nuts; and sometimes in the spring they were obliged by scarcity of food to dig groundnuts, which they roasted in the ashes. Maple syrup they could make only in small quantities until the white men came and brought them kettles; their boiling before this time being done chiefly in wooden troughs, by dropping in hot stones. Neither did they know how to make bread of their corn until taught by Europeans. Their food was eaten from the troughs in which it was cooked, or from wooden bowls. They had, too, a rude sort of earthern ware, but it appears to have been quite soft and fragile. Neither chair nor table was found in their cabins, and they sat or lay on mats and skins on the bare ground, or on a low platform of bark, or of hemlock boughs about the sides of the cabin.

11. Here the little Indians, dirty and fat, rolled and ran about, while the small pappoose cooed and cried on its cradle of bark. At sunset the maidens went forth to dance on the green, clad in their choicest garments, that they might attract the eyes of the bold young warriors. Perhaps the daughter of the chief was with them, the green crest of the heron contrasting in her black hair with the scarlet feathers of the tanager, her armlets and leggins of soft deerskin marked with bright dyes, her moccasins gay with porcupine quills, and her skirt bright with embroidered threads; while strings of the white teeth of the sable and otter gleamed upon her dusky bosom.

12. Very often indeed a young brave became enamored of a comely maiden. When this happened he told his parents, who then held a talk about it with her parents. If her parents proved favorable, he then sent her a present,—a deer, a beautiful bird, furs or beads. Lest she should be unwilling when asked to live in his wigwam, he must now pay other attentions. So in the shades of the evening he took his station near her cabin, and did his best to charm her listening ear by his singing, or the rude music of his fife; or, if he was not musical, he must please her at the merry makings of the young by his wit or feats of strength and agility. When she accepted him as her sanup (husband) he made more presents; and then the desired guests were invited to the wigwam of her parents. Then followed feasts and dances for two or three nights, the young couple keeping beside each other until the frolics were over. Then the savage bridegroom led home his bride; who thenceforth devoted herself to preparing his food, making his clothes and keeping his wigwam fire alive.

13. Foot-races, wrestling, quoits, ball playing, and a sort of draughts were frequent amusements; and they were much addicted to gambling by every possible means. The Indians were much given to smoking, also; and the offer of a pipe of tobacco was a token of hospitality and peace. At all feasts the guest must eat all that might be put in his bowl, no matter how many times it was filled or how unlike it he felt; otherwise he would give offense to his host. So many a poor Indian often went back to his wigwam with a pain in his stomach.

14. Many people suppose the Indians to have been very healthy; but this is a mistake. The Indian had fewer diseases than the white man, but these were more generally fatal. They doctored chiefly with sweating, astringents, salves and washes. They also had vegetable teas for ordinary kinds of sickness. But their

knowledge of medicine was very limited; and any intelligent country housewife of the present day far surpasses them in skill. Yet, being natives of the country, they were able to instruct the settlers in the uses of numerous plants. If a savage was very ill the "powwow" was called upon. This was the Indian medicine-man, or physician. His method of treatment was very mysterious to common Indians, and was supposed to have supernatural power. Drums were beaten, he made strange gestures, uttered wild cries,—sometimes over the patient, at others, shut up in a wigwam alone. He also carried at his waist a small bag containing bones, sticks and stones, which were thought to have virtue as charms against evil spirits, diseases and misfortunes.

15. The Abnakis believed in a good spirit, *Tantum*, or *Tanto*; and in an evil spirit, which they called *Mojahondo*; but in general these were confused in one, and called by the name of the good spirit. *Hockomock* was another word used by some Indians, which the settlers took to signify the devil. At every new moon they worshipped the evil spirit for fear, because they believed he had power to kill them, and to send storm, pestilence, drought and famine.

16. Sometimes certain old men in each tribe, who kept in mind their treaties and traditions, were appointed to teach them to the young. Beside the chiefs who were war leaders, there were others who presided over the village and regulated petty matters, somewhat like our police justices. Both these were generally called *sagamores*. Over all was the *sachem*, who was chosen for his wisdom; though, usually, he was the son of the sachem or of a chief. Yet his authority was not absolute, all important matters being decided in council. These were composed of the chiefs and old men; and, sometimes, the aged squaws were present also. There was perfect order on these occasions; when one was speaking all others kept silent, and even

after he had ceased he was allowed several minutes in which to recollect anything he might have omitted without intention. It was considered very unmannerly to interrupt another, even in ordinary conversation. Thus we see that in some respects these ignorant and cruel savages set us a good example.

17. The language of the Abnakis is easy of utterance, and quite smooth and agreeable to the ear; but its words are few and unfitted for nice distinctions. For instance, in the Tarratine dialect *thou* or *you* is "keah," but "keah-olet-haut-tamoria" means no more than *thy will*; and their word for *to-day* consists of eight syllables, and many other ideas are equally difficult of expression.

Names of places are generally descriptive, as *Mattawamkeag*, from *matta*, much,—*wampa*, white, or clear,—*keag*, or *kik*, earth; and *Anasagunticook* (tribe)—properly, *Amasacontecook*,—from *namaous*, fish,—*konte*, stream,—*cook* from *kik*, place; meaning, The region of the fish river. For heaven they use the word, *spumkeag*, i. e., above the earth. "Metungus" is *father*, a man is "sanumbee," and *boy* is "skeenooses." If a Tarratine should inquire after your health he would probably say, *Pah-que-num-se-eld*.

18. Their dialects were constantly changing, for they had no written characters to preserve the form of their words; so that when modern natives have been asked the meaning of some phrase long ago recorded by the English or French they have been unable to give it, but yet recollected the words as "old Indian." Still they very generally conveyed information by means of rude drawings, often leaving these records on trees and pieces of bark at points visited by them; and these were readily understood by others of the tribe, who came after. A rock at the sea shore at Machiasport furnishes an interesting example of this kind of writing; and it is probably the most extended Indian inscription in New England.

THE INDIANS OF MAINE.

19. In the earliest days of English settlements when an Indian signed a treaty, deed or other writing, it was usually by a rude figure of some animal,—as a deer, beaver, tortoise, snake, heron, hawk, or eagle. This was called the *totem* and was the family "coat of arms"; and in some tribes they seemed to believe that they had descended from these animals. It was often the case that a great hunter or warrior received a name descriptive of his character or exploits; therefore we may conclude that these "totems" only represented some remarkable ancestor, whose distinguishing title had become the name of a numerous clan.

Under what general name are the Indians of Maine classed? What does this name signify? What were the distinctive names of the Indian tribes of Maine? Where did each dwell? What remarkable mounds are found on the Damariscotta River? What became of the Wawennocks? Of what materials did they make their weapons? What vegetable did they raise? How did they boil their food before they had kettles? What sports and games had the Indians? What is said of the diseases of the Indians? By what means did their pow-wows pretend to cure diseases? Did the Indians believe in good and evil spirits? What were the titles of their chiefs? Which was superior in authority? By what means were important matters decided? What was their practice in speaking and conversation? Did they have any letters or written words? By what means did they sometimes convey information? What are "Totems"?

CHAPTER IX.

1. I have now given you an account of the Indians as they were when the English first came to the country; but from that time their habits and customs began to change. The traders soon supplied them with domestic utensils, cloths and guns; so that they were able to obtain game and cook their food with more ease, and to dress themselves more comfortably. The French mingled with the natives like brothers; and some of them, with their usual easy habit, even took Indian women for their wives. Very soon, French Jesuits were in all their villages; and before the year 1720 they had nearly all become Roman Catholics. Therefore, in any war that arose between the English and the French, the Indians, if they took any part, were sure to be on the side of the French. Neither did the Jesuits confine themselves to the religious instruction of the natives, but were the ever willing agents of the French government to incite the Indians to hostility against the English settlers.

2. The authorities of the colonies were quite aware of their danger, and made prudent laws to restrain the settlers and natives from wronging each other. None were allowed to settle or to hunt and fish upon the territory of the natives unless the right was first obtained of them; and the sale of intoxicating liquors was forbidden, according to the wish of the chiefs. Yet the English made crafty bargains for their land, obtaining deeds of extensive tracts before the ignorant savages understood fully the effect of such writings. Often, too, the traders would sell them rum; for this yielded a large profit, and they could also make better bargains for furs when their owners were a little in

THE FIRST INDIAN WAR COMMENCES. 69

drink. The natives, at long intervals, sometimes revenged their wrongs by killing cattle or burning buildings; yet the tribes in most cases were quite ready to pay the damages when the acts were traced to their members.

3. Doubtless a principal reason for the continued peaceable conduct of the natives toward the English was found in the wars among themselves, and the pestilences with which they were often visited.

In 1614, when Captain Smith visited the coast, the native population of Maine must have been nearly thirty thousand. In the war which happened soon after, the Wawennocks had been almost destroyed, and the Tarratines also lost severely. Then the plague came, working fearful havoc from Penobscot to Cape Cod. Following these were the wars with the Mohawk Indians, which raged at intervals for above half a century; while the small pox became a frequent scourge. From these causes their number had fallen before the year 1675 to about twelve thousand.

4. Some of the tribes did not at first join in the hostilities against the English. Among these were the Penobscot Indians, and all those at the eastward, and the Pennacooks in New Hampshire. Passaconaway, a sachem of the Pennacooks, was noted for his sagacity and cunning. He made his Indians believe that he could restore the ashes of a burnt leaf to their original form, raise a live serpent from the skin of a dead one, and change himself into a flame of fire. When he became old he called his tribe to a great feast, and there made to them his farewell address. "Hearken," said he, "to the last words of your father and friend. The white men are the sons of the morning. The Great Spirit is their father. His sun shines bright about them. Never make war with them. Sure as you light the fires the breath of Heaven will turn the flames upon you, and destroy you. Listen to my ad-

vice. It is the last I shall be allowed to give you. Remember it and live."

5. Wonnolancet, his son, was now sachem of the tribe; and as long as he lived their friendship with the English remained unbroken.

Rowles, the sagamore of the Piscataqua Indians, likewise saw that the white men would become the masters of the country. He lived in Berwick on intimate terms with the settlers. When he became old, and could no more go out of his dwelling, he sent to the principal men of the town this petition: "Being loaded with years, I had expected a visit in my infirmities,—especially from those who are now tenants on the land of my fathers. Though all these plantations are, of right, my children's, I am forced in this age of evils humbly to request a few hundred acres of land to be marked out for them and recorded as a public act in the town books; so that when I am gone they may not be perishing beggars in the pleasant places of their birth. For I know a great war will shortly break out between the white men and Indians over the whole country. At first the Indians will kill many and prevail; but after three years they will be great sufferers, and finally be rooted out and utterly destroyed."

6. But Squando, sachem of the Sokokis, had never been friendly to the English; and about this time an incident took place which made him a most bitter enemy. His squaw with her little child was crossing the Saco River in a canoe, when a party of sailors saw them and determined to have some sport. They had heard that Indian children swam from instinct; so they upset the canoe, tumbling the poor mother and her infant into the water. The child sank to the bottom; the mother dived after it, and succeeded in bringing it up alive. Soon after this affair it sickened and died. Squando believed that its death was owing to the cruel treatment of the white men; and he vowed to be revenged. This chieftain was the

most remarkable Indian of his time. Sometimes his conduct was quite humane and generous toward the settlers, and at other times very barbarous. He was not only the sachem, but the pow-wow of his tribe, and made his people believe that he had revelations from the spirit world. At one time when he wished to incite them to war against the English he said to them: "An angel of light has commanded me to worship the Great Spirit, and to stop hunting and laboring on the Sabbath; and God himself tells me he has left the English people to be destroyed by the Indians."

You perceive that the prophecies of these sachems did not agree; but it was not then so easy to decide which was false.

7. At length the alarm sounded. In July, 1675, the first blow of King Philip's war was struck. The Massachusetts authorities immediately sent the news to those of Maine, with the advice that the Indians should be deprived of their guns and knives. Some of the leading residents of Sagadahoc, or Lower Kennebec, immediately visited the Indians near them, and prevailed upon them to give up a few of their guns. They gave them many presents, and so won their favor that Mo-ho-tiwormet, the old Canibas sachem, made a dance in honor of the agreement of peace between them. The Androscoggins acted differently. They had for a long time felt very revengeful towards Thomas Purchas, who was a trader at the head of New Meadows River in Brunswick, because they believed that he had cheated them in trade. One of their sagamores declared that he had paid an hundred pounds for water from Purchas' well. His Indians must have drunk much rum to have the water in it reach that amount. It is no wonder that they wasted away.

8. It happened one day early in September that Mr. Purchas and his boys went off, leaving the

women unprotected. While they were gone a party of Indians came to the house, pretending that they wanted to trade; but as soon as they found the men were away, they fell to plundering the store and buildings of whatever they wanted. While they were thus engaged one of the boys was seen returning on horseback. Before reaching the spot he discovered the Indians, and halted. A stout fellow started out towards him with his gun under his blanket; but the boy, perceiving his purpose, wheeled his horse about and fled. He carried the alarm to the coast; and a party went up the river with a sloop and two boats to bring away whatever the Indians had left. Mrs. Purchas somehow escaped; but the men with the vessel found more Indians at the settlement, and were driven off with loss.

9. On the twelfth of September the savages burned the house of John Wakely, near the mouth of the Presumpscot River, in Falmouth. The smoke and flames were seen at Casco Neck (Portland); and a party started at once for their relief. They were too late. The bodies of seven persons lay among the smoking ruins, half burned and shockingly mangled. It proved that two others, a girl of eleven years and a young child, had been carried away. None knew what became of the child; and the poor girl, (whose name was Elizabeth) now left without father, mother, brother or sister, was forced to traverse the wilderness through long and tedious months in company with the murderers of her relatives.

10. Soon after this bloody affair, a friendly Sokokis came to John Bonython at Saco and said to him privately, "A strange Indian from the westward and several Anasagunticooks have been at my wigwam, and are persuading all our brothers to lift the tomahawk against the white people." Bonython warned his neighbors; and that very night they all retired for safety to the house of Major William Phillips, on the

Biddeford side of the river, near the falls. The next morning the attack was made. The first notice was Bonython's house in flames; then an Indian was seen skulking behind a fence. Major Phillips had been looking at the flames, and as he turned from the window a bullet pierced his shoulder. The savages were ambushed all around the house! When Major Phillips disappeared so suddenly from the window the Indians, supposing him to be killed, set up a great shout. The English were watching from every side of the house, and instantly fired at the shouters; and several of them fell badly wounded. At dark the savages set fire to a small house, and to Phillip's mill; then they came up crying, "Come now, you English coward dogs; come put out the fire, if you dare." The English didn't come; but they sent out their leaden messengers wherever an Indian exposed himself.

11. At four o'clock the moon set; and then the savages contrived another mode of attack. They built up on the forward end of an ox-cart a tier of lumber, then filled the body with shavings, birch bark and sticks. A number of them took hold of the tongue, where they were protected by the screen of lumber, and pushed the cart toward the house. They meant to set the house on fire, and kill the people as they ran out! Fifty persons were crowded into this building,—most of them women and children. The cart was steadily approaching —nearer and nearer it came. Already the tiny tongues of flame gleamed upward through the mass; and the voices of the besieged grew hushed with fear, or some excited girl screamed in frenzy. But the cart comes steadily on,—one wheel drops into a gutter, and the cart swings about. The savages who hold the tongue are in view; and the muskets of the English ring out in the still night. Several of the assailants dropped to the ground, and the remainder ran away, leaving their load of burning sticks to light up the fields.

The savages were discouraged; for they had killed none, while six of their number were dead, and fifteen, including their leader, badly wounded. In the morning not an Indian was to be found; and a day or two after, Major Phillips and his company reached the settlement at Winter Harbor in safety.

12. When it was known at Newichawannock (South Berwick) that the Indians had attacked Saco, Captain Wincoln and sixteen volunteers, with noble spirit, set out for Winter Harbor to render all the aid possible. They had just landed at the mouth of the river, and were proceeding towards the village, when a large body of savages rushed out of the woods upon them. Wincoln and his company took refuge behind a huge pile of shingle blocks, firing with such effect that they kept at bay a hundred and fifty savages. The report of the guns was heard at the village, and a party of nine men started out to join the reinforcement,—for such they knew it must be; but the savages ambushed their path and shot down every man.

13. The next attack was at Newichawannock, on the house of John Tozier, who had gone with Captain Wincoln, leaving his family unprotected. His was one of the outermost houses of the settlement; and in it were gathered at that moment fifteen women and children. A young lady of eighteen was the first to discover the Indians. She had only time to warn the family, when the savages reached the house. Fearful that the weak door fastenings would give away, she staid and held them until the hatchets of the savages had broken through. They dashed in the door; but the family had escaped from the other side of the house, and were running towards the garrison. A part of the Indians pursued them, catching two children who were hindmost. One of these, only three years old, they killed on the spot; and the other they kept in captivity six months. But the heroic girl at the door,—the savages were so angry at finding the

THE FIRST INDIAN WAR COMMENCES. 75

house empty that they beat her to death, as they thought. After they had gone she revived, and lived to recover from her wounds. I wish I knew her name, for no personage in this history would more brightly ornament its pages.

14. The next day the Indians appeared again, and burned the dwelling and storehouse of Captain Wincoln, then escaped in the darkness of night. It was now the golden month of October; but in Maine much of the crops remained ungathered; and the scarlet forests seemed to the affrighted settlers but tokens of fire and blood. October 7th was observed as a day of fasting and prayer on account of the great calamities. The Indians celebrated it at Newichawannock by shooting a man off his horse, and robbing two boys of their guns and clothing. Again on the sixteenth they assailed it in force, killing Richard Tozier, and making his son a prisoner. The commander of the garrison, Lieut. Roger Plaisted, perceiving Indians in the distance, sent out nine men to reconnoiter. The savages saw them coming, and hiding themselves, shot down three of the party before they could escape. Lieut. Plaisted, with twenty men and a team, started to bring in the bodies of their slain companions. They went silently past the house where Tozier had been killed, and reached the place of the ambush; the corpses were placed in the cart, and they turned toward the garrison with a feeling of security; for they supposed their numbers had frightened the savages away. Vain thought! A multitude of dusky figures rushed into view from behind fences, logs and bushes, pouring a volley of bullets upon the startled company. The oxen ran toward the garrison, and most of the men followed; but Lieut. Plaisted with his son and another valiant soldier disdained to fly. Repeatedly the Indians called upon Plaisted to surrender,—for savages as they were, they greatly respected courage; but the intrepid man refused to

yield, and he was literally cut in pieces by their hatchets.

15. The savages soon after went farther down the river, burning and killing wherever they dared. As they were making an attack upon a house at the mouth of the river, a cannon was fired at them from the Portsmouth battery, on the opposite side, causing them to run off in great alarm. A light snow had just fallen, and a force in pursuit was able to follow them very rapidly. In a few hours the savages were overtaken on the borders of a great swamp, which, loaded as they were, they could not pass. They dared not venture on a fair fight; so they threw off their plunder, and plunged through the swamp. In passing through Wells they killed three men and burned a house; but it was their last depredation in Maine this year.

16. Three months had passed since this savage slaughter and destruction began, and in that brief time eighty persons had been killed between the Piscataqua and Kennebec. Yet the Indians had lost a larger number, though they had every advantage. They never fought in open battle, but chose their own time and place for attack; and, being familiar with the country, their scattered bands could easily elude pursuit. A large force was now raised to assail the hostile tribes in their winter fastnesses. The soldiers were not ready to march until the tenth of December; but the snow had then fallen to four feet in depth, and the campaign was abandoned. The Indians now desired peace in order that they might hunt; for on account of the war they had raised less corn than usual, and had nothing else to live upon. So a treaty was made with the Sagamores, by which the Indians agreed to return all the captives without ransom. Between this time and the next summer many were restored; and among the rest Squando brought in Elizabeth Wakely, the poor girl who was

made an orphan by the massacre at Presumpscot River.

What nation mingled familiarly with the Indians? **In the wars between the English and French which side did the Indians always take?** Did the English colonies endeavor to deal justly with **the Indians?** What was the number of the Indians in Maine in 1675? What great sachem warned his tribe not **to war against the English?** . In what year did **King** Philip's war begin? **What settlement was** first attacked **in Maine?** Where did the Indians commit shocking barbarities? How long did the **siege of Major Phillip's** garrison in Biddeford continue? What **took place at Winter Harbor?** What **noble action was** performed **by a young lady in Berwick?** What **brave officer was cut in pieces by the savages a few days after?** How many persons were killed in Maine by the Indians this year? What was the loss of the Indians?

CHAPTER X.

1. If the English had been magnanimous toward the Indians it is quite possible that the war in Maine would have closed in the same season it began. Though **a treaty had been made, and a** few prisoners returned, yet **the fears of** the settlers all the winter filled **the air with rumors** of treachery and bloodshed. Perhaps some incidents occurred **to make these rumors plausible;** for Major Waldron, **one of the Indian commissioners,** issued general warrants **by which every man who** held one could seize any **Indian who might be** accused of killing a white man, **or who had** conspired **against the** peace, or refused to obey **the** authorities. Among others, several shipmasters obtained copies **of these warrants, and** began to seize Indians all along **the coast. One came** to Pemaquid for this purpose, where the **peace had never been**

broken. The English besought him to depart, but he would not; and they warned the Indians against him. Yet he finally caught several, and carried them away to a foreign port and sold them for slaves. Of course the natives were very angry at these outrages. To pacify them Abraham Shurte and Capt. Sylvanus Davis met the chiefs in council at Teconnet (Winslow). Mr. Shurte was a noble and venerable man, who had long been the chief magistrate at Pemaquid; and it was mostly owing to his judicious course that the natives at the eastward had remained peaceable. The Indians demanded that their brothers who had been stolen away should be restored to them, and that the English should sell them sufficient ammunition to procure game for food. These were reasonable demands, but the agents were unable to comply with them; and the council broke up without profit.

2. On August 12th, 1676, King Philip was killed, which ended the war in Massachusetts and Connecticut; but many of his tribe escaped and mingled with the Indians of Maine. These brought with them an intense hatred of the English; and, joining with the most violent of the Abnakis, they quickly excited the hesitating tribes to renewed hostilities. Early in August one of the refugees known as "Simon, the Yankee-killer," made himself familiar at the house of Anthony Brackett, at Back Cove in Falmouth, now Portland. A few days after, Mr. Brackett lost one of his cows. When Simon was informed of the misfortune, he said, "I can show you the fellows that killed the creature;" and very soon he went away. Mr. Brackett suspected treachery; and the settlers at once sent messengers to Major Waldron at Dover for aid. Before their return Simon came back at the head of a party of savages, saying to Mr. Brackett, "Here are the Indians that took your cow." They immediately fell upon the family, consisting of Brackett, his wife, five children and a negro servant.

FIRST INDIAN WAR CONTINUED.

Having bound these, they went to the other houses in the vicinity, killing and taking captive thirty-four persons. The remainder of the inhabitants escaped to Munjoy's garrison on the hill, and from here they soon removed to Bang's Island. Two days after this attack a party of natives came at nightfall to the house of Richard Hammond at Stinson's Point in Woolwich, who gave the squaws permission to lodge on the kitchen floor. A girl of the family became so alarmed by certain tokens of malice and treachery among the squaws that she ran out of the house; but some of them brought her back and tried to allay her fears. A little after, she escaped again from the dwelling and hid in the cornfield. By and by she heard a great tumult in the house,—heavy blows, shrieks, and the yells of warriors, whom the squaws had let in. At this the girl left her hiding place and fled to the nearest settlement on the mainland, twelve long miles away.

3. From Hammond's a party of savages went up the river, where they took several prisoners, while another party crossed to Arrowsic, and concealed themselves near the fort of Messrs. Clark and Lake. It was Sunday morning; and when the sleepy sentinel left his post and entered the gate, the lurking savage was at his heels. The sentinel was struck down, and the Indians were quickly masters of the fort. Mr Lake, Captain Davis and two others, who were in an upper room, got out through a back passage, and rushing to their boat, made for an island on the east The savages followed swiftly, firing upon them and wounding Captain Davis. On reaching the shore he crept up the cliff, and hid among the rocks; where the sun, shining in the faces of his pursuers, dazzled their eyes so that they could not see him. Lake was overtaken and killed, but the other two escaped. Davis laid in his hiding place two days; then crawling to the water's edge, he rolled himself into a canoe, and

drifted away unseen. All the shore from the Kennebec to Pemaquid was now alive with savages, and the inhabitants got away in boats and vessels as best they could,—first to **Monhegan** and other islands, thence to **Boston and neighboring** towns. Soon the smoke of burning dwellings arose on every hand, and few buildings were left unharmed. The cattle of the settlers roamed untended in the great pastures, affording the Indians plenty of meat; but above all they preferred horse-flesh.

One day Francis Card, who had been captured in Woolwich, was sent with another prisoner to find a horse and drive him in to be killed; but they found a canoe instead of a horse, and quickly made their escape. Simon, the Yankee-killer, had gone to other scenes of violence, leaving the family of Anthony Brackett to follow, not supposing that they could by any means escape; but they found on the shore, a leaky birchen canoe; and Mrs. Brackett repaired it so well that they all embarked, and reached Scarborough in safety.

4. A few families of those who had been driven from Casco Neck had gathered on Jewel's Island, unwilling to go far from the pleasant places they had chosen for their homes; but here, too, the savages found them. One day as the women were washing their scanty clothing along the gravelly marge of the sea, and the children playing happily about, the report of a gun suddenly signalled the presence of danger. The men were out in their boats catching fish, as usual; and it was a lad at the house who had fired the gun. The brave little fellow had actually killed two Indians with the shots that gave the alarm. Some of the men now came rapidly to shore, and, making a sudden charge, drove the savages to their boats. In this affray the English lost two killed, and five made prisoners.

5. The General Court now found that something

must be done, or the Indians would soon carry the war into Massachusetts; so one hundred and thirty English and forty Natick Indians were enlisted, and put under the command of Captain William Hawthorn. These arrived at Dover, New Hampshire, on September 6th, where they met the soldiers under Majors Waldron and Frost. Four hundred other Indians had also gathered there. Most of them were of the neutral Pennacooks; but others belonged to King Philip's defeated forces; while some were known to have been concerned in recent depredations in Maine,—and were the very savages whom these troops expected to fight; and it was difficult to prevent the soldiers from falling upon them at once. Probably they had come there at Major Waldron's invitation for the purpose of making a treaty; for he protested to the troops that they were relying upon his honor and fidelity.

6. Finally he proposed an expedient which, he thought, might preserve his honor with the Indians and still satisfy the soldiery. So the next day the Indians were invited to join with the English in a sham fight. After they had gone through several military manœuvres Major Waldron ordered a grand round of musketry. The Indians promptly discharged their guns, while the English, who were in the secret, did not empty a musket. They immediately surrounded the astonished savages, and made prisoners of them all without the loss of a life. The Pennacooks and other friendly Indians were set at liberty; but the others—about two hundred—were marched to Boston. Here several were proved to have taken the lives of the English since the treaty, and were therefore put to death; while the others were carried to foreign countries and sold as slaves. This affair was long known as "Waldron's Ruse." It was a trick that the Indians never forgot nor forgave; and they wreaked on him a terrible vengeance.

7. Captain Hawthorn the **next day set** out with a small company for **Casco Neck, to** rebuild **the fort.** One day seven of **the** inhabitants, who had **now** returned, went **to** Peaks' Island to kill some sheep. While thus employed they were attacked by savages, and **took refuge** in **an** old stone house. They defended themselves bravely; but by the **guns** of the **savages and the** stones thrown down upon **them from the walls, all were** killed except one, who **soon afterward died of his wounds.**

The next day, in Wells, James Gooch was shot from his horse by the Indians, as he returned from divine service; and his wife, who rode on the same horse, was cut in pieces with their hatchets. On the following day **they burned** the **settlement** at Cape Neddock, in York, **killing and carrying away** captive forty persons. The **Indians came and went** with such rapidity and secrecy that **Captain Hawthorn's** troops were unable to meet them; **so** on the twelfth of October they returned to Berwick. Two days after their departure one hundred and twenty Indians attacked the fort **at** Black Point in Scarborough, where the inhabitants who remained had taken refuge, which **was immediately** abandoned.

The **leader** of the savages was a **shrewd** Tarratine **sagamore** named Mugg. He knew the garrison was **strong, and induced** the commander, Henry Jocelyn, **to come out and hold a** parley with him. Mugg proposed easy terms of **surrender; and while** they were **talking the subject over, managed to draw** Jocelyn to **a distance from the garrison.** On returning **to the fort he was** astounded **to find** that all the occupants except his own servants had fled to the boats. Mugg therefore secured the fort unharmed, much to his gratification; for the Indians desired the place for an encampment.

8. About this **time** Captain Fryer was sent **to** Richmond's Island **to bring** away goods; but the sav-

ages set upon his men as they were carrying the goods to the vessel, and all were killed or made prisoners. They were offered release for a certain additional quantity of goods; and two of the English were sent for the articles. They returned within the time named, but the Indians who had been left to guard the prisoners, took the goods and kept the men.

Mugg next led his band against the garrison at Wells, and sent a prisoner to demand a surrender.

"Never," replied the commander, "never shall the gates be opened until every one within is dead."

This determined reply showed Mugg that he could not hope to get possession of the fort except by severe fighting, and he made no attack; but his Indians killed two or three men whom they found outside. They then cut the throats of thirteen cattle; and taking out their tongues, retired to the woods to make a dainty meal.

9. The cold weather was now coming on, and it was supposed that the Sokokis would soon be gathered in their winter quarters at the great fort on the Ossipee River; and on the first of November Captains Hawthorn and Sill set out with their companies to attack them. After two months of severe toil and hardship, they returned without having seen a single Indian.

Before the troops had been gone a week, Mugg himself came into Piscataqua bringing Captain Fryer, who was dying from his wounds. He told the authorities that the prisoners taken at Richmond's Island should be restored without ransom; and offered to negotiate a treaty. He was taken to Boston, where, on November 6th, he signed a treaty in behalf of his master, Madockawando, sachem of the Tarratines. The terms of this treaty were that all acts of hostility should cease, all English captives, vessels and goods be restored, full satisfaction rendered for damages, that his tribe should buy ammunition of those only whom the governor should appoint, and that the Indians of Penobscot should take up arms against the Androscoggins and other eastern natives, if they persisted in the war.

"In proof of my sincerity and honor," said Mugg, "I pledge myself an hostage in your hands till the captives, vessels and goods are restored; and I lift my hand to Heaven in witness of my honest heart in this treaty."

10. It was certainly a strange treaty for a victorious leader to make, as all its stipulations were in favor of the English. A vessel was sent to Penobscot with him to have the treaty ratified by the sagamores, and to bring home the captives. The treaty was agreed to, but only some eighteen or twenty prisoners were restored, though there must have been more than fifty at this time among the Indians. Mugg now set out for the Kennebec for the purpose of inducing the Canibas tribe to join in the peace. He pretended to be in much fear of harm for having made so easy a peace; saying to the captain of the vessel, "If I do not return in four days you may conclude I am certainly bereft of life or liberty." A week passed, yet nothing was heard from Mugg; and the vessel went back to Boston with the treaty and the captives.

11. There was still a fear among the settlements that peace and safety were not secured. Few of the prisoners were restored, and Mugg's conduct was suspicious; besides, it was believed that Indians from Narragansett were in Maine inciting the natives to resume the war. At length it began to be quite certain that hostilities would be resumed in the spring unless some decisive steps were taken; therefore in February of 1677, Majors Waldron and Frost were sent eastward with an hundred and fifty men to see what the savages were about, and to obtain further pledges of peace.

The troops landed at Mare Point in Brunswick;

meeting there a party of Indians led by Squando, **the Sokokis** sachem, and Simon, **the Yankee-killer,**—with **whom they had a skirmish. Unable** to obtain any captives here, **the** troops re-embarked and went **to** the Kennebec. Here a party was sent to Merrymeeting Bay in search of the Canibas Indians, while Waldron kept on to Penobscot with the remainder.

12. About the last of the month **he met a company** of Tarratines at Pemaquid. At the **first interview** they agreed to deliver up some prisoners whom they had received from the Canibas, for twelve beaver **skins each and some** good **liquor. Major Waldron** and five men **were to** bring **the** articles **in** the after**noon;** and both they and the **Indians** who met them **were to be unarmed.** Only three captives were **brought.** Waldron suspected treachery, and looking about he espied the point of **a** lance under a board. This led to the discovery of other weapons. Seizing one, he brandished it in their faces, exclaiming, "Perfidious **wretches! you intended to get** our goods and **then** kill **us, did you?" For a** moment the savages **were confounded;** then they rushed upon him **and** tried to wrest the weapon from his hands. He waved his cap **to** the ship, and bravely continued the **struggle.** His companions armed themselves from a **pile of** guns which they had uncovered, while other **Indians came to join** in the **affray.** A re-enforcement which had started from the **vessels** at the waving of the cap, now reached the shore,—and just then a stout squaw seized her arms full of the hidden guns, and ran away with them into the woods. Finding themselves **overpowered,** the **natives** fled, some into **their** canoes **and others into** the woods. The boats attacked the canoes, sinking **one and** disabling others, and killing several of **the Indians. A** pow-wow and two sagamores—Mattahando **and the bloody** Megunnaway—**were killed,** and a **sister of** the sachem Madocka**wando was** taken prisoner. The whole force now re-

turned to Boston, with the exception of forty men under Captain Davis, who remained as a garrison at the mouth of the Kennebec. This expedition did more harm than good; for the natives were not pacified, but rendered more revengeful.

13. In the spring the General Court decided to employ the Mohawks in the war; though many good people thought it wrong to seek the aid of the heathen. The Mohawks were the hereditary enemies of the eastern Indians; and the first thing they did was to kill some of a friendly tribe, not knowing the difference between friends and foes. Among others who fell by their hands was a sagamore called Blind Will; but the English did not feel very sorry for his death, because of his duplicity. Finally these heathen allies were dismissed; but the news that the English were bringing the Mohawks to fight them went like the wind through the tribes from Piscataqua to Cape Sable, exciting them to the highest pitch of activity.

14. The garrison at Kennebec, sometime in March, attempted to bury the bodies of those slain on Arrowsic Island seven months before; but the Indians were watching them, and nine were killed before they could escape in their boats. This point was soon after abandoned; and now there remained in Maine only the settlements of York, Wells, Kittery, Newichawannock and Winter Harbor. On the seventh of April the savages killed eight men while at work in their fields in York; and the next day they were heard from in Wells, where they prowled about in large and small parties, killing and burning, all through the month.

15. Black Point had now been garrisoned anew; and on May 16th it was again attacked. After three days a sharp shooter in the fort brought down the Indian leader, and the siege was soon after abandoned; but the English had lost four men, one of whom was tortured to death. On the twenty-eighth of June

FIRST INDIAN WAR CONTINUED.

Captain Benjamin **Swett and** Lieutenant Richardson **with a force of** English and friendly Indians arrived to **aid in the defense of** this place and Winter Harbor. The next day they marched out in search **of** the enemy. They soon came upon a party, which immediately retreated, leading the whole pursuing force between a swamp and a dense thicket about two miles from the fort. The party was only a decoy. The moment the English reached the most exposed point they heard the terrible war whoop, and a volley from a host of ambushed savages laid many **a brave man** low. Soon Lieutenant Richardson fell; **and the fight** became **hand** to hand.

16. It was now plain that the English were greatly outnumbered; yet Captain Swett, with great bravery **and coolness,** repeatedly rallied his old fighters to **cover** the retreat of the new recruits, and to bring off **the** wounded. He had received many wounds, and **was** becoming weak. **The** savages, **seeing his** condition, grappled him, and, throwing him **to the ground,** cut him in pieces before the eyes of the garrison. With him fell **forty** English, and twenty friendly Indians,—just **two thirds of** the number he **led into** action.

The **chief who had been shot from this garrison in May, which** had caused **the Indians** to withdraw, **proved to** be Mugg, the Tarratine. He was a savage more than usually brave and cunning. You will remember that he made a treaty for his tribe **the** year before, and was sent to persuade the Canibas **to** join in the peace. He pretended to be very much afraid that they would kill him for his services to **the** English; but I suspect that he was as much opposed to a permanent peace **as they were,** for he even made suggestions to them for the next season's campaign. "I know how we can even burn Boston and drive all the country before us," **said** he. "*We must go to the fishing islands and take all the white man's vessels.*"

17. Accordingly, when the time of year came for Bay fishing, the savages proceeded to execute this plan. In the daytime they prowled along the shores, spying out their prey; and in the darkness of night they slid out noiselessly in their light canoes, boarding the motionless vessels, and killing or capturing their sleeping crews. In the month of July they secured about twenty vessels, each of them having a crew of from three to six men. When these captures became known, a large ship was sent out after them. She was supplied with plenty of cannon and small arms, and manned by forty seamen and soldiers. It was expected that this vessel would somewhere encounter the Indian fleet, which she would capture or sink, and at the same time destroy a multitude of savages. She came upon the vessels,—one here, another there,—some aground, and others beating against the rocks,—but not an Indian in any of them. The vessels were so large they could not be navigated by paddles; and the sails flew and flapped about, while the vessels went in any direction but that which their dusky sailors desired; consequently they soon abandoned the prizes in fright and disgust.

18. Manhattan had now been regained by the English, and again become "New York"; and Sir Edmund Andros was sent over as governor. He saw how the eastern settlements were overrun by the savages; and, fearing that the French might take possession of the Duke of York's province, he sent a strong military force to Pemaquid. The Indians were much discouraged by the failure of their naval project, and the sight of so large a force broke their courage down entirely; and the Tarratines very soon made a treaty with the commander, and gave up their captives and some booty.

The next spring the commissioners of Massachusetts and the sagamores of the Sokokis, Androscoggins and Canibas met at Casco (Falmouth) and made a treaty. The agreement was that all captives should be restored without ransom, and **that the inhabitants should possess their lands on condition of** paying to the natives a peck of corn annually for each family. This closed the first Indian war, which had raged three years. In this war two hundred and sixty inhabitants of Maine were known to have been killed **or** carried into captivity from which they never returned; while more than half the settlements **were** laid waste.

What excellent magistrate lived at **Pemaquid? When did King** Philip's war close? What fugitive **from Philip's forces led the** attack on Falmouth? What places **at Sagadahoc were captured** by the Indians soon after**?** What **took place at** Dover soon after these **events**? What happened at Peak's Island while Capt. Hawthorn **was** rebuilding the fort at Casco Neck? What chieftain led the attack on Black Point and Wells? For what point did a large force set out to meet the Indians? Who came into Piscataqua to make peace a few days after? Where did Major Waldron go **in** February to meet the Indians? What happened this **spring at** Arrowsic Island? What two brave English **leaders fell at Black** Point this season? What noted sagamore was killed by a shot from the fort in May? What was Mugg's plan for attacking the settlements? What events put an end **to the war? How many** settlements had been destroyed?

CHAPTER XI.

1. Several years before the first Indian war a Frenchman called Baron Castine had come to Biguyduce, on the eastern side of Penobscot Bay, and opened a trade with the natives. He had originally come to Canada in command of a regiment; and when that was disbanded, feeling himself aggrieved, he plunged into the wilderness far away from all his kindred and nation. Here he soon married a daughter of Madockawando, sachem of the Penobscot Indians, and himself became a sagamore of that tribe. Twice during the war the Dutch drove him away from his settlement; and in 1676 the English drove the Dutch away. Then, as the Dutch liked the region so well, and there were too many at New York, Governor Andros settled several families of them about Pemaquid.

2. In 1687 Andros was appointed governor of New England; and, taking a tour eastward in the spring of the next year, he, also, made a descent upon Castine's settlement. He found there a fort, dwelling house, trading house, and chapel; but Castine himself with all his people had cautiously retired to the woods. Like Castine, Andros was a Papist; so he touched nothing in the chapel, which was very richly decorated, but carried away all else that was movable,—furniture, firearms and goods. On his return he met some of the Tarratines at Pemaquid, and told them not to fear or follow the French, offering them his protection. "Tell your friend Castine," said Andros, "if he will render loyal obedience to the King of England, every article taken from him shall be restored." In order to make sure of the good will of the Indians, he made them presents of clothing, and treated them with ardent spirits.

FIRST FRENCH AND INDIAN WAR.

The colonists did not have much confidence in the peace-making of Governor Andros, and wanted to prepare for war; but he would not allow them. A little more than two months later the war broke out.

3. It was about the middle of August, 1688, that the Indians waylayed two men in North Yarmouth as they were out looking for their oxen. Other savages then approached a party who were at work on the garrison house, and soon commenced a fight with them. The English retired to the river, where they were partially protected by the high, steep bank, and made a brave defense until their ammunition was gone. The people living on the other side of the river had become aware of the fight. One of these, Captain Walter Gendell, perceiving that his countrymen had ceased firing, seized a bag of ammunition and hastened in his boat to their relief; but as he reached the shore he was shot fatally by the savages upon the bank. He had just strength enough to throw the ammunition to his friends, and say, "I have lost my life in your service,"—then breathed his last. With this fresh supply the English beat off their foes.

4. At midnight the Indians repaired to Lane's Island, a short distance out in the bay; where they held their horrid carousal, butchering the two men whom they captured before the fight. The settlers considered it imprudent to remain any longer at North Yarmouth, and soon removed to the islands; being fiercely attacked here also, they finally fled to Boston.

Early in August a band of near a hundred Indians, unknown to the inhabitants, hung about the village of Jamestown at Pemaquid, and at length captured a man passing from there toward the Kennebec. Learning from their prisoner the condition of the settlement, they proceeded to make an attack. One party followed Judge Gyles, who, with fourteen men, had gone to work on the farms at the falls three miles above; while the others entered the village, and succeeded in getting possession of several dwellings, and from this shelter made their assault on the fort.

5. At night the garrison were summoned to surrender: the cool reply was, "We are weary and want sleep." They expected, doubtless, that the party from the farms would return as soon as the darkness was sufficient to cover them. The night passed, but there were no tidings of the absent men. Two days more the garrison held out, and all hopes from Gyles and his men were given up. Weems, the commander of the fort, had fallen, and his little company found themselves obliged to yield. They were allowed, according to the stipulations, to retain their arms, and depart in a sloop which lay in the harbor. The Indians then destroyed the fort and houses, and departed with their spoil and prisoners.

6. It was soon after noon of the first day of the siege when about forty warriors led by a chief named Moxus came upon Gyles' party. The savages at once gave them a volley; then with demoniac yells rushed upon them. A few only escaped, the larger number being either killed or captured. Judge Gyles was mortally wounded, and his sons James and John taken prisoners. In answer to a taunt of Moxus, the old man made reply: "I am a dying man, and ask no favors but to pray with my sons." This having been granted, the poor old gentleman was led aside and dispatched with a hatchet. Soon after this the boys met with their mother and two little sisters, also captives; but these were redeemed within a few months. John remained in captivity nine years, enduring many hardships and abuses. At last he was purchased by a French trader, and restored to his surviving relatives. Afterward he served the government as interpreter and as a soldier for many years. His brother fared worse. After three years of captivity he attempted to escape, but was retaken, and put to torture on the heights of Castine.

7. In consequence of the fall of Jamestown at Pemaquid, the coast east of the Kennebec was now deserted; and it remained without inhabitants for nearly thirty years. Governor Andros still pursued his peace policy, setting the Indian captives at liberty, and attempting to treat with the tribes at several times and places. Not meeting with the least success, the governor took a violent turn the other way; and, raising eight hundred men, he sent them eastward to wreak terrific vengeance on the refractory savages. By setting out late in November, they suffered greatly during the whole campaign from cold and exposure; and failed to kill or capture a single savage, or even to see one of them.

In the spring the Massachusetts people revolted against Governor Andros, and sent him a prisoner to England; for King James II., who appointed him to office, had abdicated the throne, and William and Mary were king and queen of England. The government chosen by the people of New England was again revived; Deputy Governor Danforth of Massachusetts being governor of the province of Maine.

8. The new government sent peaceful messages to Baron Castine and to the Tarratines, hoping that these and the well-manned garrisons might prevent the renewal of hostilities. The hope was vain. My readers will remember the affair at Dover in the first war, called "Waldron's Ruse." That evil seed now bore its dreadful fruit. On the evening of the seventh of June, 1689, two squaws came to the garrison at this place, and begged for lodgings. Their request was granted. At the most silent hour of night, when all others in the garrison were sunk in repose, the treacherous squaws opened the gates; and two hundred savages who had been crouching outside, rushed in at the moment. The commander of the garrison was the same Major Waldron who, twelve years before, had broken his faith with the Indians, and made

four hundred of them prisoners. But his fighting days were now well nigh over, for he was eighty years of age. The Indians quickly found the apartment where he and his young wife lay asleep. The door was broken; but, wakened by the noise, the old hero sprang from his bed and drove his assailants back through two rooms with his sword. As he turned back for his pistols he was stunned by a blow upon the head; and in a moment he was in the grasp of the savages. They dragged the white-haired old man into the hall, and bound him into his own arm chair, which they had placed upon the long table. Often for many years past, had he sat at this table as justice of the peace, settling the disputes of both the English and the Indians. It was a wild group that now gathered in that room, beneath the ruddy glare of the torches,—that brave old man, his white hair and loose garments waving in the midnight wind,—and about him the cruel faces of the painted savages.

9. "I cross out my account," cried they, as each of the two hundred in turn drew his knife across the body of their victim. When his flesh was filled with gashes, they cut off his nose and ears, and thrust them into his mouth; and, to close this scene of vengeance, they tumbled the dying man over upon his sword held erect upon the table. So died the noble Major Waldron, and the revenge of the savages was accomplished. Then they set the village on fire, killed twenty-three of the inhabitants, and carried away captive twenty-nine others, whom they sold to the French for servants.

The Indians now ranged through the provinces of Maine and Sagadahock; in the daytime waylaying the traveler upon his road and the husbandman upon his farm, in the darkness prowling about the blockhouses and stockades, to surprise the unwary inmates; so that before the summer of this year was past, all the country eastward of Falmouth was deserted. At the last of August Major Swaine was sent eastward from Massachusetts with near six hundred men; with whom he drove the Indians from Scarborough and Falmouth, though at the expense of nearly half of Capt. Hall's company.

10. About three weeks after, Benjamin Church, who had been very successful in King Philip's war, was put in chief command in Maine. At **Fort Loyal**, on Casco Neck, (Portland) he met a daughter of Major Waldron, who had just been rescued from the Indians by a Dutch privateer, then in the harbor. She told Major Church that the Indians, who had brought her into the bay, numbered near seven hundred; and that several Frenchmen were with them.

Church determined to be ready for them; and at daylight he posted two companies of English and Indians under Captain Hall among some small trees near the head of Back Cove, about half a mile northwest of the village. Before the Major had finished his breakfast Captain Hall discovered the savages on the opposite side of the cove, and immediately crossed and attacked them. Church now learned that nearly the whole stock of bullets was too large for the guns; and he had them cut up into slugs as quickly as possible. Messengers were sent to the cove with a supply for Captain Hall, but the tide was up, and they dared not go over. In this dilemma an Indian of Hall's force, called Captain Lightfoot, threw down his gun and forded the stream to meet the messengers; and taking a knapsack of powder on his head and a kettle of bullets in each hand, he waded safely back; so the companies were enabled to maintain their position.

11. Meantime Major Church had gone up the stream in order to cross the bridge and fall upon the rear of the enemy. Just beyond the bridge the savages had built breastworks of logs and bushes, behind which they were hiding. Church ordered his men to scatter and rush across; but before they could

reach the breastworks every Indian **had fled.** Before Church could find them, those **in front of** Captain Hall had also retreated, **escaping** into a cedar swamp at the west.

After **this repulse the** Indians were not seen again **for the season, though** the forces ranged as far east as **Kennebec;** therefore when winter came **on,** Church **returned to** Massachusetts, leaving sixty of **his soldiers to garrison** Fort Loyal. Through the season of snows **the** Indians were occupied as usual in procuring their necessary food, and the settlers of Maine had rest; but with the opening of the spring the war was renewed with increased vigor.

12. At daybreak of the eighteenth of March, **1690,** the inhabitants **of Newichawannock** (Berwick) were aroused by **the yells of** the savages at their doors. The attacking party consisted of fifty-two French and Indians under M. D'Artel of Canada, **and** Hopehood, a chieftain of the Kennebec. The people defended themselves bravely, but thirty-four were killed, while fifty-four, mostly women and children, fell into the hands of the savages, and were carried into captivity. There were at this time about twenty-seven **houses in the** village, which, together with the barns, mills, **and many** cattle, were destroyed.

13. **In** the May following, four or five hundred **French and** Indians **came** into Casco Bay from the **Kennebec and Penobscot in a** great flotilla of canoes. **Probably they were** alarmed by **the fleet of Commodore Phipps, who** had **just sailed past** this coast **on** his way to Acadia; for they **did not** make their attack at once, but encamped somewhere in Falmouth, ravaging among the cattle of the se:tlers. Meantime a force of one hundred militia from the western towns, together with a part of the garrison of Fort Loyal, were sent out in search of them. While they were absent thirty young volunteers from the garrison ascended Munjoy's Hill, to see if any savages **were lurk**

ing in that vicinity. On this hill, about half a mile from the fort, was a long green lane leading to a house at the edge of the woods. As they passed through this lane they noticed that the cattle were staring strangely at the fence; and, suspecting that Indians might be hidden there, they rushed towards the point with a loud "huzza." Very dearly did they pay for their rashness; for the watchful savages poured upon them a volley which brought fourteen of their number to the ground. The remainder fled to the village, closely pursued by the French and Indians. These assailed with great fury the **houses where the people** had taken refuge, and killed a great many of them; but in the night those who were left escaped to Fort Loyal. The next morning the enemy plundered the village and set it on fire. They next attacked the fort, but the cannon kept them at such a distance that they could do little harm. But they soon found a deep gulley not far away where the guns could not touch them; and here they began to mine toward the garrison. After several days an underground passage had been carried very near the walls of the fort; and its surrender was demanded. The commander was mortally wounded; and, as the enemy offered fair terms and kind treatment, **the garrison** capitulated. Madockawando, the Tarratine, with his son-in-law, Baron Castine, were the chief Indian leaders; and the whole was under the command of a Frenchman named Burneffe. The leaders made little attempt to restrain the savages; and the wounded, together with many of the women and children, were brutally murdered, and the others treated in a most barbarous **manner.**

14. Fort Loyal having fallen, all the garrisons as far west as Wells were now abandoned; and again the Indians ranged victoriously over Maine, making captives and burning buildings in every quarter. Many of these captives were detained for months in the wilderness; made to carry the packs of plunder through

rough woods and tangled swamps, over rugged hills, in rain, snow and cold,—poorly clad and often half starved,—and still urged on by dreadful threats and the points of the Indians' weapons.

What Frenchman lived at Biguyduce at the time of the first Indian war? Who was appointed governor of New England in 1687? In what year did the second Indian war break out? What noble deed was performed at Yarmouth, and by whom? What place east of the Kennebec was captured by the Indians? How long did the region east of Sagadahoc now remain without inhabitants? At the abdication of James II. what happened in New England? Can you give an account of the massacre at Cocheco, or Dover? Who was placed in command of the forces in Maine in 1689? Give an account of his engagement with the Indians at Casco Neck. Who led the attack on Newichawannock the next spring? In what bay did the Indians next appear? Who were the leaders of the attack on Fort Loyal? What was the most easterly settlement now remaining?

CHAPTER XII.

1. Soon after the capture of Fort Loyal the French withdrew from Maine; for Sir William Phipps was giving them employment enough in their own territory.

Phipps was a Maine boy, the son of a gunsmith at Woolwich on the Sheepscot River, where he was born in the year 1650. He had twenty-five brothers and sisters, being himself the tenth child. When he was about sixteen years of age his father died, leaving little else than a small farm for the support of his numerous family. William continued to work on the farm until he was eighteen, when he was apprenticed to a ship carpenter for four years. At the close of his apprenticeship he went to **Boston** and worked at his trade, and learned **to read and write**. A year or two later he married; and soon after this he went back to his old home on the **Sheepscot** River, and built a ship **for some** Boston men. The vessel was completed just as the first Indian war broke out. He had purchased a cargo of lumber to take to Boston when he delivered the ship to its owners; but, seeing the inhabitants in **distress** and in danger of destruction by the savages, he abandoned his lumber **at a great loss**, and, taking the afflicted people on **board, carried them away to** a place of safety.

2. After building vessels **and making** voyages **for several years** he learned that **a Spanish** ship laden **with treasure** had been sunk **near the** Bahama Islands. He told his story to the Duke **of** Albermarle, who aided him in obtaining **one of the** king's ships, in which he sailed in **search of the** wreck. The first voyage was unsuccessful, but on **the second he found it lying under forty or fifty feet of water.** He obtained from it thirty-**four tons of silver, beside gold**, pearls and jewels, **worth in all $1,350,000. His part of this amounted to $70,000.** For the fair manner in which he treated the crew, and the honest division he made of the spoil, the king made him a knight; **and** the Duke and Duchess of Albermarle sent his wife a golden cup worth four thousand dollars, as a special mark of esteem.

At home, when the expedition against Acadia was planned, he **was** thought to be the fittest person to command it; and so he was made commodore. He sailed from Boston early in May, 1690, with a frigate of forty guns and eight other vessels. He took possession of the country, captured the authorities, and, at the close of the same month, returned to Boston, bringing sufficient of the enemy's merchandise **to** pay **the** expense of the expedition.

3. The success of Phipps encouraged the colonists

to send an expedition against Canada, which started early in the next August—the sea forces only being under his command. The land forces were to march from New York by way of Lake Champlain, and meet the fleet on the St. Lawrence. But the army met with discouragements and turned back; and Phipps, not receiving the promised aid from England, was repulsed before the strong fortifications of Quebec. On his return a great storm wrecked many of the vessels, and scattered the remainder so that they came into Boston one by one, some of them not arriving for nearly a month after. The colonies had counted on success, and had expected the spoils to pay the expense, as before; and there was no money in the treasury to pay the men, and very little specie among the inhabitants.

Then for the first time in America, paper money was contrived. In December the General Court of Massachusetts issued what were called "Bills of Credit," with which the public debts were paid. It soon depreciated so that one dollar in specie was worth four dollars in bills; but they afterward increased in value until that they were worth as much as the coin.

4. A few weeks after Phipps set out for the St. Lawrence Major Church was sent again into Maine. He landed at Maquoit, and marched directly to the falls at Pejepscot (Brunswick). Not finding any Indians, he continued up the river. A little past noon of the next day he came in sight of the cataract at a place called by the Indians *Amityonpontook*, now known as Lewiston Falls. Before they came to the Little Androscoggin, which was still between them and the Indian fort, they were discovered by a savage near the river. In order to surprise the Indians, Church was obliged to act with all possible speed; and, while one company staid with the baggage, the other two, with Church at their head, waded the

river, and ran swiftly towards the fort. But the Indian they had seen was there before them; and just as they burst in the south gate the savages rushed out at the north, and retreated down the hill to the large river. But Church's men had cut them off from their canoes; and some of them were shot in the water, while only one gained the opposite bank—for the current here was very strong, it being just below the falls. The larger number of Indians, however, had run under the cataract, and hid in the rocky caverns behind the falling waters, and thus escaped. Several prisoners were taken at the fort, among whom were the wives and children of Worumbee, the sachem of the region, and of Kancamagus, a Pennacook chieftain. "Tell the sagamores," said Church, as he departed, "that they may find their wives and children at Wells."

5. On his return he had a skirmish with a body of savages at the mouth of the Saco, and another at Cape Elizabeth,—in both of which the enemy was beaten. In October these chiefs with several other Indians, came to Wells, and were much gratified to receive again their wives and children.

"The French have made fools of us," said they; "we will go to war against you no more; we are ready to meet your head men at any time and place you appoint, and enter into a treaty."

Accordingly, on the last of November, six sagamores met the commissioners at Sagadahock, where they surrendered a few prisoners and signed a truce. The truce was to continue until the next May, when they were to bring the remaining prisoners to Wells, and make a lasting peace.

6. Yet it was a dismal winter to the people of Maine; for they had known too much of Indian treachery to feel at ease respecting the next season. Every town east of Wells had been destroyed; and only the settlements of Wells, York, Kittery and the

Isles of Shoals now remained. The settlement in Wells was near the beach, where there were several houses of hewn timber, with flankers and watch towers—a little village of block houses. In some of these the upper story was largest, projecting over the lower story; while others had the upper story turned so that the corners projected beyond the sides of the lower story. This was for the purpose of firing down upon assailants, if they should come close to the building. The sides were also pierced with long, narrow openings for the guns.

7. In May, 1691, the time set for the treaty, Mr. Danforth, President of the province, with several other members of the government, came to Wells to meet the Indians. None appeared; but Captain Converse found several lurking in the neighborhood, and brought them in. When asked why the sagamores were not present according to promise, their answer was, "We no remember the time. But still we now give up two captives; and we promise, certain, to bring the rest in ten days." They departed, and though the officers waited, nothing more was seen of them.

On the ninth of June thirty-five soldiers came to reinforce the garrison at Wells; and in half an hour after their arrival the place was attacked by two hundred Indians under the famous Moxus. Being repulsed here they went to Cape Neddock, in York, where they killed the crew of a vessel, and burned the houses.

8. Two or three weeks later, four companies under Captain King started in search of the savages, meeting them at Maquoit Bay, in Brunswick, where he had a sharp skirmish. During the remainder of the season the Indians shunned to meet the English forces, but hung about the coast and remaining villages, burning exposed buildings, and shooting down or taking captive lone men, women and children.

Early in the morning of February fifth, 1692, the inhabitants of York, while yet in their beds, heard the report of a gun. It was the Indians' signal of attack. Between two and three hundred savages, led by Frenchmen, instantly fell upon the unarmed settlers; and in half of an hour, more than a hundred and sixty of the inhabitants were helpless captives, or lay bleeding on the cold snow. There were four strongly fortified houses in the settlement, and the people who found shelter in these alone escaped; and when the savages demanded a surrender, their answer was, "Never, till we have shed the last drop of blood."

GARRISON HOUSE AT YORK, BUILT ABOUT 1645.

9. So after plundering and setting fire to the remaining houses the Indians went away, carrying with them nearly a hundred prisoners. The sufferings of these from hunger, cold and fatigue must have been

very great; yet there was one pleasant incident in this terrible affair. In Captain King's expedition from York eastward in the summer previous he left unharmed four or five Indian women and their children whom he found at Pejepscot; and for this the savages now sent back to the garrison several elderly women and young children.

The garrison at Wells at this time consisted of only fifteen soldiers under Captain Converse; and on the ninth of June two sloops came in with supplies and a reinforcement. About an hour after their arrival the cattle ran in from the pastures, frightened and bleeding. By this the settlers knew that there were Indians in the vicinity, and at once made all possible preparations for safety. The next morning at daybreak five hundred French and Indians appeared before the garrison. They were led by Madockawando, Egeremet, Moxus, Worumbee, and other sagamores, together with Labrocree, a French officer; all being under the command of M. Portneuf, who had been the leader at the destruction of Falmouth.

10. They learned from a prisoner captured outside of the fort, that it contained only thirty soldiers; and, being confident of success, they apportioned among themselves the prisoners whom they expected soon to have. Then with hideous shouts, they commenced an attack, which was continued all day; but still the garrison held out. Meantime they constructed a rough breastwork of timber and hay, from which they fired upon the vessels; setting them on fire several times with their fire arrows. But the crews put out the flames with wet mops on long poles; and their bullets pierced through the breastwork so often that the enemy was forced to leave it. Then they built a shot-proof breastwork on wheels, and rolled it towards the shore. One wheel sunk in the soft earth, and as a Frenchman applied his shoulder to lift it out a shot from the vessel brought him down; then another who

took his place shared the same fate, and this, too, **was** abandoned.

11. A scout of six men had been sent out to look for Indians only a few hours before they appeared. The next morning after the attack these approached the fort just at daylight, on their return. The corporal, discovering a party of Indians close by, cried out, "Captain Converse, wheel your men round the hill, and these few dogs are ours." The savages, thinking that Converse was at their heels, fled in great haste; and the scout got safely into the fort.

The enemy, probably ashamed of this flight, **soon** after advanced in full force **to attack** the fort. One of the soldiers now sighingly suggested a surrender.

"Utter the word again," said Converse, "and you are a dead man. All lie close; fire not a gun until it will do execution."

12. The enemy came up firmly, and, arriving **within** range, gave three wild shouts, then poured a volley upon the fort. Those in **the garrison exerted** themselves to the **utmost,—even the** women bringing ammunition, and the brands to discharge their little cannon; and for a few moments the walls blazed with fire from **the muskets and cannon, causing the enemy** to retreat in disorder with great loss.

Failing to prevail against the vessels by means of breastworks, the French and Indians now constructed a raft; and heaping it high with combustibles, they set it on fire, and pushed it off. The tide bore the burning mass directly toward the vessels; but these, having been lashed together for better defense, could not be **moved out** of the way, and their destruction seemed inevitable. But a kind Providence, just at the **critical moment,** sent **a breeze, and drove** the raft away **to the opposite shore, where** it burned harmlessly out.

13. The enemy before **the fort now** sent a flag of truce, demanding a **surrender and inquiring** what terms were desired.

"I want nothing but men to fight," replied Captain Converse.

"Then if you, Converse, are so stout, why don't you come out and fight in the field like a man, and not stay in a garrison like a squaw?" said one of the Indians.

"What fools are you? Think you my thirty are a match for your five hundred? Come upon the plains with only thirty, and I'm ready for you."

"No, no; we think English fashion—you kill me, me kill you—all one fool. Not so; better lie somewhere and shoot 'em Englishmen when he no see;— that's the best soldier."

14. The Indian bearing the flag threw it down and ran away; and the enemy began to fire again, keeping up a scattering discharge until midnight. In the morning they were gone. They had not killed a man in the garrison, and but one on board of the vessels. In revenge for the death of Labrocree, one of their leaders, they put their only captive to torture. They scalped him, slit his hands between the fingers, and his feet between the toes, cut deep gashes in his body, and stuck the gaping wounds full of lighted torches; then they left him to die by degrees.

15. In the spring of 1692 the king issued a new charter for Massachusetts and Maine, even including Acadia; and under it appointed Sir William Phipps as governor. The new ruler had a warm regard for his native place, and was resolved that it should be better defended than formerly; therefore in the autumn of the same year he built a great stone fort at Pemaquid. While this was in process of construction the brave Church, now colonel, with one company of the men, ascended the Penobscot again in search of the natives. He came to Seven-hundred-acre Island, near which they dwelt in large numbers; but they discovered his approach and escaped in their canoes. Yet he captured a few of them, and secured quantities of corn, together with moose and beaver skins.

16. He soon after ascended the Kennebec, where he had a smart fight not far from Swan Island. Here a part of the Indians were driven into the woods, while others fled in their canoes up the river to their fort at Teconnet, in the present town of Winslow. Church followed them; but as soon as he was discerned approaching, the savages set fire to their huts and ran away into the forests. This exploit closed Church's third expedition eastward.

In the autumn M. Iberville, then newly made French commander in Acadia, came to Pemaquid with a body of French and Indians to capture the place; but when he saw how strong the fort was, he gave up the project in despair — while the savages stamped the ground in rage.

17. The next spring the intrepid Captain Converse was made major; and the garrisons of Maine and Sagadahock, together with three hundred and fifty new levies, were put under his command. He built a stone fort at Saco, and hunted the Indians to the mountains, scouting as far east as the Penobscot. The Indians were also in fear of an incursion of the Mohawks, while the French had been obliged to leave them in order to defend their own settlements; therefore early in August, 1693, thirteen sagamores, representing all the tribes from Saco to St. Croix, came to Pemaquid and made a treaty of peace. They agreed to restore all their captives without ransom, to buy their supplies at the English trading houses, and gave up all claims to the possessions of the English inhabitants. But they were immediately dissuaded by the French from surrendering the prisoners and from carrying the treaty into effect in other respects.

18. A jesuit priest now resided in each of the four principal native settlements in Maine; and these were ever the ready agents of the French government in their intrigues. Very soon the Indians were again engaged in open hostilities; and within a few weeks

they made another descent upon **Cocheco, which was now the second time destroyed.** They continued to kill, capture and burn; **and** though strenuous efforts were made to **obtain a new** treaty, every attempt proved a **failure.** In February, 1696, the sagamores Egeremet, **Toxus and** Abenquid, with a number **of their followers,** came into the fort at Pemaquid to procure **an exchange** of prisoners; but by order of **Captain Chubb, the** commander, they were treacherously attacked by the garrison, and two of the chiefs with several of their followers killed, and others thrust into confinement; only Toxus and a few others of the most athletic escaping. This was in retaliation for an attack upon a party of his soldiers in the neighborhood **the autumn** before, by which **four of them were** killed **and six wounded.** I am sorry to say that even the Puritans **at this** period **seem to have** imbibed somewhat of the brutality **of the savages, for** the General Court offered a bounty of fifty pounds each for Indian scalps, and the same for captive squaws and children. Yet we must remember that there was no **other** convenient way for the soldiers to prove **the** number they had killed in order to get their **bounty. Certainly** war is a brutalizing occupation.

19. **In July, 1696,** Iberville came against Pemaquid **with three** ships of war, two companies of French **soldiers, and two hundred** and fifty Indians in canoes. On **the way he had met and beaten an** English armament **in the Bay of Fundy; and he now confidently** demanded **the surrender of the fortress.**

"I shall not **give up the** fort though the sea be covered with French vessels, and **the** land with wild Indians," replied Captain Chubb, pompously.

This fort, you remember, was the one built by Governor Phipps, and was of stone, very large and strong **for those** days. It mounted fifteen heavy guns, and **was** garrisoned by ninety-five soldiers,—having also an abundance of arms, ammunition and provisions; so that the commander thought he was much more than a match for the enemy. A rattling fire of musketry was kept up until dark; but during the night the French landed some cannon and mortars on the other side of the little bay. By the next afternoon they had them in position, and threw several bombs into the fort. This was something Captain Chubb had not considered; and it frightened him and his garrison so much that he surrendered at once—only stipulating for a safe passage to Boston. There Chubb was tried by a court martial; and being found guilty of cowardice, lost his commission. Two years later the **Indians found out his residence, and** killed him, in **revenge** for his treachery toward the flag of truce.

20. A squadron of armed vessels was sent by the colonies in pursuit of Iberville's fleet, but it was too late; and they captured only an officer and twenty soldiers, who had lingered behind in a shallop. At the last of August Colonel Church again went **eastward**, ascending the Penobscot as far as Oldtown, **but without** meeting any large number of Indians. **He** also visited the Bay of Fundy, where he took valuable spoil**; for this** region had **now** been **recovered by the** French.

The next year **Major** March was sent eastward **with five** hundred men to chastise the **Indians. On the** ninth of September, as his forces were landing at Damariscotta, the Indians rushed out from an ambush, and giving the war-whoop, poured a fearful volley of bullets upon the troops. The English instantly rallied and answered with a well-aimed **fire**, then charged **with bayonets; and the savages ran** away, leaving their dead upon the field.

21. **In December, 1697, news came that** peace had **been** made between England and **France** by the treaty **of** Ryswick; and this long **war** drew to a close.

Peace was not definitely settled with the Indians until January, 1699, when a treaty was made at **Mare**

Point, in Brunswick. This was the second Indian war, sometimes called the old French and Indian war, and Baron Castine's war; also William and Mary's war, from having occurred during their reign. It had lasted above ten years, and in that time about four hundred and fifty English had fallen, and two hundred and fifty been carried into captivity.

What noted man was born in Woolwich? For what was he knighted? What naval expedition did he command? In what year did Major Church make his famous expedition up the Androscoggin? What place was attacked soon after the time set for the treaty? Describe the disastrous attack upon York. Describe the attack on Wells the next year. Whom did the king appoint governor of New England in 1692? What did Governor Phipps do for the protection of his native region? Where did Major Church meet the Indians at this time? Who prevented the Indians from carrying out the provisions of the treaty made at Pemaquid? Did Iberville's second expedition against Pemaquid meet with success? What happened at Damariscotta the next year? What treaty operated to close this war? How long had the war lasted? How many English had fallen? How many had been carried into captivity?

CHAPTER XIII.

1. While the people of Maine were suffering from the attacks of the French and Indians, those of Massachusetts were afflicted by **the** witchcraft delusion, in which many good, **as well as** some bad people were put to death. About the year 1650 two or three persons in Massachusetts professed themselves witches, and were therefore hanged. I suppose they had some nervous disorder, or perhaps mesmerism and clairvoyance were **at the** bottom of much of this mischief. More cases of the kind happened in 1688; but it was not until the spring of 1692 that the delusion came on, which spread like a contagious disease all through the towns, and proved such a terrible calamity. Governor Phipps had not meddled with the matter, though his friend, Rev. Cotton Mather, was among the **foremost** in these prosecutions; but while **the governor was away in** Maine, his **kind-hearted wife signed an order for the release** of a lady who was in prison **for witchcraft. Then** Mistress **Phipps** also was accused of being **a witch.** This was the situation of things when the governor returned. It opened his eyes; and he soon put a stop to the terrible work.

2. Phipps soon after went to England, where he died in 1694; the Earl of Bellamont being **his successor.** The Earl had for some time been governor of New **York,** and his administration in New England also proved quite popular. He did much service to our fishermen by destroying or driving off the petty pirates **that preyed upon them.** It was this governor who commissioned **the notorious** Captain Kidd to cruise against pirates; but when Kidd himself turned pirate the Earl was the first to proceed against him.

The Earl of Bellamont was **succeeded in 1703 by** Joseph Dudley, a native **of** Massachusetts. Another war had now **arisen between** England **and** France; and Governor Dudley, wishing to keep the Indians from **joining the** French, invited them to meet him at **Casco Neck. On** the twentieth **of** June, **1703, the day** appointed for the **meeting,** the **governor was on** the spot with a retinue of members of the legislature, and a guard of soldiers; and around them gathered the delegates of five native tribes. The Pennacooks from New Hampshire, and the Sokokis from the borders of Lake Sebago and the head waters of the Saco and Ossipee rivers, streamed out of the woods, radiant in war paint and feathers; the **Canibas from** Sagadahock, Teconnet and Norridgewock, and the **Tarratines** from lordly Penobscot, were there with **scarlet robes and** shining weapons; while two hundred and fifty Androscoggins glided over the bay in a flotilla of sixty-five canoes. In the midst of this savage concourse a tent was spread, where the governor and his attendants and the sachems and sagamores made their talk.

3. The Indians seemed desirous **of** delaying **the** interview; and the English, suspicious **of** their intentions, scattered themselves among the savages for **greater security.** When all were seated the governor **stood up, and said to** the chiefs, "I have come to you **commissioned by** the great and good queen of England. I would esteem you all as brothers and friends. **Yes, it is even** my wish to reconcile every difficulty that has happened since the last treaty." After a few minutes of silence one of the chiefs named Captain Simmo made this reply:—"We thank you, **good** brother, for coming so far to talk with us. It is a great favor. The clouds fly and darken, but we still sing with love the songs of peace. Believe my words: so far as the sun is above the earth are our thoughts from war, or the least rupture between us."

4. Then the chiefs presented the governor with a belt of wampum, and the governor made them several **handsome** presents in return. The company then left the tents and visited two tall heaps of stones made at a former **treaty, to** which the Indians had given the significant name, *Two Brothers.* Other rocks were now added to the heaps, while the Indians made over them the most solemn protestations of friendship. The day closed by a grand discharge of musketry, the Indians firing first. It was now seen that their guns were loaded with bullets; showing that they, too, had prepared themselves against a **surprise.**

Many inhabitants of Maine, **since the news of another war came,** had decided **to** remove to **safer regions;** but, reassured by this treaty, they now concluded to remain; while some from the older colonies southward, attracted by the excellent forests and the fertile soil, began to make preparations to settle in the province.

5. It afterward became known **that** three days **after the treaty a** body of French **joined** the **natives, —which explained clearly** why some of the Indians **wished to delay the talk.** They were too late to prevent the making **of the** treaty, but **not too** late for **its** breaking; and within two months of Captain Simmo's sounding speech, the wampum pledge, and the pretty allegory of the "Two Brothers," these same tribes were in the full tide of war. Yet there had already been opportunity for a party of English to commit an outrage at Penobscot. Baron Castine had gone back to France, and his son known as "Castine, the younger," **succeeded to the** establishment at Bignyduce. A **lawless band, visiting the place under** the mask of **friendship, gained access to the** premises, and robbed **the unsuspecting half-breed** of all his most valuable **goods.**

6. Baron Castine, you remember, married the daughter of Madockawando, sachem of the Tarratines,

and, consequently, was himself a sachem **after the death of his father-in-law.** When the Baron returned to his native country, **his son** succeeded to the chieftainship; **and at** his father's death he became a baron **of France. He was also** a military officer under **the king, and had a handsome uniform; but he** seldom **wore it,** preferring to appear in the simple **dress of** his **tribe.** He might have complained to the king **of the** outrage which had been committed upon him, and demanded French troops to enable him to obtain satisfaction of the English; or he might have roused his tribe to action to avenge **his** injuries; but instead of **this** the magnanimous chief only expostulated with the Massachusetts rulers about the injustice of his treatment. The **act was regarded by the government as base treachery; and the authorities promised** to punish **the offenders and to** make ample restitution. Castine, **the younger, was** ever the friend of peace; and though a portion **of the** Tarratines, urged by the French, engaged in hostilities against the English, they did so without his consent. We must here **dismiss young Castine** for the present, but he **will again appear in this history.**

What delusion occurred in **New** England during the second Indian war? What opened the **eyes of** Governor Phipps in regard **to the delusion?** Who succeeded Phipps as governor of New England? **What were the most** noted occurrences during the administration of the Earl of **Bellamont?** What **war broke out in 1703? What tribes engaged in the treaty?** With what ceremonies did **the treaty conclude?** How **soon after** this did the war **break out? What** outrage **was** perpetrated just before? What **can you relate of** Castine, the younger?

CHAPTER XIV.

In August, 1703, the war with the French **and Indians** called Queen Anne's war commenced. **Six or seven large parties of the enemy fell at once upon Wells, Cape Porpoise (Kennebunkport), Saco, Scarborough, Spurwink and Purpooduck in Cape Elizabeth, and Casco Neck, now Portland.** In **this** attack Wells **lost thirty-nine** killed **and taken captive,** while **Cape Porpoise** was wholly **destroyed.** The garrison at Winter Harbor was overpowered by numbers, but the fort at Saco was able successfully to resist the attack. At Scarborough, just as the garrison was almost exhausted, a reinforcement arrived; and the savages **withdrew,** having already suffered **severely. At Spurwink** twenty-two of the settlers **were killed or** taken **captive.** Purpooduck **had no garrison, and there** was **not a man at** home **when the attack was made.** Only eight persons were carried away prisoners, twenty-five being butchered on the spot.

2. The first knowledge the garrison at **Casco Neck** had that Indians were in the vicinity, was the approach of a small party of them led by Moxus, Wanangonet and Assacombuit. They held out their empty hands to show that they were unarmed, then sent a flag of truce to the fort to invite the commander to an interview; pretending that **they** bore an important message. Captain March, the commander, went out with **two old men to** meet them. At the first **word uttered every Indian drew a hatchet from under his mantle, and rushed upon them, killing the two old men** at once**; but** March, being **a man of** great courage and strength, wrested a hatchet from **an** Indian, with which he parried the blows of the others. In a few

minutes a party from the **fort reached the spot, and the savages ran away,** leaving Captain March **unharmed.** The foe seemed quite disconcerted by the failure of their **plot to kill or** capture the commander of the **fort; yet they still** continued in the neighborhood, **burning houses and** butchering cattle. On the return **of the other parties** from their work of destruction, **they gathered at** Falmouth; and the attack **on Fort Loyal commenced.** They had captured three small **vessels in** the harbor, and were attempting to undermine **the** fort as before, when fortunately Captain Southwick arrived in an armed galley. He **at once** retook the vessels, and scattered the Indians in their **two** hundred birchen canoes, like **leaves before the wind.**

3. The attack **on the** settlements **so soon after the treaty,** took them **by surprise, and** they **suffered accordingly,** more than **one hundred and** fifty **persons having** been killed within **a few days.** A troop of horse was **now** stationed at Portsmouth, and another in Wells, ready to move at a moment's notice wherever the savages might appear; while a force of three **hundred and sixty** men marched for Pigwacket **(Fryeburg) and another** party to the Ossipee Ponds **in New Hampshire, to** assail the savages at their headquarters. **Still large** numbers **of** Indians hung about the coast, **capturing** boats and small vessels, burning houses, **butchering cattle, and** murdering and carrying **away captives men, women and children.**

One morning a party of twenty men started out **from** the garrison at the Neck in Scarborough to collect and drive in the cattle which had been left to feed where they liked through the summer. It was supposed that the Indians had all left the vicinity, and **the** party went on in utter carelessness. Their leader, Richard Hunniwell, had no arms whatever except a **pistol.** Soon after they left the garrison **one** of **his companions asking** him why he had not taken his gun, he jocosely replied, that if a gun was needed he might take it from the first person killed. They little thought as they approached the western end of Great Pond that in the alder thicket beside it two **hundred** Indians were hidden! But they were there; and as the unsuspecting settlers passed by, the Indians took deliberate aim, and nineteen of the party fell before that fatal discharge. One alone escaped to the garrison to tell the dreadful story.

4. The men who came to bury the bodies found that of Hunniwell horribly mangled. The savages had in this way glutted their vengeance on the man they so much hated and feared; for he had killed a great number of their people. His wife and child had some years before been murdered by them, kindling in his mind such enduring hatred that he would kill an Indian wherever he met him, in war or peace. On one occasion he entered a house where two of them were warming at the fire. He could not keep quiet, but continued to pace the floor; for his murdered wife and babe seemed before his eyes. Two guns stood in a corner of the room; and he took up one of them, and putting it to his shoulder, moved it from side to side, as if taking aim at birds on the wing. Presently the Indians' heads came in range, and he fired and killed them both.

Soon after the slaughter in Scarborough, the savages attacked Berwick, but were repulsed with considerable loss. Late in the season, Captain March with three hundred men penetrated the wilderness to the Indian stronghold at Pigwacket, where he made the first captures of this war, killing six of the enemy and taking prisoners six more. During the winter several private parties in Western Maine went out on snow shoes after Indians, but very few were taken. The Sokokis had gone far up into New Hampshire; from whence in February they fell upon Deerfield and other of the outermost settlements in Massachusetts.

5. The following spring the farmers **dared not go into their fields to plant**, and the only cultivated places were the lands immediately around the garrisons. As Berwick was **an** important point, ninety-five Pequods and Mohegans **from Connecticut were** placed there for its protection. The Maine Indians were at **first somewhat frightened by** these, but they soon became **as bold as ever**.

In May some French privateers appeared upon **the coast;** and the government again sent Colonel Church **eastward** with a force of five hundred and fifty men in fourteen transports, having also thirty-six whaleboats **and a** scout shallop. Ascending the Penobscot, he captured several French and Indians, among whom **was** the **wife of** Castine, **the** younger, with her children. He next visited Passamaquoddy Bay, where he captured **Gourdon** and Sharkee, two French officers **who had** married Indian **wives; and** who were at this time engaged in raising a party of savages to go against the settlements.

From here Church proceeded with his flotilla **to the Bay** of Fundy, where he destroyed several villages of the French. Port Royal was found **too strong to be assailed** successfully; so he returned without attacking it, **having** taken an hundred prisoners and much spoil, **and lost only six men.**

6. The Indians committed few depredations on the **settlements** during the remainder of the season; for Church's expedition **had driven them** away **from** the **coast to their** winter fastnesses at the head of the **rivers.** In the midst of the winter a force of two hundred and seventy men under Capt. Hilton was sent against Norridgewock. The snow was four feet deep, and the troops were obliged to travel almost the whole distance on snow shoes. But the Indians discovered **their** approach, and when the force arrived they found **the** village deserted. So they turned back again; and after enduring many hardships, reached their starting

point without loss ; yet having accomplished **nothing** except the **burning of the** Indian village.

Through the summer and autumn of the next year [1705] the **French privateers still haunted our coast,** taking many of **our** vessels ; while the Indians were continually in ambush **about** the settlement, where they were too successful in killing and capturing **the** poor, distressed inhabitants.

Thus the war continued for two years more ; **the** savages lurking **about,** killing and capturing a **few unwary persons, and** keeping the **settlers** from **working** their farms.

7. In January **of 1707 Colonel Hilton marched** toward Casco in search of a body of **Indians who had been** seen about the settlement. Striking a trail, they soon came upon four **warriors, and a** squaw with her pappoose. The squaw **in her** fright told where eighteen other Indians lay asleep ; and Hilton with his men, coming upon them suddenly**, killed or captured every one.**

In the summer another expedition consisting of one thousand men under **Colonel March** was sent against **Acadia in the** expectation **of subduing it to the** English. He was unsuccessful, and **Maine soon** had to suffer in consequence ; for the triumph of the **French** encouraged **the** Indians to renewed depredations. Yet they met with no very brilliant success. The most noted engagement of the year was at Winter Harbor, where one hundred and fifty Indians in fifty canoes, attacked two sail boats in which were eight men belonging in the garrison and settlement. After a fight of **three** hours the Indians succeeded in **capturing one boat, and killing one man ;** but they **lost nine of their own men and had several others wounded.**

In the **two following years very little** damage **was** done by the Indians, except in **hindering the cultivation of the land,** lumbering and other **industrial operations.** Steps were taken on both sides **to bring about** a peace, yet no treaty was made; for the Indians paid little attention to treaty obligations, if inclined to war.

8. In the spring of 1710, a fleet with a regiment of mariners arrived from England to aid in the conquest of Acadia. To these were joined regiments of troops from New England, the whole force being under the command of General Nicholson. The province was unable to withstand such an armament as this; and, after one day's bombardment, Port Royal surrendered, and Subercase, the French governor, yielded up his province. By this easy victory the whole of Acadia fell into the hands of the English, ever after to remain in their possession as New Scotland; being divided, many years later, into the provinces of New Brunswick and Nova Scotia. Major Livingston, a brave young officer, was at once sent to Canada to inform the governor of that country of the English possession of Acadia, and that the inhabitants were accounted prisoners of war, and would be treated as such unless the French ceased to incite the savages to hostilities against the English. Livingston journeyed by the way of the Penobscot, and thence by land through the unbroken wilderness to the St. Lawrence. With him went that friend of peace, Castine, the younger, to guard him against savage rage, and to procure guides and supplies.

Yet neither this event, nor the desire of some of their chiefs for peace, prevented large numbers of the Indians from continuing their treacherous warfare. Therefore on his way home from the conquest of Acadia, Colonel Walton with one hundred and seventy men scoured the coast in search of savages. At Sagadahock he captured a sagamore and his family and some of his tribe. Soon after, another message came from the Indians, desiring peace; yet parties of them still continued to maraud. The next year twenty-six persons were killed in Maine, by attacking solitary families, or waylaying venturesome travelers. Their last hostile act in this war was in the autumn of 1712, at Wells.

9. On that day a joyous company were gathered at the home of Captain Wheelwright, to witness the wedding of his daughter with young Plaisted of Portsmouth. The ceremony was over, guests made their gratulations, and were preparing to depart, when it was found that two of the horses were missing. Several persons started in search of them, but, going near the place where the Indians were in ambush, two of them were shot down and others made prisoners. The report of the guns informed the neighborhood of the presence of Indians; and a dozen men started across lots from the garrison to intercept the enemy, while Captains Lane, Robinson and Hurd, with the bridegroom and several others, vaulted upon the remaining steeds and galloped eagerly to the rescue. In a few minutes these, also, fell into an ambush. Captain Robinson was killed outright, and the others were unhorsed; but every one of them, except the now unhappy bridegroom succeeded in escaping. In the mansion where a few moments before, peace and happiness had reigned supreme, were now consternation and rage, the wailing of widowed women, and the anguish of the lovely bride. After a few days, however, the bridegroom regained his liberty; but it cost his father three hundred pounds, as a ransom.

10. In 1713, peace was made between England and France, by the celebrated treaty of Utrecht; and now no longer incited and aided by the French, the Indians sought peace in earnest. Accordingly on the eleventh of July, the governor, with twenty councilors and many other gentlemen, met the delegates of the hostile tribes at Portsmouth in New Hampshire. The Indians acknowledged their offence, and begged for the pardon and favor of the English. Then a written treaty was made, by which the Indians agreed to yield

to the English settlers all the lands occupied by them, and to observe the regulations which had been made by former treaties in regard to trading, hunting and fishing. Each sagamore signed the document by making the figure of the quadruped, bird or fish, which was the totem of his family.

When the ceremonies were over, some of the authorities went to Casco Bay, where they found Moxus, a Penobscot sagamore, with a large body of Indians waiting to learn about the treaty. It was read aloud to them by the English, and explained by the interpreters; and when the reading was finished the Indians huzzaed in approval. Then the English authorities distributed to them the usual presents. The next day Moxus came to the English desiring more ; saying that the young Indians had stolen the presents away. This was very strange ; for the Indians, especially the younger men, always treat their sagamores with the greatest respect. Yet Moxus did not sign the treaty, though he pretended to be chief sagamore of the tribes from Penobscot to St. Croix ; but the English knew him to be a very subtle Indian, and did not believe his statements at all.

Upon what places did the Indians make a simultaneous attack? What treacherous attempt did they make at Fort Loyal? What afterward happened at Scarborough? Who were the next year stationed for the defense of Berwick? Where was Colonel Church sent the next year? Where was Capt. Hilton sent the next winter? What was done by the French and Indians in the two years following? What was the result of Colonel March's expedition against Acadia? Who commanded the expedition against Acadia in 1710? How long thereafter did the country remain in possession of the English?

CHAPTER XV.

1. As soon as Queen Anne's war was over there was a rush of settlers to Maine; and mills began to be built and villages to spring up all along the coast from Piscataqua to Penobscot. This was very pleasing to the English; but the Indians watched with jealousy the damming up of the rivers and the destruction of the woods, by which their hunting and fishing grounds were continually narrowed. The French Jesuits, who resided among the natives, were ever watchful for the interests of France, and used every occasion to embitter the minds of Indians against the English. The natives did not understand the nature of the writings called "deeds," believing that their forefathers, in giving them, had intended only to convey the use of the lands during their own lifetime; therefore the Jesuits easily persuaded them that every new fort, mill, or dwelling was an intrusion upon their rights.

2. An English society for the education of the heathen had before attempted to give the Indians some religious instruction; and the General Court of Massachusetts now voted to pay seven hundred and fifty dollars annually for missions to the Indians, with board and lodging for the missionaries. So there were at various times missionaries on the Androscoggin river at Brunswick, at Fort Halifax on the Kennebec, at St. Georges and Penobscot; while provision was also made for a school master to reside at Brunswick, and fifty dollars were voted for books and rewards for the young Indians who might become his pupils. It was thought best as a matter of duty to remove, if possible, the false teaching of the Jesuits; and it was also believed that this would be the best

method of pacifying the Indians. According to Bomazeen, a sachem of Norridgewock, the priest of that place had instructed the Indians that "the Virgin Mary was a French lady, and that her son, Jesus Christ, was murdered by the English, but had since risen and gone to Heaven; and that all who would gain his favor must avenge his blood." Perhaps the wily chief spoke falsely, but the English believed him.

3. This provision for missionaries was made in 1717; and the next year Governor Shute with his council met the natives at Arrowsic. The governor presented the sagamores with an English Bible, and another translated into the Indian tongue, telling them that they contained the true religion.

"All people love their own ministers," said the chief speaker, in reply. "Your bibles we do not care to keep. God has given us teaching, and if we go from that we offend God."

It was found that they could not be moved from their devotion to the Jesuits; and the remainder of the discussions was on the land rights of the English and Indians. A part of the Indian talk made on this occasion was nearly as follows:—

4. "Indians and white men have one Great Father. He has given every tribe of us a goodly river, which yields us fine salmon and other fish. The borders of our rivers are wide and pleasant. Here, from ancient time, our people have hunted the bear, the moose and the beaver. It is our own country, where our fathers died, where ourselves and our children were born;— we cannot leave it. The Indian has rights and loves good as well as the Englishman;—yes, we have a sense, too, of what is kind and great. When you first came over the waters of the morning we took you into our arms. We thought you children of the sun, and we fed you with our best meat. Never went a white man cold and starving from the cabin of an Indian. Do we not speak truth? But you have returned us

evil for good. You put the burning cup to our lips; it filled our veins with poison; it wasted the pride of our strength. Ay, and when the drunken fit was on us, you took advantage—you made gains of us. You made our beaver cheap, then you paid us in watered rum and trifles. We shed your blood; we avenged your affronts. Then you promised us equal trade and good commodities. Have Christian Englishmen lived up to their engagements?

They asked leave of our fathers to live in **the land as** brothers. It was freely granted. The **earth is for the** life **and the** range of man. **We are told that our** country, spreading far away from **the sea, is** passing **away to** you forever,—perhaps for nothing, **because of the** names and seals of our sagamores. Such deeds **be** far from them. They never turned their children from their homes to suffer. Their hearts were too full of love and kindness,—their souls were too great. Whither shall we **go**? There is no land so much our **own,—none** can be half so dear to us. Why **should we flee before our destroyers?** We fear them not. Sooner, far, will we sing the war song, and again light up our council fires. So shall the great spirits of our sires own their sons."

5. Yet the old men and many others were opposed to war at this time; for they feared to be driven away from their cornfields and their pleasant villages, to undergo the sufferings of a wandering life. So they promised to inquire into the injuries committed by their brethren, and presented the English with a lot of beaver skins, as a pledge of their fidelity. They also placed four young Indians **in their hands to** be **held as hostages** for the good **behavior of the tribes; and these were** taken to Boston **and educated.**

Three years later ninety **canoes** of Indians came early in the month of August to Sagadahock. They bore the French flag, and were well armed and clad. There were also several Frenchmen with them, among whom were Castine, the younger, and the Jesuit, Ralle. The leaders of this company visited Arrowsic and delivered to Captain Penhallow, in the name of the tribes, a message warning the settlers on that river that if they did not remove in three weeks the Indians would come and destroy their cattle, burn their houses and kill them all; "for," said they, "you have taken away the lands which the Great God has given to our fathers and us."

6. This, no doubt, meant war; and immediate measures were taken for defence. The Indians did not immediately come to put their threat into execution, but, as usual, watched for a favorable moment. In December a force was sent under Colonel Westbrook to Norridgewock, to capture Ralle, who was the chief instigator of the savages against the English. They reached the place undiscovered, for the braves were mostly away on their winter hunt; but before the soldiers could surround the village, Ralle had escaped to the woods. No blood was shed or captive taken by this expedition; but the troops brought away a dictionary of the Abnaki language, written by the Jesuit, the result of many years of study.

7. Castine, the younger, having been in the company which made the threats against the Sagadahock settlements, was soon after seized and carried to Boston, where he was kept a prisoner several months; but as no evidence could be found against his peaceful character, he was set at liberty in the spring. The government at this time sent presents and peaceful messages to the tribes, in the hope of softening their feelings toward the English, in order to avert, if possible, the threatened destruction of the settlements.

All means proved useless; for in June, 1722, the savages fell upon the settlement on the northern shore of Merrymeeting Bay, killing or carrying away into captivity nine entire families. They soon after attempted to surprise the fort at St. George's River but only succeeded in burning a sloop and taking a few prisoners. In July another attack was made on the same fort, under the lead of a Romish priest. This time they undermined a portion of the walls; but a rain caused the banks of the trench to fall in upon them; and, having lost twenty of their number, while the garrison lost only five, they gave up the siege and retired. The savages were now on the war path in all directions; and vessels were captured, houses burned, and settlers murdered or carried into captivity from every quarter.

8. About the middle of July, 1722, Fort George, in Brunswick, was attacked, and the village burned. The news reached the mouth of the Kennebec within a few hours, and Captain Harmon with thirty-four men immediately started up the river in pursuit of the perpetrators. Late in the night they discovered fires on the western shore of Merrymeeting Bay, in what is now the town of Topsham. They happened to land at the very spot where eleven canoes were drawn ashore. They ran directly to one of the fires, and, blinded by the light, actually stumbled over the sleeping savages. They had been torturing a prisoner, and had kept up their dancing and carousing until a late hour, and were now in a drunken, stupid sleep; and the whole number were killed on the spot without the loss of a man to the English. Another party, lying at a little distance from the first, were aroused by the tumult; but after firing a few guns, they fled into the woods and escaped.

9. In September four or five hundred warriors, chiefly St. Francis Indians from Canada, and Micmacs from Nova Scotia, made a sudden descent upon Arrowsic. The garrison was prepared for them, and in a few days drove them from the island; but in the meantime they had killed fifty head of cattle and burned twenty-six houses.

In August, 1723, sixty-three Mohawks, including

many principal men, came to Boston in response to numerous invitations from the authorities, to make a treaty against the eastern Indians. They were received by the Lieutenant Governor, who presented them with a belt of wampum; and they, in return, gave him pieces of plate curiously engraved with the figures of a turtle, bear, wolf, hatchet and other figures — totems of their several tribes. The authorities also gave the Indians a fat ox, which they killed with their arrows; and then they held a feast, which closed with songs and dances.

10. The tribes could not be induced to take up the hatchet, but gave their young men liberty to enter the service of the English; yet only two accepted the offer. These were sent to Fort Richmond, on the Kennebec. A few days after their arrival they were sent out on a scout in company with a small party of English. They had gone scarcely three miles when the two Mohawks said they smelt fire, and refused to go further without a reinforcement. A messenger went back to the fort and brought thirteen more men; and, again advancing, they came upon thirty of the enemy. In the brief conflict that ensued, two of these were killed; while the remainder retreated to their canoes in such haste as to leave their packs on the ground. The English lost their leader, Sergeant Colby, killed, and two others, wounded. But the Mohawks had already become sick of the service, and soon after this affair returned to Boston.

11. In September, 1723, Colonel Westbrook was sent eastward with two hundred and thirty men in search of the enemy. He ascended the Penobscot river in boats to the vicinity of Marsh Bay, where he landed, and continued up the river through the woods. After four or five days they came upon a large fort not far from the present site of the city of Bangor. They entered it without resistance, finding it abandoned, and every article of value removed.

The fort was found to be seventy yards in length by fifty in breadth; the walls, which were fourteen feet high, consisting of stockades, or strong wooden stakes driven into the ground. Inside the walls were twenty-three good wigwams, the dwelling of the priest, and a chapel twenty by sixty feet in size, and handsomely furnished. Committing these to the flames, they returned down the river, and searched other parts of the coast with no better success.

12. The next year the Indians killed and carried into captivity from twenty to thirty persons; four men and three children being captured at one time while engaged in picking berries in the town of Scarborough. There were skirmishes at Casco Neck, and on the Kennebec; and the Indians made another fruitless attack on the fort at St. George's River.

In the winter a third expedition was sent to Norridgewock under Captain Moulton to capture Ralle. Again he escaped them; but they secured his books and papers, and retired without doing any further injury. Among these papers were letters from the governor of Canada directing the Jesuit "to push on the Indians with all imaginable zeal against the English."

13. The fort on St. George's River, being the most advanced post of the settlers received the particular hatred of the savages, and the attacks it suffered during the war were both frequent and severe. It was on a beautiful May morning in 1724 that Captain Josiah Winslow, the young commander, set out from the fort with sixteen men in two whale boats,—proceeding down the river, and thence to the Green Islands in Penobscot Bay. It was the season for fowling, and they expected to find Indians somewhere on the route, snaring or shooting sea-fowl. None were discovered, however; and the party returned the next day to St. Georges'. But the wary savages had seen their hunters, and now lay in ambush along the bank

of the river. Captain **Winslow's boat** was near the middle of the river, **and some distance in** advance, the other having lingered, against the request of Winslow, to look **for** ducks **along** the shore. Suddenly the Indians opened **fire upon the imprudent crew,** but it was **briskly returned. Captain Winslow, seeing** that the **crew was outnumbered and in great danger, turned back to their assistance.**

14. **Thirty canoes** containing ninety savages **immediately** shot out from **the shore,** and **with a** terrible **whoop** fell upon the devoted **crews.** The English **saw that** there was no hope of **escape, and every man** determined to sell his life dearly. **In a brief time** nearly all were dead **or** mortally **wounded. Winslow's boat had floated ashore,** and **he sprang upon the bank, though his thigh was shattered by a ball. An Indian met him, and for a few moments they fought hand to hand; but Winslow beat off his foe.** By this time the savages **were** pressing upon him from all sides; but the brave young soldier killed another, supporting himself on one knee, before they could dispatch him.

Did the natives fully understand how their lands had become the property of the English? What threat did a party of savages make at Arrowsic? What did the government do the next spring? How many families did the Indians take captive on Merrymeeting Bay? At what date was Brunswick burned? Where did Capt. Harmon find the Indians? What tribes made an attack on Arrowsic in September? What did Col. Westbrook find near the present site of Bangor? What was accomplished by the third expedition to **Norridgewock?** Give an account of the fight **on St.** George's River.

CHAPTER XVI.

1. In the summer of 1724 another and final expedition was sent against Norridgewock. It was led by Captains Moulton, Harmon, Bourne and Bane; and consisted of two hundred and eight men. This force left the fort at Richmond on the nineteenth day of August, ascending the river in seventeen whale boats. The next day they arrived at Teconet, where they left their boats with a guard of forty men. The remainder of the journey must have been made on the eastern bank of the river, and they consequently passed the site of the village of Skowhegan in the forenoon of the twenty-second day of the month. At a little past noon they discerned the smoke of the Indian settlement. Captain Harmon with sixty men made a detour towards the cornfields opposite and above the mouth of Sandy River, while Captain Moulton with the residue of the troops went directly towards the village. They moved in the utmost stillness, noting the wigwams, the chapel, the dwelling of the priest, the trees marked by hatchets, the broad stones tossed by the Indians in their sports; but there was not a human being in sight. They were within pistol shot of the cabins, when an Indian looked out and saw them. Instantly he gave the war whoop, and sixty warriors sprang out to meet the English.

2. The first volley of the savages did not harm a man, but the guns of the English made fearful havoc. The Indians stayed only to fire a second volley, then rushed to the river. Some jumped into the canoes, in which they tried to escape, using their guns for paddles, while others attempted to ford or swim across. Still from two wigwams shots continued to be fired

upon the soldiers. One of the **two** Mohawks with the expedition fell, and **his** brother rushed forward and broke in the door **whence** the shot came. Within was an old sagamore **named** Mogg, who, scorning to fly, devoted the **remnant** of his strength to destroy the foes **of his race.** In the other wigwam was Ralle, **the** Jesuit; and he also fell fighting at **his post, being shot through the head** by Lieutenant Jaques.

3. Thus died the zealous and intrepid missionary **of the** Abnakis. He was in the sixty-seventh year of **his age,** and had lived at this village nearly thirty-five **years.** In this solitary place his hours, he writes, **were** crowded with employment. Mass was held every morning, and following **this** the children and others **were instructed in the catechism.** His own **household labors occupied a large portion** of the remaining hours **until evening; when the dusky** congregation again gathered **for vespers. The scene** is well described by Whittier **in these lines:—**

    "Well might the traveler stop to see
      The tall, dark forms that take their **way**
      From the birch canoe on the **river shore,**
      And the forest paths, to that chapel **door;**
      And marvel to mark the naked knees
    And the dusky foreheads bending there,
    While in coarse white vesture, over these
    In blessing **or in prayer,**
      Stretching abroad his **thin,** pale hands,
      Like a shrouded ghost the Jesuit stands."

4. To **him came** the Indians, old and young, to make their complaints, to tell of their joys and sorrows, or to receive his advice — which they always heeded; for they loved him as a father. Their affection for him is shown by this incident, narrated by himself: — Once when encamped with **a party** of the tribe at a long distance from the village, there came tidings that the English **were near;** and all immedi-

ately started for home. A few hours later another Indian came to warn the party. Finding the camp deserted, he concluded that the English had captured them; and he, also, started for the village, leaving on the way information of the supposed calamity for those who might come after. He did this by fastening to a stake a piece of white birch bark, on which he had drawn with charcoal a rude picture of some Englishmen surrounding a priest, one of whom was in the act of cutting off his head —hats signifying that the wearers were English, and the long robe indicating the priest. Shortly after, a party of Indians passing up the river, saw the bark on the top of the stake.

"There is a writing," said one; "let us see what it is."

5. As soon as they looked at it they cried out, "Ah! the English have killed them who were quartered with our father, and cut off his head." Immediately they began to pluck out their long hair; and, sitting down on the spot, remained motionless and silent until morning. This was their customary form of mourning when suffering the severest affliction. The next day they resumed their journey. When within half a league of the village they halted, and sent forward one of their number to see if any English were in the neighborhood.

"I was reading my breviary by the river side," says Ralle, "when the messenger appeared upon the opposite bank. As soon as he saw me he cried out: 'Ah! my father, how glad I am to see you. My heart was dead, and now that I see you, it revives. The writing told us that the English had cut off your head. How rejoiced I am that it told us false.'"

When the Indians urged him to retire to Quebec till the war was over, he replied, "What do you think of me? Do you take me for a cowardly deserter? Alas, what would become of your religion, should I abandon you? Your salvation is dearer to me than life."

6. Notwithstanding all his piety, he could coolly deceive them to secure their devotion to his religion. My young friends will remember what the old chief said the priest taught them about the Virgin Mary being a French woman, and about our Saviour being put to death by the English. On another occasion Ralle pretended to have received a letter from an Indian who was dead, in which he wrote that he was burning in the most horrible fire; and he showed them a letter written in the Indian tongue. The corner where the signature should have been was torn off; for if the name of a deceased relative of any member of the tribe had been given, there would have been trouble between the priest and that family.

In regard to this remarkable character, Mr. Sparks says, "So far as the patient toils of the missionary and love for the darkened soul of the Indian are concerned, we may place the names of Eliot and Ralle in a fellowship, which, indeed, both would have rejected, but which we may regard as hallowed and true; for they both belonged to the goodly company of those who have given their lives to the beautiful labors of pious benevolence.

7. "Whoever has visited the pleasant town of Norridgewock, as it now is, must have heard of "Indian Old Point," as the people call the place where Ralle's village stood; and perhaps curiosity has carried him hither. If so, he has found a lovely, sequestered spot in the depth of nature's stillness, on a point around which the waters of the Kennebec sweep in their beautiful course, as if to the music of the rapids above; a spot over which the sad memories of the past, without its passions, will throw a charm; and where, he will believe, the ceaseless worship of nature might blend itself with the aspirations of christian devotion.

He will find that vestiges of the old settlement are not wanting, in the form of hatchets, glass beads, and broken utensils, turned up by the plough, and preserved by the people of the neighborhood; and he will turn away from the place feeling how hateful is the mad spirit of war in connection with nature's sweet retirements."

MONUMENT OF RALLE, NORRIDGEWOCK.

8. But I must return to my narrative, though feeling as if I should ask pardon of my gentle readers, for bringing them again to the horrors of the bloody battle field. Captain Harmon and his party, who had gone in the direction of the cornfields, did not join the other troops until near evening, when the fighting was quite over. That night the English slept in the wigwams of the Norridgewocks. In the morning, after the troops had left the village, the vengeful Mohawk turned back; and soon chapel and wigwam were wrapped in flame.

On the twenty-seventh of the month the companies

arrived at Richmond on their return; the Mohawk shot by Mogg being the only man lost. Thirty Indians had been left dead on the field, among whom were five sagamores—all noted warriors; and it was believed that more than fifty were killed or drowned in the river. The Canibas tribe never lifted its head after this blow, and was no more counted among the red man's nations. The remnant lingered a while about their old dwelling places on the banks of their pleasant river; but not many years later most of them removed to the St. Francis, whither their kindred tribe, the fated Wawennocks, had gone before them.

In what year was the final expedition against Norridgewock? Who led the attack upon the village? How long had Ralle been with this tribe? What incident shows their regard for him? What deceptions did he use with the Indians? Who set the village on fire? What became of the remnant of this tribe?

CHAPTER XVII.

1. In the autumn following the fall of **Norridgewock** Colonel Westbrook with three hundred men scoured the country to the eastward of the Kennebec, and Captain Heath soon after ascended the Penobscot; but neither met with the Indians or destroyed any of their settlements.

In December, and again in February, Captain Lovewell made successful excursions into the region north and east of Winnipesaukee Lake; and in April, 1725, he set out on the expedition **which terminated in the famous "Lovewell's Fight."**

It was on the sixteenth of April that Captain **Lovewell** with forty-six volunteers set out from Dunstable, Massachusetts, to hunt for Indians about the headwaters of the Saco River, which was the home of the Sokokis. The chief pilot was an Indian named Toby; but he was obliged to return on account of lameness. After marching about one hundred miles another **of** the party became disabled by reason of an old wound; and his kinsman was sent with him **back to the settlement.** By the time the **force reached Ossipee** Pond, in New Hampshire, another **man** fell seriously ill; and **the** whole company stopped **there** and built a small stockade fort. Here they left the sick man, with the surgeon and eight of the most weary ones; so that there now remained only thirty-four men, including the captain, to continue the march. **About** twenty-two miles to the northeast lay the body of water **now** known as Lovewell's Pond, in Fryeburg; and thither this brave little band took its way.

2. On the night of the seventh of May they encamped by **a brook** that **runs into** the pond **near the northwest corner;** while only two miles northward, on the bank **of** the Saco, was Pigwacket, the principal village of the Sokokis. The next morning while they were at prayers the report of a gun was heard. Passing another small brook, they came upon a level plain at the north of the pond, and discovered an Indian standing on a point that ran into the pond on the east. It was now believed that the savages had discovered **them,** and that this lone Indian **was** a decoy **to draw them into an** ambush. Captain Lovewell **inquired of his little company** whether it was **prudent to venture** an engagement with the enemy in his own country, or to make a speedy retreat. One of them answered boldly and firmly, "We came out to meet the enemy; we have all along prayed God we

might meet them; and we had rather trust Providence with our lives,—yea, die for **our country, than** try to return without **seeing** them, if we may,—and be called *cowards* for **our pains."** To this the rest willingly and **fully assented.**

Therefore, leaving their packs among **the brakes in the midst of the plain,** they went cautiously **forward, crossing on their way** another stream, since known as **"Battle Brook."** In a short time they met the Indian returning toward the village. Several fired upon him, **and he** instantly fired in return, wounding Captain **Lovewell** and one of the men; but Ensign Wyman **fired** and killed him. In the meantime **a** party of savages **led by Paugus and** Wahwa, going, **or returning between the village and the** pond, had **come upon the** packs **which were left on the plain; and,** counting them, they found **themselves** three times as strong as **the** English.

3. **It** was now about ten o'clock; and Lovewell's **party** turned **back in** the way they came. They **passed over** the **brook and** were crossing the plain to resume their packs, when the savages **rose** in **front and rear, and rushed toward them with guns presented, and** yelling like demons. Lovewell and his men **with** determined shouts ran to meet them. In the **volley that** followed **many** Indians fell, and they were **driven back** several **rods.** They turned again with **fierce cries; and** three more rounds were fired at close **quarters, some of** the combatants being **not more** than **twice the length of their** guns apart. **Captain Lovewell was** mortally wounded; but, leaning against a tree, he continued **to** fight; and he was seen with a gun in his hands ready to fire, when he was too far gone to speak. Others did the **same.**

4. Eight were **now** dead besides the captain, and **several** others badly wounded; **and** the enemy attempted to surround **those** who remained. Ensign Wyman, who had taken command, ordered them to

fall back to the pond; which was done in good order. **On** their right was Battle Brook, on the left, a rocky **point; in** front, on one side a belt of tall pines afforded a partial shelter, while on the other they were further protected by a deep **bog.** Here for eight terrible hours the savages beset them on front and **flank.** They howled like wolves, they barked like dogs, **they** roared and yelled like demons in their rage; **yet the** intrepid little band was not dismayed, but encouraged each **other with cheers,** and answered the **savages with** shouts **of defiance.**

5. The chaplain of this brave company was Johnathan Frye, a youth **not yet** twenty-one, but already **greatly beloved for his piety and** excellence. He had fought bravely with the rest until the middle of the afternoon, when he received a mortal wound. Unable to fight longer, he betook himself to prayer for his comrades;—and God, we know, has sometimes made prayers more effectual than arms. At **one time** in the **afternoon the** savages withdrew to a little distance, and seemed to be "powwowin**g**"; and **Ensign Wyman crept up and** fired **into** the group, **killing one who seemed to be a leader.** Afterward some of the Indians came toward **the** English and **held up ropes,** shouting, "Will you have quarter?"

"Yes,—at the muzzle of our guns," replied the heroic men. They preferred to die by bullets rather than by torture, or in a cruel captivity; but, chiefly, they were determined to stand by each other to the last.

6. The fight was long, and some of their guns became foul with **so much** firing; **and John** Chamberlain went down to the water **to wash** his piece. **Just then an Indian came down for the** same purpose, not more than **a gunshot off.** In hate and fear they **watched each other's motions as** the cleansing was performed. They finished together, and commenced to load.

"Quick me kill you now," exclaimed the Indian.

"May be not," answered Chamberlain, thumping the breech of his **gun** heavily on the ground. His old flintlock primed **itself,** and a moment later his bullet crashed through **the brain** of the huge savage, whose bullet whistled harmlessly up in the air. Many **histories state that this** Indian was Paugus, a chief greatly **dreaded by the English.** There is, however, a ballad **written at the period,** which says:—

> "And yet our valiant Englishmen
> In fight were ne'er dismayed,
> But still they kept their motion,
> And Wyman captain made,—
> Who shot the **old chief, Paugus,**
> Which did the foe defeat;
> Then set his men in order,
> And brought off the retreat."

7. There was **no way of** escape from the spot as **long** as the foe hung about them; and they were entirely without food since the morning—the Indians having secured their packs; yet never a word **of surrender** escaped their lips. Just before **dark the savages** retired from the field, taking with them their own **wounded, but** leaving the dead bodies of Lovewell's **men unscalped.** The English remained on the ground **until about midnight,** when **it was** thought best to attempt **a retreat.** Ten of their number were already **dead, fourteen** wounded, one missing, and only nine **uninjured. Solomon** Kies, exhausted by fatigue and **loss of blood from three** wounds, had crawled slowly and painfully **to** the edge of the pond, with the intention of throwing himself into the water at some spot where the savages would not find and mangle his lifeless body. Providentiall**y he** spied **a** birch canoe near by, which he managed to enter; and, lying there almost unconscious, he **was** slowly drifted by the wind **to** the western side of **the pond.** After a while he

recovered his strength a little, so that he finally reached the fort at Ossipee Pond.

8. Painful as it was, two of the mortally wounded had to be left. When the moon rose the others started on the retreat; but, after traveling a mile and a half, four more sank to the ground unable to support themselves longer. These were Lieutenant Farwell, Chaplain Frye, and privates Davis and Jones; and, at their request, their companions went on without them. After resting awhile they felt stronger, and went on again a little distance, then rested again; and thus continued for several days. But they grew weaker and weaker; and, first, Frye was left, then Farwell sank to rise no more,—Davis alone reaching the fort. Jones followed down the Saco river, arriving after many days at Biddeford, emaciated almost to a skeleton by hunger, pain and loss of blood.

9. Ossipee Pond was scarcely more than twenty miles from the scene of the battle, but so weary were the men and so indirect their route, that it was four days before the first arrived at the fort. They found it deserted. A man of the company had run away at the beginning of the fight; and, coming to the fort, he told the men of the fall of Captain Lovewell and others, and of the great number of the Indians. The little garrison had no doubt that every one remaining had been killed or captured, and supposed that the savages would next fall upon the fort; so they at once abandoned it, and started for the settlements.

It was Wednesday when the remnant of Lovewell's brave band reached the fort. They were in a half-starved condition, having had nothing to eat since the morning of the preceding Saturday, except a few roots and the bark of trees. Here they found some bread and pork left by the deserters; so they were saved from starvation. After a short rest they started for home, where they were received with great joy — almost as persons restored from the dead. Colonel

Tyng with eighty-seven men at once started for the scene of the fight. He found the bodies of the twelve who had been killed, and buried them at the foot of a great pine, carving their names upon the trees about the battle ground.

VIEW OF LOVEWELL'S BATTLE-GROUND.

10. The Indians were struck with such dread by this fight, that they immediately retired into some unknown wilderness, and were found no more in their old haunts until the war was over. It is supposed that about fifty warriors fell in this conflict, among whom was their principal leader, Paugus.

The next month Captain Heath, probably desirous of emulating the heroes of Norridgewock and Pigwacket, set out again for the Penobscot. Since the burning of their village by Colonel Westbrook, the Indians on this river had built another a few miles above the Kenduskeag, at a place now called "Fort Hill," which is within the present limits of Bangor. It had between forty and fifty wigwams, together with several cottages with chimneys and cellars, and a Catholic chapel. The Indians were on the alert; and again their invaders found only deserted dwellings. These they set on fire, and departed.

11. The tribes were now disposed **to make peace; but so many things happened to disturb the negotiations, that the conditions were not settled until the fifteenth** of December, 1725. Only four sagamores then signed **the treaty;** and it was not until the next summer **that the conference was held for its** ratification. **By this treaty,** trading houses were to be kept on the principal rivers for the convenience of the Indians; while the settlers were confirmed in their lands, **and** all the English captives **were to be** released without ransom. This war is known as "Lovewell's War," or the "Three Years War"; **and the number** killed and carried into **captivity during its progress, including** settlers, **soldiers and seamen, was about two hundred.**

12. On the thirtieth of **July, 1726, about forty** sagamores, **with the Peno**bscot **sachem, Wenemovet,** at their head, appeared at Casco **Neck; where Governor Dummer, with** a large number **of** councillors and representatives, and a fine train of young gentlemen, had already been waiting nearly a fortnight. These chiefs represented the Tarratines, Canibas and Androscoggins, and brought a letter and two belts of **wampum** from the St. Francis Indians, in Canada,— **indicating their wish** to join in **the treaty. The conference lasted a full week; and every** paragraph of **the treaty was read to them and repeated** distinctly by their **interpreters; after which it** was explained and discussed. **It was** ratified in **the** meeting house, (a very good place to make a treaty of peace) and signed by Governor Dummer and others on the part

of the English, and by Wenemovet and twenty-five of the sagamores; and then the business ended with a public dinner.

13. This affair was long celebrated as "Dummer's Treaty"; and the peace that followed was the most lasting of any since the Indian wars commenced; for it was better understood by them than any of the former treaties, while they had just had the importance of keeping their agreements impressed upon them by a severe chastisement.

When did the famous battle known as "Lovewell's Fight" take place? Where did Lovewell build a fort? Where is the pond beside which the fight occurred? When the leader inquired of his men whether they would fight, or retreat, what reply did they make? What happened when they returned to resume their packs? After the fall of Capt. Lovewell who took command? How long did the savages keep up the attack? What remarkable personal encounter took place in this fight? Who were left at night in possession of the field? What had been the loss of the Indians? What became of the remainder? What celebrated treaty closed this war?

CHAPTER XVIII.

1. The inhabitants of Maine had suffered frequent and long distress by the savage wars, yet they clung to their freeholds as a most precious heritage. This freehold right to the land upon which they lived, no rents to pay, no feudal service to render to some lord proprietor,—this was something few or none of them had enjoyed in England. From this cause, doubtless,

arose in a large degree that love of country, which was so distinguished a virtue of our forefathers.

The hardships of those early days no pen can properly relate. The paths of the settlers were ambushed, they were shot down in the fields, they woke in the silent hours of night to find their buildings in flames, and the hatchets of the savages breaking down the doors of their dwellings; none could tell when or where the prowling foe would strike. Consequently many families spent weeks together in the garrison, daring to cultivate only the nearest fields. But with the return of peace the farms soon teemed with plenty, while the ringing saws beside the dashing cataracts turned the dense woods into marketable lumber.

2. Soon after the close of Lovewell's war the General Court laid out a tier of back towns, and divided them into lots, with which to reward the soldiers, and supply farms for immigrants. The old settlements were greatly pleased at this; for they had stood for nearly a century in single file between the ocean and the forest; and in case of another war these new towns would be a bulwark against their old enemies.

Many settlers came from Massachusetts and New Hampshire, but foreign emigrants came slowly; for the authorities acted with severity toward these, and would not knowingly admit any person of bad morals or shiftless habits. There was a law at this time that the stranger, or the captain who brought him, should secure the country for five years against being chargable for his support; yet if he could prove himself skilled as a mechanic, mariner or farmer, and was of unblemished character he was admitted without any bond; because such as these make valuable citizens for any country.

3. You will recollect that in Gorges' charter the best trees were reserved for the king's navy—and just so they were in all the charters and grants. There was a great extent of forest in Maine, and a

great length of sea-coast; and many owners of sawmills and vessels chose rather to cut up the trees which the king claimed than those to which they had an undoubted right. The king soon found this out; and in 1699, when the Earl of Bellamont was made governor of New England, John Bridges was sent over as surveyor or keeper of the king's woods. He went through the forests bordering on the coast and rivers, seeking out the tall pines suitable for masts, and the noble oaks, good for plank and to make strong knees to strengthen the vessel,—marking them with the royal "R." But the owners of territory considered themselves wronged by this grasping claim on all their best trees; and the crafty lumbermen hewed off the stamp and sent the fine logs rolling down to their mills. So the surveyors watched the mills, where they often came into conflict with the millmen, and sometimes got very roughly handled by these sturdy sons of the forest—who laid their fists upon the intrusive surveyor and his aids with as hearty good will as they had lain their axes against the king's trees.

4. In 1729 Colonel David Dunbar was appointed surveyor of the royal woods. The king, George II., also granted him the territory between the Kennebec and Penobscot rivers, under the name of the Province of Sagadahock; but reserved to himself 300,000 acres of the best pine and oak. In return, Dunbar was to settle the province with good, industrious Protestants. Now the king had no right to make a grant of this territory; for, by the charter of William and Mary, it belonged to Massachusetts, which had expended much money for its protection against the French and Indians. But Dunbar took possession, garrisoning the fort at Pemaquid with British soldiers from Nova Scotia. He laid out several towns and brought in his settlers, to whom he conveyed the land by perpetual lease, the rent being only a peppercorn, annually. He found a great many persons already occupying his

province, who denied his claim, holding their possessions under the original patents. Some of these would not yield to his demands; and he sent an armed force, who burnt their houses and drove them from their lands, even threatening them with imprisonment for insisting on their rights. After three years, however, the province was taken from him and restored to the rightful owners. It was not Dunbar's fault that he had no genuine right to the province, but the king's, who commissioned him. Yet he did the country much service by the numerous and excellent settlers whom he brought in; and, on the whole, nobody suffered much wrong. His settlers were mostly the Scotch-Irish, from the north of Ireland, and Presbyterian in religion. Some of this people had nearly a century before settled about Saco, while others still made their homes at Brunswick and Topsham on the Androscoggin, and at Bath and other places on the Kennebec. Soon after the restoration of the province of Sagadahock to the patentees, Samuel Waldo brought from Germany many families of the religious sect called Lutherans, and founded the town of Waldoboro, in the present county of Lincoln.

5. Governor Belcher of Massachusetts had been one of the most earnest opposers of Dunbar's claim to the province of Sagadahock, and when the latter became lieut.-governor of New Hampshire he made a great effort to have Belcher removed. By making the jealous king believe that the governor was favoring the colonies at the expense of the royal interest, he at last succeeded. So Governor Belcher lost a good office. But he got a better one afterward; for the king soon learned that he was really a faithful and upright officer.

Among the friends of the good governor was the celebrated George Whitefield, who came to the country during the last years of his rule. Whitefield, you know, was an evangelist; and in his day he was reckoned the "prince of preachers." Young Ben. Frank lin one day went to hear him, fully determined to contribute nothing to the charity for which the "wonderful preacher" pleaded. Ben was an exceedingly cool young man; but as the sermon went on he put his hand in his pocket, and thought he would give his copper coin; pretty soon he concluded that he would give the silver; but when the plate came round he pulled out his purse and said, "Take it all." Whitefield first preached in Maine in 1741; and again in 1745 he visited York, Wells, Biddeford, Scarborough, Falmouth and North Yarmouth,—stirring up the religious feeling of the people. I suspect there was great need of it, though Maine had been blessed by many faithful ministers.

6. The Rev. Samuel Moody was the most noted clergyman of this day in Maine, having been minister over the first parish in York above forty years. When settled there he refused any stipulated salary, preferring to live on voluntary contributions. His parish, therefore, faithfully provided for him, and he knew nothing of what he was to receive until it was placed in his hands. With all his eccentricity, he was a man of ardent piety and great usefulness.

Puritan preaching was usually grave and severe; but theirs was a period of violent men and stern necessities, and they felt that the laws of God must be declared without fear or favor. Though the Christian graces were not so well displayed by them as should have been, yet the fruits of their ministry were seen in the virtuous lives of their hearers, and of the generations which came after.

7. For many years it was the law in Massachusetts and the province of Maine that none except members of the Puritan church should be voters; and while this union between Church and State continued, all other sects within their borders suffered persecution. But after many years people of all shades of belief were admitted to full citizenship; then the stern Puri-

tan became the milder Congregationalist, and persecutions ceased. In Episcopal churches the form of worship was very nearly the same as it is to-day, except that the English "Book of Common Prayer" was used instead of the American,—which was not prepared until our country became an independent nation. The method of worship in Congregational churches was also the same in its general plan as now, though on account of the old customs there was a striking difference in several particulars. The churches were roughly built, like the houses. **Many were not plastered, and** until long **after the** Revolution few **were warmed, even in the coldest winter** weather; for the **strict "professors"** of the day thought **it** wrong to have **a fire** in the house of God. So they sat and suffered, **until** it became the practice to use hot bricks and stones for the hands and feet. The next thing was **foot-stoves,** which **were** filled with wood coals, and **must have** made **the people feel quite** drowsy from **the oppressive and unwholesome air** which resulted. **The services were very long; the** sermon usually **occupied above an hour and often two, and** the **prayers fully half as much. So in the cold weather the minister** was often **obliged to beat the** sacred desk **most** unmercifully to **restore warmth to** his purple **and benumbed fingers.**

8. Puritan ministers always wore black gowns and flowing wigs in the pulpit; and one would hardly be surprised that their sermons were dignified and severe rather than sympathetic and winning. It is not strange that under these **circumstances** the little **boys were often inclined to play, and even** the heads **of families sometimes nodded!** Of course this **conduct could not be tolerated; and** all through the sermon **and prayers the deacon or** tythingman kept watch, or **walked** softly about, rapping the heads of **the** naughty boys with the knob **on the end of his long stick,** or tapping **the** heads **of the** men when they

snored; but when the women forgot to keep their eyes open, he only tickled their faces with the feathers on the other end of his staff.

9. Books were scarce and expensive in those days; and, when the hymn was not familiar, the minister read off two lines, which were sung by the congregation; then other two lines were read, and sung —and so on through the hymn. After a while printed tunes came into use; and then the chorister had to be more particular about pitching the tunes,—so they had for this purpose little wooden whistles, which they called pitch pipes.

The Puritans reckoned the Sabbath to begin at sunset on Saturday, and to close at sunset on Sunday night. Within these hours no labor was allowed, except what was needful for the health of the body. All recreation or traveling for business or pleasure was strictly forbidden; and people who staid away from meeting were by law subject to a fine. In good Puritan families on this day the children and servants recited the orthodox catechism; for this, also, was required by the law.

10. From the year 1638, when Harvard College was established, every town of fifty householders was ordered to hire a teacher the year round; and a town of one hundred householders had its school where children were taught their a, b, c; and where, also, boys could be fitted for college. Probably none of our well trained boys and girls ever heard in school hours such buzzing as they had in these ancient schools all the time. The country in those times seemed so large that most families talked loud, having no fear that they would be overheard by any neighbors except the bears and wolves; while the children had no idea that they could study without pronouncing the words at least in whispers; so, I suppose, when they buzzed the liveliest the teacher looked for the best lessons. Often two or three would be seen studying

from the same volume, as one book of a kind frequently answered for a whole family; for classes were very few, but large. There were other sounds in the room besides the smothered tones of the student; the sound of the birch that made the jacket smoke, the "spat" of the broad ruler,—which was sometimes pierced with holes, for the kindly purpose of raising blisters; while over all arose the sob of the sensitive, the whine of the base, or the groan of the plucky. But there were busy fingers as well as lips; and the rustle of sheets and pillow cases, and the "whip" of the stout, swift thread on the the back seats answered to the click of the knitting needles, where the stockings and suspenders grew in the hands of both boys and girls. Often in cold weather the cut and split of the firewood fell short; then the big boys had to take their turns in making the fresh chips fly from the great, green logs piled up beside the door.

11. In the long winter evenings there were the spelling school and the singing school, where pleasure was joined with instruction; and the husking and the apple bee, where pleasure went hand in hand with profit. And when the parties separated, the favorites walked home together in the calm moonlight; and often then, as now, a pair would linger on the doorstep for a few tender whisperings, and the soft chirrup of a good night greeting. But the law was very watchful to prevent unsuitable matches; and if an ardent youth or an older and more designing man attempted to win the affections of a girl under eighteen unbeknown to her parents or guardians, he thereby became subject to a fine. Yet most of the young people either fell in love or grew to love each other, got married and lived happily. Land was cheap and lumber abundant in those days; and any healthy and industrious young couple could soon make themselves a comfortable home,—as, indeed, they can at the present day.

12. The first houses were built of logs; notches being cut on the opposite sides at each end, so that they would lock at the corners and lie close along the sides. But after the Indian wars were over, wherever the sawmills provided lumber, frame houses were built, which were covered with great broad boards; being made water tight on roof and wall by shingles split out of the great blocks with mallet and frow,— and old men say that never since have shingles lasted as those did.

In passing through our State even at this day we shall see that many houses, mostly very old, set at every angle with the roads; yet we might be sure that most of them faced the south. This happened because the houses were often built before the roads were made; but the south was always there. So the sun gave the chief rooms a cheerful aspect at all hours, while at noon it shone squarely through the little windows, telling the busy housewife what was the time of day.

13. Then there was the great fireplace, of brick or stone, four—aye, often six feet wide at the back; deep and high enough, too, for the children to sit in the corners and see the stars glimmering through the huge throat of the chimney. Within the fire-place also hung joints of pork, slowly turning to bacon in the smoke; while from the bare beams overhead were suspended strings of pared and quartered apples, and the curving strips of pumpkin,—which through the long winter and spring, turned to delightful pies, or made more savory the great loaves of "rye and Indian" bread.

On hooks near the chimney hung the guns, the big powder horn, and, perhaps, a spontoon, or a halberd. Possibly a coarse engraving or two of bible scenes, or more frequently, King Charles' "Twelve Good Rules," hung upon the plain wall of wood or plaster. Opposite the fireplace, and always reflecting its light, was the "dresser," on which **stood the table** ware of bright **pewter, crockery, or** smoothly **turned** wood. About the **room were long** benches and movable stools, **a broad** stout table **and,** possibly, a few chairs.

14. There was **the** little treadwheel with its distaff and spindle, for flax spinning,—and near by was the larger wheel for wool and cotton; while farther **away,** or in another **room,** stood the great, square **wooden** frame of the hand **loom,** where the family clothes **were** woven. Here, **during** the long **summer afternoon,** the **industrious mother or buxom daughter sat** flinging the **swift** shuttle from **side to side of the stout** web, **and her** buskined foot upon **the** treadle reversed at every moment the mazy warp, while the swinging beam **beat** close the imprisoned thread of the woof. Cloth of wool for blankets, cloaks and coats, sheets of **linen** and cotton, strong and serviceable,—each came in **its** turn from this **true** and **original** "manufactory."

At first all the shoes were brought from England; then the skins of moose and deer, and, later, those of **their** own domestic **animals, were used by the shoemakers;** while soft-dressed **deer skins were frequently** worn for coats **and leggins.** In summer, **farmers and** mechanics **had** their **tow** cloth suits for **every day wear,**—for winter, their woolens, and for Sunday, their "full-cloth" and linen,—generally the product of the industry and skill of their own wives and daughters.

15. The villages of Maine were as yet too small and scattered for much display, and the dress and **ceremony** of fashion were rarely seen except **in one** or two towns, until after the revolution. The people of this period loved better a cordial and comfortable sort of life; and when the thrifty housewife went out **to visit a neighbor, it** was often **with** distaff of flax in **hand and the** diminutive spinning **wheel on** her arm. And sometimes all the ladies of **a parish** would **visit their minister's house, and hold there a spinning bee**

as a benefit to their worthy host and his excellent wife.

The good ladies attended each other's afternoon tea parties, bringing each her own cup and saucer of china, —if she was so fortunate as to have one; for these were generally heir-looms,—part of a set which the mother or grandmother had brought over from her English home, and divided and subdivided among daughters and granddaughters. It was often with other household stuff as with china; in many a plainly furnished house might be seen a carved chair, a fine table or buffet, seeming quite out of place amid the rough furniture made on the spot.

The early settlers of our State were usually of good parentage, many of them being impoverished branches of noble families —here becoming sons and daughters of the soil; whose names, by and by, should emerge again to fame by the noble deeds of their children.

What right had the settlers in Maine which few of them had possessed in England? What regulations were made by the **General Court** in regard to immigrants? What can you tell of the **king's woods?** To whom did the king give the territory between the **Kennebec** and Penobscot in 1729? Who held a previous right to that tract? What people did **Dunbar** bring in as settlers? What celebrated preacher visited Maine in 1741 and 1745? What was in general the character of **Puritan** preaching? What was at first the **Puritan law** in regard to voters? What were the laws in regard to the observance of the **Sabbath**? What were some of the customs of those days?

CHAPTER XIX.

1. In the spring of 1744 France joined Spain in the war which she was carrying on against England. As soon as the French subjects in America heard of this, they began to plot against the English colonies. Nova Scotia was now in the possession of the English, and here the French and Indians made their first attacks. Yet Cape Breton Island was still held by the French; and Louisburg, the chief town, naturally a strong position, had been so strongly fortified that it was called the Dunkirk and the Gibraltar of America. The possession of this place would be of great advantage to the English; and in the spring of 1745 an expedition was sent against it. As the principal leaders of this enterprise were citizens of Maine, I shall give a particular description of the siege.

2. The armament consisted of four thousand men, and thirteen vessels, with transports and store ships, carrying in all about two hundred guns. The commander in chief was William Pepperell, of Kittery; who had for several years been colonel of the Yorkshire militia. He was a gentleman of unblemished reputation, by occupation a merchant; but he had a taste for martial affairs, and was familiar with Indian warfare. The second in command was Samuel Waldo, of Falmouth, who was commissioned Brigadier General. Others were Lieutenant Colonel Jeremiah Moulton, noted for his success in the destruction of Norridgewock; and Lieut. Colonel William Vaughn, of Damariscotta, the originator of the enterprise. The commander of the fleet was Captain Edward Tyng, of Falmouth, who had distinguished himself the year before by capturing a French privateer, much larger than his own vessel. Mr. Whitefield, the great

preacher, was consulted by General Pepperell in regard to the expedition, and gave as a motto for the flag the words, *Nil desperandum, Christo duce.*

3. The movement had been kept so secret that the force arrived within sight of Louisburg before the French were really certain that they were to be attacked at all. Off Louisburg the fleet captured a French brigantine laden with supplies for the garrison. Commodore Warren with four British war ships soon after joined the colonial flotilla, and during the siege six other ships of war arrived; so that in all the fleet mounted some four hundred and ninety guns. The first movement against the city was made by Lieut. Colonel Vaughn. Landing four hundred and fifty men in the woods, he marched in the night to the northeast side of the harbor, where he set on fire some buildings containing naval stores and a great quantity of wine and brandy. The grand battery of the French was about three fourths of a mile from these, and such volumes of smoke were carried into it by the wind, that the gunners became terrified; and, spiking their cannon, fled to the city. In the morning Vaughn took possession; and, drilling out the spiked vents, turned the guns—great 42 pounders—upon the city. Then more troops were landed and other batteries constructed, one after the other,—each new one nearer than the last. Yet to do this the guns and ammunition had to be dragged over a morass where oxen could not pass, the men going up to their knees in the mud; and all the work was done on foggy days, or in the night time, when the enemy could not see to fire upon them.

4. A summons of surrender was sent to Duchambon, the governor; but being refused, the work was still pressed on until a battery was erected within two hundred and fifty yards of the west gate. The next day after this was completed, a French ship hove in sight, and was decoyed into the midst of danger;

where, after a few shots, she surrendered to Captain
Tyng. She proved to be the *Vigilant*, a sixty-four
gun ship, laden with military stores, and bringing five
hundred and sixty men. A few days later a flag of
truce was sent ashore with a letter requesting the
enemy to give his English prisoners better treatment.
The messengers were accompanied by the captain of
the *Vigilant*, who informed the authorities how
kindly the French prisoners on board the vessels were
treated. His appearance was the first knowledge the
French had of the capture of his vessel with its troops
and stores, on which they greatly relied; and they
were in great dismay. Their works were already
badly damaged by the fire of the batteries, even the
magazine and the central battery being greatly injured, while the western gate was broken down.

5. The fourteenth of June was the anniversary of
the king's ascent to the throne; and at twelve o'clock
the English fired a grand salute, the guns of the fleet
and batteries being discharged together. The French
perceived that everything was now ready for the bombardment and assault, and the governor sent a flag of
truce offering to surrender. A capitulation was
agreed upon, by which the French troops were sent
home to France, under parole not to fight against the
English for twelve months. On the 17th of June the
English troops marched into the city. They were
filled with surprise at the strength of the fortifications;
the wall on the side next the shore being above thirty
feet high, with a ditch in front eighty feet in width;
while in the various batteries were nearly one hundred heavy guns and mortars. The garrison consisted
of two thousand soldiers. The French loss in this
siege was above three hundred killed and many more
wounded, while the loss of the English was but one
hundred and thirty. One vessel had been lost in a
storm; but, to offset this, the prizes taken amounted
to nearly a million pounds sterling. Yet it all went

to the British; but the colonies, after soliciting parliament for seven years, obtained an allowance of 200,000 pounds.

6. The news of this victory filled France and England with astonishment, and America with gladness. Bells were rung, bonfires blazed, and a public thanksgiving was held throughout New England. Pepperel., the commander of the land forces, was made a baronet; and the British commodore, Warren, who came to the siege unwillingly and late, was raised to the post of admiral; while Tyng, to whom belonged all the honor of the naval exploits, received the offer of post-captain in the British navy; but declining this, he had only his pay and the applause of his countrymen as his reward.

SIR WILLIAM PEPPERELL.

Though the Indians east of the St. Croix were now in open war with the English, the Tarratines still remained peaceful. They had every reason for it. Since Governor Dummer's treaty the authorities had frequently met them for conference, feasted them, made them presents, and had even bestowed pensions on some of the chiefs. Yet for a year previous to the fall of Louisburg frequent acts of mischief had been committed by some tribes in Maine. They seemed to have a fondness for breaking down fences and setting the cattle upon the growing corn; while now and then a beast was killed or a building burned.

7. It was supposed that the Androscoggin and Norridgewock Indians were the guilty parties; and the Penobscot tribe was called upon to furnish warriors to aid in chastising the guilty tribes — this being a condition of Dummer's treaty. A high premium was offered them for scalps, with an additional sum of five pounds for captives, in order to save life. Yet the constant reply of the sagamores was that their young men would not take up arms against their brethren. During these twenty peaceful years since Lovewell's war a generation of young savages had grown up. They had heard from their sires the story of the white man's wrongs upon their race; and they burned for vengeance, and to win honor and renown among the tribes for their valiant exploits. The French supplied them with arms and ammunition; and neither the persuasions nor the presents of the English authorities could deter them from their bloody purpose.

8. The first blow fell on St. George's Fort, which was attacked by a body of Cape Sable, St. John and St. Francis Indians on the 19th of July. Not making any impression upon it, they burned a mill and several dwelling houses, killed many cattle, and departed, having captured but a single prisoner. Meantime a party of young warriors from Penobscot and Norridgewock marked Fort Frederick, at Pemaquid, for their prize. Coming near the fort they met a woman whom they shot in the shoulder, then made prisoner. This was only about three hundred yards from the walls; and the sound of the gun, together with

the shrieks of the wounded woman, alarmed the garrison,—who immediately gave the savages a telling volley. In the smoke and confusion the woman broke away from her captor and escaped to the fort.

9. The foiled braves now set their hideous faces westward, appearing a few days later at North Yarmouth. Their first approach was discovered by a dog; and, turning back, they committed other barbarities eastward. Again they laid an ambush at Yarmouth. Unconscious of their presence, three men approached their hiding place; and one was instantly killed, another was made prisoner, while the third escaped. The Indians now scattered themselves along the ridge between the two forts, and fired upon the men as they rushed out of the houses below to repel the attack; but they speedily retreated to the woods when the English bullets began to whistle about them.

It was now considered more than imprudent to work on the farms except in large and well armed parties; for people away from the garrison were liable to be shot down at any moment.

10. But it was on St. George's River that the savages were the most numerous and watchful; for these settlements were the furthest advanced upon the territories of the tribe best able to resist such encroachment. Here a whole party, consisting of several men, were killed and scalped only a short distance from the garrison; two men going down river in a boat to collect rockweed were taken and carried to Canada; two women while milking their cows close to the garrison were surprised, and one of them captured, while the other narrowly escaped to the fort.

So many had been drawn from Maine by the Louisburg expedition that scarcely as many men as there were families remained for defense; and one hundred and seventy-five soldiers were drawn from Massachusetts to reinforce the garrisons. This raised the number in military service in Maine to about six hundred; and scouting parties now frequently traversed the region in the rear of the towns from Berwick to St. George.

11. At length another demand was made upon the tribes at Penobscot and Norridgewock in a somewhat different form. It was that they should deliver up the parties guilty of the recent outrages in the East, or hostages for them, or else furnish at least thirty fighting men within fourteen days — otherwise the treaty was to be considered broken, and war declared. The tribes made no response; therefore on the 23d of August government declared war against all the eastern tribes. The bounties offered for each Indian captive or scalp taken were one hundred pounds to a soldier in public service, two hundred and fifty pounds to a person receiving provisions and not wages, and four hundred pounds to a volunteer having neither pay nor rations. Though by these inducements many small companies were drawn into occasional service, the depredations of the savages were not wholly prevented. One inhabitant fell here and another there, all along the coast; and, though scouting parties were constantly out, few Indians were taken — the most successful party being that of Lieutenant Proctor, who had a skirmish near St. George's River, in which two Indian chiefs, "Colonel Morris" and "Captain Sam," were killed, and "Colonel Job" taken prisoner.

12. During the winter a rumor that the French were preparing to join the Indians and fall upon some of the towns, caused a further addition of about four hundred men to the garrisons from Massachusetts, together with four small field pieces and a swivel. But no attempt was made by the enemy; and, though greatly distressed, the inhabitants had not to mourn other friends fallen, or property destroyed.

What war commenced in 1744? Who at this time held Cape Breton? What town upon this island was very strongly fortified? Who were the leaders of the expedition against Louisburg? What motto did Whitefield give for the expedition? Give a brief account of the siege. To whom did the credit of these achievements belong? What reward did Pepperell receive? Who after this supplied the Indians with arms and ammunition? What fort was first attacked? What Indians attacked Fort Frederick? To what place did the savages next proceed? Why was war declared against the eastern tribes?

CHAPTER XX.

1. In the following spring the Indians renewed their depredations in greater force and more vengeful mood. In Gorham several persons were killed or captured while at work in their fields. A Mr. Bryant and his son being surprised by them, the two ran different ways, and the father was overtaken and killed. The boy getting out of their sight, plunged into the brook. He pushed his head above water among the roots of a tree, so as to breathe; but he was so well hidden that when the Indians arrived at the spot they were unable to find him. They then went to Mr. Bryant's house, and killed four children, and took off their scalps. One of the savages pulled the baby from its cradle by the feet, and dashed its head against the fire-place before the eyes of its mother. Then he tossed it into a kettle of water that was boiling on the fire, shouting with fiendish glee, "Hot water good for Indian dog, good for pappoose, too." This horrible act was in revenge for its mother's cruelty in throwing hot suds upon him more than a year before. Then the savage danced about her, pointing with bloody fingers at her

husbands' scalp in the girdle of the chief. They carried the widowed and bereaved woman away with them to Canada, where she was sold to the Frenchmen.

2. In May a large body of Indians attacked Waldoborough, burning the dwellings, killing many of the inhabitants, and taking many prisoners. They kept up this sort of warfare until winter, almost every town losing inhabitants, buildings and cattle. The people were forced to remain in the garrison houses, and could only plant and gather their crops under a strong guard, and at times they dared not even milk their cows, though these were kept in pastures adjoining the garrisons. There had been so many wars that the two races had now learned each other's devices; so that while fewer of the settlers were killed, the savages, on their part, came so secretly and fled so swiftly that the English could not often meet or overtake them. The dogs of the English generally showed great antipathy to the Indians, growling, barking and bristling with rage whenever any of these people were near. They could scent them at a long distance, too; and often gave timely warning of their approach. Therefore these animals became a great advantage to the settlers; and the scouts, also, found their keen scent of much use in following Indian trails. The Indians soon came to fear the white men's dogs, and the killing of them by the savages was often found a precursor of hostile attacks.

3. The French were now planning to recapture Louisburg and Nova Scotia; and in the autumn of 1746 a fleet of seventy ships with upwards of three thousand land troops was sent for this purpose. Several of the largest ships were so much disabled by a storm that they had to be sent back; and on landing at Chebucto, (Halifax) it was found that nearly one-half the troops had died of scorbutic fever, while the remnant were so weak that they could not endure the least fatigue. A force of seventeen hundred men had

8

been sent from Canada to act with the fleet; but, discouraged by its not arriving at the time agreed upon, all except four hundred of them had returned. The Duke D'Anville, commander of the expedition, was so overcome by these disasters that four days after the arrival he died of chagrin. In a council of war held by the officers after his death, the vice-admiral proposed to return at once to France, but Jonquiere, the governor of Canada, and third in command, wished to attack Annapolis. A majority joined with the governor; and the vice admiral fell into a delirious fever, and threw himself upon his sword. When off Cape Sable, on the way to Annapolis, the fleet was again overtaken by a storm, and so scattered that the vessels were obliged to return to France. The Indians caught the fever of the French, and it raged fearfully among them, and great numbers of them died. Thus Providence itself seemed to war against the designs of the French, utterly defeating their great fleet, and destroying their troops without the aid of man.

4. The next spring the garrisons in Maine were increased by five hundred men, but the country was already swarming with savages. Thirty men under Captain Jordan were stationed at Topsham, but with this exception the inhabitants from Kennebec to Wells were left to their own defense. A few volunteer companies were raised at various times; that of Captain Ilsley of Falmouth being among the most useful. Yet these received neither pay nor rations; their only reward being the bounties for the Indians and French captured or killed.

In May a second fleet sent from France to retrieve the misfortunes of the first, was met and defeated by a fleet of the British; so that the hopes of the French in America were again doomed to disappointment. Yet the French and Indians made attacks upon the forts at Pemaquid and St. George's, though without success; and predatory bands harassed the settlers until July,

1748, when the peace of **Aix-la-Chapelle** closed the war. Early in the spring of the next year a delegation of chiefs appeared at Boston, desiring to make a treaty; and again a treaty was made.

5. In December, 1749, a quarrel happened between some Indians and English in which one of the Indians **was** killed. The guilty parties were placed in prison to wait their trial; yet, being incited by the French authorities, the St. Francis tribe the next season sent a band of warriors into Maine to glut their still unsatisfied vengeance. They were joined by some **young** Canibas fighters, swelling the party to about **one** hundred. Their first attack was in September, 1750, upon Fort Richmond, in the present town of that name. The garrison consisted of only fourteen men; but while the greedy savages were killing cattle and burning houses in the vicinity a reinforcement reached the fort. **As soon as the** Indians learned this, they gave up **the attempt,** and departed down the river, destroying property and killing or capturing all who came **in** their way.

6. One party attacked **Wiscasset, setting some of** the houses on fire, and taking **two prisoners.** Another party **went to** Parker's Island, **at the mouth** of the Kennebec. Coming to **a** house just within call of the fort they were discovered, and dared not approach nearer; for they feared the cannon with which the garrisons were now generally supplied. The owner of the house was at that time its only occupant, but he fought bravely against his savage assailants. When at length they had **cut down** the door with their hatchets, he escaped through a window in the rear. Being **cut off from the fort, he ran** toward the **river and** plunged in, **with the intention of swimming to** Arrowsic Island. The Indians pursued him **to the shore;** and two **of** them, springing nimbly into a canoe, continued the chase. They came rapidly up with him, and could almost reach him with their pad-

dles; but he suddenly **turned upon them and upset the canoe, then resumed** his **course,—leaving the discomfited savages floundering in the water.**

7. **Passing from the** Kennebec region, **the Indians visited Falmouth, Gorham** and Windham, committing **the usual acts of** destruction, and carrying away twenty **or thirty prisoners. On** their return to **Canada they came** upon **the camp of** two hunters, named **Snow and Butterfield, in** what **is** now the town of **Paris. Startled by a hideous** yell, the two **men** looked up to **discover a pack** of savages close upon **them.** The foremost **wore** upon his head a hood formed of a hawkskin, **the wings and** tail reaching down to his shoulders and back. **He was the chief.** Snow **was sitting down with his gun in his lap, picking its flint, at the moment he discovered the Indians; and he deliberately rose and aimed at the leader. He had been a captive once, and found the** experience too **painful** to **be repeated; so he determined to fight to the death.** There was a flash and a report; and the haughty form of the chief pitched forward and lay stretched upon the ground. The infuriated Indians instantly poured a volley upon **the bold** hunter, and he fell dead beside his **companion, pierced** through and through with bullets.

8. **So much** alarm **was created** by this incursion, **that one hundred and fifty men were** detailed from **the Yorkshire regiment to scour the** woods between **Saco and St. Georges', and the forts were** restocked **with ammunition, in readiness for the savages,** should **they come again. But this raid proved the** last; though a few revengeful individuals **continued to** rob, murder and **burn,** wherever they dared, until the summer of 1751; **when a** new treaty settled all difficulties and confirmed **the peace.**

What settlement was attacked by the Indians **in** the spring of **1746?** What place was attacked in May? For what purpose did the **French** send a powerful fleet to America in 1746? What happened to this force? What happened to the fleet sent out by France the next year? What treaty closed this war? What was done by a band of Indians from St. Francis River? What happened on the return of this party? What was the conduct of the Indians from this time until the treaty of 1751?

CHAPTER XXI.

1. Hardly had the afflicted settlers of Maine joined again the broken links of business, when the actions of the French filled them with fresh alarm. Among the captures of the last war were two families of children, taken in Frankfort, now Dresden. Their fathers visited Canada in search of them, finding the children in Montreal, to their great delight. But now the French governor interfered, and would not let them go. This was in violation of the treaty and of humanity; and when the afflicted parents returned and made the facts known to Governor Shirley, he sent a messenger to Canada, who brought the children away by authority.

Then the French began to form settlements along the river Chaudiere, which has its source near the head waters of the Kennebec; and the Indians on this river resorted to the French for supplies. In Nova Scotia their actions were warlike, but the first positive act of hostility was the murder of some English settlers on Lake Erie. The messenger sent to protest against these outrages was George Washington, now appearing for the first time in national affairs; but all the reply he could obtain from the French commander was that the territory was French, and that he had orders to expel all intruders.

2. There were unsettled questions about boundaries, both on the east and north of Maine and in the valley of the Ohio River; and these were now under discussion at Paris. In the meantime France was pushing her settlements and forts in every direction, with the evident intention of holding all she had and getting all she could. There were Louisburg, on Cape Breton Island, which had been restored to her by the last treaty, four forts in Nova Scotia — though by the same treaty this province had been ceded to England; on the St. Lawrence were the strong cities of Montreal and Quebec — while southward were Crown Point on lake Champlain; Ticonderoga, between lakes Champlain and St. George; Fort Frontenac, at the outlet of Lake Ontario; Fort Niagara, just below the great falls; and Fort Du Quesne, [du kane] on the site of the present city of Pittsburg, in Pennsylvania.

3. The greatest efforts were made by the authorities of Maine to keep the natives peaceful, conferences being held with them, and many valuable presents given; so that at the last of these conferences, held in July, 1754, the Indians, in seeming good faith, placed five young savages in the hands of the English as hostages for the good behavior of the tribes. Three of these were Canibas, and two Tarratines; and they were taken to Boston to be educated.

Yet the authorities thought well of the old adage, "In time of peace prepare for war"; so they strengthened the old forts and built several new ones. The first, called Fort Halifax, was situated at the junction of the Sebasticook River with the Kennebec, in the present town of Winslow. It was a quadrangular structure of hewn pine, one hundred feet long and forty feet wide. It contained two block houses, and was mounted with several small cannon and a swivel.

LAST BLOCK HOUSE OF FORT HALIFAX.

4. The proprietors of the Plymouth Patent had built a fort a year before at Cushnoc, (Augusta) on the eastern side of the river, which they named Fort Western. It was constructed in nearly the same manner as Fort Halifax, but was not quite so large, and had only four guns. This year the same proprietors built another within the present town of Dresden, about a mile above the northerly end of Swan Island. This they named Fort Shirley, in honor of the governor. It was formed of stockades, and enclosed a parade ground two hundred feet square, together with two block houses. Another small fort was built at the second falls of the Androscoggin, in the present town of Lisbon.

On the sixth of November, 1754, before the fortifications were entirely finished, the Indians attacked a detachment of the garrison at Fort Halifax, as they were hauling wood. The **governor** immediately sent them a reinforcement of **one hundred** men with five cohorn mortars, **while six** companies of minute men were ordered **to be in** readiness to march at the **short**est notice; **but no further** attack was **made at this time.**

5. **Early in the year** 1755 occurred **the famous defeat of General Braddock** by **the** French **and Indians, when Colonel George W**ashington **behaved so gallantly. The** war soon **raged** from **the eastern to the western** settlements, **on land** and water; and **two thousand** men were raised, chiefly **in** Massachusetts **and Maine, to drive** the intruding French **from Nova Scotia.** Forty-one small vessels **conveyed them to** Chignecto **Bay, at the** northeastern **extremity of the** Bay of **Fundy, where** Colonel Monkton, **a British** officer, joined **them with a few pieces** of **artillery and** about three **hundred men. Monkton took the chief** command, **but the New Englanders did the fighting.**

A strong **fortification on the Missiquash River, well** garrisoned with **French troops, was attacked** by them **with** such spirit **that** the **French fled to** Beau-sejour, **a fort** farther up **the river. This** fort mounted twenty-**six guns, and was** supplied **with** plenty of ammunition **and soldiers; but** after **a siege** of four days **it** was **surrendered. The troops soon** appeared before the re**maining forts, all of which surrendered** in **turn. It was an easy victory; and the total loss** of **the English in the campaign was only twenty men.**

6. **Much the** larger **portion of** the inhabitants of **this** province lived about the bays of Minas and Chig**necto, where** were several populous villages. But the **people were of** French parentage, **and** would not take **the oath of allegiance,—**and from **this cause they were** generally spoken **of as the French Neutrals. They were a** peaceful people **when left alone; yet, longing to be under** the government **of their own nation, they were always** ready to **rise** in **rebellion at the bidding**

of French authority. This rendered them an exceedingly dangerous community to the English; therefore it was now decided by the British authorities of the province, that they must be removed. So the Acadians were forced to leave forever their pleasant homes, with their houses and lands, their flocks and herds,—and were scattered among the English colonies from Maine to Louisiana. The poet Longfellow has in "Evangeline" told us their touching story.

7. Meanwhile the Indians flitted like shadows among the settlements of Maine. There was scarcely a town where houses were not burned, and men, women and children killed or carried into captivity. Fifty men scouted constantly from the Piscataqua Ponds to Saco River; fifty more from New Boston (Gray) by way of Sebago Pond and New Gloucester; ninety from New Boston to Fort Shirley, in Dresden; and one hundred from thence to St. George's River. All these could not wholly prevent the destructive rage of the savages from making many victims; but when the fate of the French in Nova Scotia became known, the Indians, alarmed for themselves, forsook the frontiers and retired to the northern wilds.

8. The Indians who had been engaged in these hostilities were the Anasagunticooks, Canibas and St. Francis. The Tarratines still remained neutral, and no hostile acts had been committed by them during the war; yet a Captain Cargill, who had raised a company to fight the northern Indians, coming upon a party of Tarratine hunters near Owl's Head on Penobscot Bay, immediately shot down twelve of them. There was no call for such a force as Cargill's in that region; neither was any care taken before they fired upon the hunters, to learn whether they were friends or foes. Cargill was very justly arrested for this act; but though he was kept in prison for two years, no Indian appeared against him, and he was at last discharged. Government did what it could to

avert vengeance for the outrage, sending a letter of condolence to the families of the slain Indians, and loading with presents a party of the tribe who soon after visited Boston.

9. The governor not long after required the Penobscot Indians to furnish a number of warriors to join the English against the hostile tribes, according to their agreement in the last treaty; threatening to treat them as enemies if they refused. They were unwilling at any time to take up arms against their brethren of the Kennebec and St. Francis, and were now especially bitter against the English; while the French, who were of the same religion, were urging them to join their cause;—yet they decided to remain neutral. So government declared war against them because they did not fulfil their treaty obligations.

The next spring [1756] the Indians again commenced hostilities against the settlements, small parties of them being heard from in every quarter, from St. Georges to Saco. New Gloucester, especially, was so perilous a place that the inhabitants were offered the value of two pounds colonial money each, if they would stay in the town through the year.

10. In Windham one morning in May ten men started to work upon the farm of one of their number, about a mile and a half from the garrison. They were all armed with guns, as usual, and had with them a yoke of oxen attached to a sled,—for carts were difficult to be got in those days. When nearly to the field two of them went ahead to let down the bars for the oxen, and were shot down by the Indians from an ambush. One of them having two balls lodged in his heart, died instantly; the other, named Winship, had one ball pass through his head near the eye, and another lodge in his arm; and he also fell. The Indians scalped them both; but Winship was conscious all the time, though feigning to be dead, so as to escape the knife or tomahawk of the savages. At the report

of the guns four of the men ran back to the fort, while the others, led by Abraham Anderson and Stephen Manchester, crept silently forward to the spot, and hid behind a great log. Manchester put his cap on the end of his gun and pushed it into view of the Indians, from behind a tree; and one of them instantly fired at it, thinking it covered a white man's head. As the Indian turned aside to load, Manchester stood up and shot him dead on the spot. The other Indians instantly gave a loud shout and ran into the woods, supposing that a large company was after them. The Indian who was shot proved to be a chief named Poland, who claimed all the lands on the Presumpscot River, and had refused to make peace with the English until they allowed his claim.

11. The two men now placed the bodies of their companions on the sled and returned to the fort. After these had gone, the Indians returned. Bending down a small tree until its roots at one side were lifted from the ground, they thrust the body of the chief underneath; then the tree, being released, sprang back and covered it up; but they had first cut off an arm, to be placed in some consecrated burying ground of the Catholic church.

It would weary you if I should relate the incidents of this year in Maine. Everywhere the inhabitants fell singly, or by twos and threes, before the lurking foe; their buildings were burned, their cattle slaughtered,—and whatever crops escaped the Indians were badly damaged by worms, while in many localities the inhabitants were wasted by disease. There had been no military successes; forts with many regiments of troops had been surrendered in the west, the expeditions up the Kennebec and Androscoggin rivers had accomplished nothing; and the people were overwhelmed with public debt. It was a terrible year.

In 1758 several events took place which quite revived the spirits of our people. The first was the capture of Fort Du Quesne, at Pittsburg, by General Forbes,—followed by that of Louisburg, which now fell the second time into the hands of the English. In the siege of the latter place the famous General Wolfe took a brilliant part; and the six hundred soldiers furnished by Maine also did themselves honor.

12. Maine raised at about the same time, three hundred men for her own defense. There was need of them; for in August the fort at St. George's was attacked by four hundred French and Indians. Fortunately the governor got wind of the movement just in time to throw a strong reinforcement into the fort; and, unable to gain any advantage, the foe withdrew in great rage. Their next attack was on the fort at Meduncook, (Friendship) where they killed or captured eight men, but failed to take the fort. This was the last notable attack of the Indians upon the English settlements; and with this season the outrages and massacres by the tribes of Maine forever ceased; and the Abnaki, Etechemin and Mikmak have ever since been peaceful subjects of the English race.

13. But the result was not yet secured. Indians and French still held their ground, the one in Canada and about the great lakes, and the other in the remote forests of Maine. Therefore, in 1759, Governor Thomas Pownal, who had succeeded Shirley, sailed up the Penobscot River, looking for a site whereon to erect a fortress. It was the season when the fine scenery of this river is at its finest; and the governor expressed his regret that this noble region had been left so long to the savages.

The place chosen for the fort was a crescent-like hill on the western side of the river, in what is now the town of Prospect. The fortification was ninety feet on each side, and the breastwork was ten feet in height. Around it was a ditch fifteen feet wide and five feet deep; and in the midst of the ditch was a high palisade, making a fatal obstacle to an Indian enemy. At each corner was a flanker thirty-three feet square, and in the center stood a block house forty-four feet square and two stories high, having a sentry box on the top. This fortification was named Fort Pownal, in honor of the governor who was its builder.

14. While the fort was being built, Governor Pownal and General Waldo with a guard explored the river to the first falls, in Bangor. General Waldo was much interested in the new fort, because it was within the Muscongus, or Waldo Patent, in which he was a large owner. The northern limit of this patent was then thought to be near the point on the east of the river where the party halted. General Waldo, walking out a little distance from the others, stopped, looked about, and made the remark, "Here is my bound." He soon after dropped down in a fit of apoplexy, and died on the spot.

Meanwhile great battles were in progress at the west; and soon the glad news came that Fort Niagara had surrendered to the English, and that General Amherst had driven the enemy from Ticonderoga and Crown Point, while a strong force was besieging Quebec. Then the tidings came that the intrepid General Wolfe had won a victory over the French on the plains of Abraham, sealing the triumph with his life.

15. A few days before the fall of Quebec, Colonel Rogers was sent from Ticonderoga with two hundred rangers to destroy the Indian villages about the St. Francis River, just northwest of Maine. For twenty-one days they marched through unbroken wilds, when, from the top of a tall pine, one of the men discovered the village three miles distant. That night the Indians held a great feast and dance; and while this was going on Colonel Rogers with two of his officers wandered through the village unnoticed. Towards morning, when the weary savages were sunk in a drunken sleep, the rangers fell upon them, killing a

large number, and putting the rest to utter rout. In the morning the victors beheld a sight which made their blood run cold; for before them, on tall poles in the midst of the village, several hundred English scalps hung swinging in the wind.

16. The fall of Quebec filled the whole country with joy, for it was the harbinger of security and peace, and of many prosperous years. The towns of Maine celebrated the event with illuminations, while a day of public thanksgiving was held throughout the British dominions.

The power of France was broken in the north, and the long-suffering settlers of Maine no more met the Frenchman as a foe. When the trying days of the revolution came, the French forces, led by the gallant Lafayette, made amends to our young and struggling nation for the evils their countrymen had inflicted on the fathers, while subjects of Great Britain.

What unsettled questions brought on the last war with the French and Indians? How far southward had the French extended their fortresses? What noted man first appeared in national affairs at this period? What forts were built in Maine about this time? Where did the Indians make their first attack in Maine? What events occurred in Nova Scotia during this war? Why was war declared against the Tarratines? What Indian village at the northwest of Maine was destroyed? What effect did the fall of Quebec have? How did the French nation atone for their injuries to our forefathers?

CHAPTER XXII.

1. After years of bloody strife the sun of the eastern tribes had set in darkness, and the power which had urged them on to useless wars was overthrown. It is with a feeling of relief that we turn from scenes of savage cruelty to scan the fair fields of peace and prosperity.

The population of Maine in 1742 (a few years before the last Indian war commenced) was twelve thousand souls,—aside from the Indians, who at the close of this war numbered nearly fifteen hundred. The towns and plantations at this date had increased to about twenty-five; extending as far eastward as St. George's River, northward to Cushnoc (Augusta), and westward to Tow-woh (Lebanon) and New Gloucester. The population of Massachusetts, Rhode Island and Connecticut had increased greatly beyond that of Maine; for their settlements had not suffered for more than a century from the incursion of an enemy, except on their extreme northern borders. But Maine was all border; her small hamlets stretching in a slender line along an hundred miles of coast, with a vast wilderness behind them. I think that Massachusetts could well afford a few men to garrison our forts; for if the settlements of Maine had been overrun, the savage foe would have carried terror and destruction into her own villages. Surely there was much of heroism in the founders of our State, or they would not have chosen to come where forests must be felled, and the rough earth swept by fire before the seed could be planted and crops grown, and where they were ever liable to sudden destruction from the revengeful and bloodthirsty savage. No wonder that their bodies grew sturdy and their manners rude! Yet if their natures were rugged, like the hills among which they dwelt, the sweetness of the valleys lived in their deep affection towards the dear ones for whom they toiled and suffered.

2. In 1760, two new counties were formed, our present Lincoln and Cumberland. The boundaries of Cumberland have remained nearly unchanged; but Lincoln included all the country northward of the Androscoggin, and eastward to the St. Croix River. Its shire town was Pownalborough; of which the towns of Dresden, Wiscasset and Alna were afterwards formed.

Governor Pownal, for whom this town had been named, was much interested for the eastern people, so, of course, they greatly esteemed him. He was popular in Boston, too, though not a Puritan; and when he embarked for England at the close of his official term the members of the government attended him to his barge. He was afterward a member of Parliament;

GOVERNOR THOMAS POWNAL.

and by opposing the acts of oppression against the colonies, proved himself a true friend of America. Sir Francis Bernard, who a few months later succeeded him as governor, was on the contrary, entirely subservient to the wishes of the Parliament and King.

The first English settlements east of the Penobscot were made shortly before the year 1762. In this year twelve townships lying eastward of that river, were granted to several hundred petitioners, a few of whom had already settled there. The chief condition of these grants was, that sixty protestant families should become resident in each within six years. One lot in each township was reserved for a church, another for the first minister who should be settled there, a third for Harvard College, and a fourth for the use of schools.

3. The years 1761-62 were long remembered in Maine for the sickness, drought and fires. In the latter year the fresh vegetation of June was shriveled and blighted, and in July the flames, breaking out in the New Hampshire woods, swept eastward through the towns in York and Cumberland counties to the sea. It was not until late in August that their devastation was checked by copious rains.

Soon after the close of Lovewell's war, Parliament made several laws, called *Acts of Trade*, for the purpose of benefiting British revenues. One was the "Iron Act," by which all mills for working iron or steel were prohibited in the colonies; so that they were obliged to export the "pigs" (or bars of iron) from their mines to England, taking in return, in accordance with another law, woolen cloths and other fabrics, and implements of iron and steel. There was still another law imposing a high import tax on the molasses and sugar which the colonists of Maine received from the West Indies in return for lumber; this and fish being nearly all they had to sell. Then the molasses and sugar had to be carried to the southern colonies to pay for their corn and pork; so that by this time little remained **to be turned into** money or other property. Now that the wars had ceased, these laws were enforced **with rigor;** and the British government began **to plan how** it might realize still greater revenues **from** America. So in 1765 Parliament passed **the** celebrated "Stamp Act," by which **all papers for** ships, transfers of property, college diplomas, marriage licenses, and newspapers must be **made of** stamped paper, which was supplied at a high **price by the** government.

4. The feeling in Maine was strong against these oppressions, though few acts of violence **were committed** on account of them; but in other parts of the country the boldest royalists and stamp-masters **were** hung in effigy, and **the** latter forced to resign their offices. In England **that** great man, William Pitt, Earl of Chatham, **said in a** speech before Parliament on this act, "Sir, I rejoice that America has resisted. *Three millions* of people, so dead to all the feelings of liberty as to submit to be slaves, would have been **fit** instruments to make slaves of all the rest."

Yet no representative of the colonies **was admitted to a seat in** Parliament; and our countrymen **boldly declared that** "*Taxation without representation is tyranny.*" In 1766 the obnoxious act **was** repealed; and the event was celebrated in Maine by bonfires and illuminations, the firing of cannon and display of flags. The next year another form of taxation was tried on the colonies; a duty being imposed upon all paper, glass, colors, **and** teas brought **into the** country. This tax was not, like **the** former, opposed **by** force; **but the** representatives of **the** colonies met together **and expressed** their detestation of British exactions, and **took** all lawful means **for the redress of** their **wrongs; recommending** the **people to a manly defense of their rights, whether it brought relief or led to warlike resistance.** Meanwhile **by means** of newspapers, orations and pamphlets, **patriots like** Samuel and John

Adams, with Otis and Mayhew, in Boston, Livingston of New York, and Gadsden of South Carolina, instructed the people in their rights and stimulated the spirit of liberty in their breasts.

5. In 1768 seven hundred British soldiers arrived at Boston to enforce these iniquitous laws. They landed under cover of the guns of their vessels, and with loaded muskets and bayonets fixed, marched up to the Common. This, of course, greatly incensed the people; and Governor Bernard, being unable to prevail on the General Court to agree to any of his measures, the next year departed from the country in great disgust. His successor, Thomas Hutchinson, was a native of Boston, and a man of learning, ability and wealth; but, hoping to receive from the king an order of nobility, he became a foe to the liberties of his country. Having a familiar acquaintance with the people, he thought he could carry the king's measures by persuasion and skilful management. So the duty was taken off most of the articles in the new tax list, with the principal exception of tea.

Such a concession might have satisfied the people at first, but it did not now; and they formed associations, the members of which were pledged to drink no tea, in order thus to make a peaceable protest against the tax. Not that they cared much for so small a matter of itself, but their eyes were now open to see the danger and wickedness of being taxed by a government in which they had no representative.

6. Soon after this a sad affair happened in Boston. General Gage had sent some of his red-coated soldiers from New York to aid Hutchinson in governing Boston. Parties of them in passing through the streets were often gazed at and followed by idle men and rude boys, who were called by the soldiers, "Damned Yankees," and "Rebels"; while the rabble retorted by shouting, "Lobsters," and "Bloody Backs." The last taunt was a very bitter one to the soldiers; for it was

in allusion to the practice of flogging which then prevailed in the British army. So the soldiers and the rabble quickly got to quarreling; and one day (the fifth of March, 1770,) the soldiers fired on a party of sailors who attacked them, killing four and wounding several others. This was the famous "Boston Massacre," which produced such excitement.

7. In Maine there had long been a bitterness between the surveyors of the king's woods and the lumbermen, which led to frequent fisticuffs; but the affair at Portland in 1771 was the first in our State which had special relation to the Revolution. The king's collector of revenue at this port was absent; and the comptroller, who was next in authority, seized the schooner of Mr. Tyng, then in harbor, for the breach of some rule or other. This act was regarded by the people of Portland as unwarrantable, and produced great resentment,—at last resulting in a mob, which treated the unfortunate comptroller with the indignities common with such gatherings.

8. As the people of the colonies refused to drink tea the merchants refused to buy it; and the tiers of tea chests grew higher and higher in the warehouses of the East India Company in England. Something must be done, or the company would suffer great loss; so in December, 1773, they sent several shiploads of the article to America. You know what happened then. Some men dressed like Indians went on board the vessels and broke open the boxes of the dainty herb, and threw them overboard, until they reached up the ship's sides and tumbled back on deck; for just at that time the tide was out, and the heaps of tea chests rested on the dock mud.

9. This affair alarmed Governor Hutchinson, and soon after he, also, left for England; and he never came back. Then General Gage was appointed governor; thus becoming the chief ruler of Maine, as well as Massachusetts, because we were then a part of the

same province. The king **and the** tory members **of his government were very** much enraged at **the spoiling of the** tea; **and Parliament** ordered the port of Boston to be closed from the first day of June, 1774. When the order went into effect the bells of Falmouth and other towns in **Maine** tolled all day in token of sympathy with the oppressed city. On the 17th, Governor Gage dissolved the General Court,—but they had already chosen delegates to meet others from the colonies in a congress at Philadelphia.

10. The people of Maine and Massachusetts **soon** after elected representatives, **who met in** Salem in October. They formed themselves **into a** Provincial Congress, and chose John Hancock as its president. They **also** elected a Committee of Safety, and a Committee of Supplies, and chose five delegates to represent Maine and Massachusetts in the new Continental Congress. They **also** made laws for the formation and drill of military companies in **every town, and recommended the people to grow more** flax, **to be made into linen, and to enlarge their** flocks of sheep, **so as to** produce more wool,—that the colonies might be prepared for the events which **seemed to be approaching.**

What was the population of Maine in 1742? How many settlements were there at this date? Why had not the population of Maine increased as rapidly as that of other New England States? What counties were formed in 1760? At what time were the first English settlements made east of the Penobscot? What happened in Maine in the year 1761-62? How did Great Britain oppress the colonies at the close of the Indian wars? What great principle did our forefathers proclaim? What noted affray took place in 1770? What was the first outbreak connected with the Revolution in Maine? What happened in Boston in 1773? What was done by the people of Maine and Massachusetts soon after this event?

CHAPTER XXIII.

1. In March, 1775, the Canseau, a British sloop of war, came to Falmouth, (Portland) for the purpose of forcing the citizens to allow the unloading of a tory vessel. She was commanded by Captain Mowatt, who afterwards proved the especial scourge of Maine. From Falmouth he went to the Penobscot, where he robbed Fort Pownal of all its guns and ammunition, and nearly broke up the rich trade here carried on with the natives.

Government had at this point taken especial care for the comfort of the Indians, having erected buildings for their use when they came to trade. It had also supplied a devoted minister of the gospel for the benefit of the garrison and such natives as would listen to his instructions. One or more ministers had also long been sustained at or near Fort Shirley, on the Kennebec; and the Indians on these rivers, being relieved from French influence, became so favorably inclined toward the colonists that neither the British agents nor their brethren in New Brunswick were able to prevail upon them to take up arms against their white neighbors.

In the very next month after Mowatt's visit the battle of Lexington was fought, giving the signal of open war throughout the colonies. The news arrived in York at evening. In the morning the citizens flocked together, a company was enlisted, armed and equipped, and the following night it reached New Hampshire on the way to Boston. Three days later Falmouth sent a company; and shortly after, Colonel Scammon of Biddeford reached Cambridge with a regiment. New Gloucester raised twenty men, paying their wages and supporting their families during their absence. Thus did our good State of Maine answer the summons of liberty.

2. The inhabitants eastward were too remote and scattered to furnish any more troops than were necessary to protect their own exposed borders; yet, as we shall see, they were not in the least behind their western brothers in courage and patriotism. When the news of Lexington fight reached Bath, the people decided that war had begun, and that all persons under British control must be treated as enemies of American liberty. It happened that a company of British were then preparing masts at the king's dock; and Colonel Sewall, with thirty other inhabitants, marched down to seize them. The workmen hastily jumped into their boats and got on board the vessels, which then sailed away down the river and escaped; but the naval agent was left in the hands of the citizens.

A few days after this affair, Lieutenant Colonel Thompson, of Brunswick or Topsham, learned that the Canseau was again at Falmouth, and that her commander, Captain Mowatt, spent much time on shore; and, raising a company of volunteers, he proceeded thither in hopes to capture him. The standard of the company was a spruce pole with a green tuft at the top, while each man had a sprig of evergreen in his cap. Having ascertained that Captain Mowatt was to dine on shore, they concealed themselves in a small wood on the east side of the peninsula and awaited his appearance. The dinner hour passed; and soon the captain, his surgeon and a citizen sauntered down near the grove, and all three were quietly taken prisoners.

3. When the capture become known on board his vessel, the officer next in command sent word to the authorities, that unless Captain Mowatt was released within two hours he would bombard the town. This created great alarm; and many began to pack their goods and send them off in carts into the country.

But Mowatt promised the town authorities that if they would permit him to go on board his vessel he would prevent the bombardment; **so** two of the leading citizens became **security to** Colonel Thompson for him, and he **was permitted to** depart, on agreement to return the **next** morning. He professed the **utmost gratitude to the** citizens for their interference in his favor; **but, once on board his sloop, he** staid there; **and sailing away,** left his sureties to pay the forfeit.

Then came the battle of Bunker Hill, where the **brilliant ranks of the** British marched up towards the **silent** breastworks, and "Old Put" rode back and forth **upon his** white horse,—when the **silent** breastworks suddenly became sheeted with flame, **and there was** rattle **of** musketry and **roar of cannon,—where the** smoke of **burning** Charleston **poured about them, and the swelling forces** of the **British still came on,** until the outnumbered patriots, with powder spent and useless guns, retired before the bristling bayonets of the enemy. **There** were Maine men who fought bravely in the **ranks** that day, and some were left lying in their gore upon the bloody field.

4. There were also desperate conflicts **at home, and successful** ones, though not on so grand **a scale. In May the Margaretta, an** armed schooner of the enemy, came **to Machias** for the purpose of convoying some lumber **vessels to the** British at Boston. Seeing a liberty pole, **the captain came** on shore and inquired who erected it. He was informed that it was done by order of the **town.** He told them it must be taken down, or he would fire upon **the** village. The citizens held a meeting and voted not to take it down. Some were dissatisfied, and another meeting was appointed for the next Monday. On Sunday the captain and some of his officers attended church **in the** village. Happening to look out of **the** window **during** the service, he saw a company of men armed with guns crossing the river on the logs. The frightened captain quickly **leaped**

out of the window and fled to his vessel. The band which had sent him off in such haste consisted of Benjamin Foster and some other bold young fellows, whose plan it had been to surround the church and seize the British as they came out. A few shots were exchanged between this party and the schooner, but she soon sailed down the river beyond their reach.

5. The next day Foster and his company were joined by six fine brothers, named O'Brien, with another company. In the course of a day or two both had set off in search of the Margaretta; Foster in a small coaster, and the O'Briens in the wood sloop, "Liberty." They found the schooner in the bay, and ran alongside with the intention of boarding. She received them with a discharge of swivel guns, muskets and hand grenades, by which several were killed. The vessels fell apart, only John O'Brien, one of the six brothers, having got on board the enemy. Seven of the British instantly fired at him, but not a bullet touched him. Then they charged upon him with their bayonets; but before they could reach him he was overboard, and swimming to his sloop. Several of the enemy had fallen by the fire of the Americans, and among them their captain; and when the vessels were again brought together the officer in command fled below in terror, and the crew yielded at once. This was the first British vessel captured by Americans; and the action brought the captors much applause.

6. O'Brien's sloop was then fitted up with bulwarks, armed with the guns of the captured schooner, and sent off on a cruise. A month later she fell in at Buck's Harbor with two vessels which had been sent out to recapture the Margaretta. These were the Diligent, a schooner of eight guns and carrying fifty men, with her tender, armed with swivels and carrying twenty men. Foster, in his coaster, came to O'Brien's aid; and the Diligent and her tender were captured

without the loss of a man. For these brilliant exploits Foster and the O'Briens received the thanks of Congress.

Only once since Mowatt dishonored his word and sailed away, had the good people of Falmouth suffered the least intimidation from the enemy; that was when a sloop of war came to help away some tories with their goods. Again in October the inhabitants were alarmed by the sight of four British vessels entering their harbor; but when they saw that Mowatt's vessel was the flag ship of the squadron their minds were more at ease; because they trusted in his gratitude for the favor they had done him five months before. Great was their consternation when, the next day, he sent a letter ashore, stating that in two hours he should open a bombardment on the town.

7. At this time the place consisted of about five hundred dwellings and stores, with many barns and stables. Some hundred of the poorer sort of houses were scattered over the peninsula to the south and west, but the main portion were clustered together in the midst of the slope towards the harbor. The place was entirely defenseless from an attack by sea; but as no provocation had been given no such event was looked for. The time allowed the inhabitants to secure their safety was cruelly short; and a committee was sent to inquire the cause of such an extraordinary proceeding. Mowatt made them this answer:—"My orders I have received from Admiral Graves, and they direct me to repair to this place with all possible expedition, take my position near the town, and burn, sink and destroy,—and this without giving the people warning. The note you have had is of special grace, at the risk of my commission."

8. The committee protested against the barbarity of the order, and urged the town's claims for the favor done him a few months ago by its citizens; but he only replied that his orders related to every seaport upon

the continent. Yet he finally said that if they would deliver him four pieces of cannon, their small arms and their ammunition by eight o'clock the next morning, he would spare them until he could hear from the admiral, who might be induced to spare the town; or if they would give him eight stands of small arms immediately they should not be molested until the hour named. They were completely at the mercy of this petty tyrant; and in order to save something from their homes to keep their families alive, they sent him the eight stands of arms. At daylight the next morning the citizens held a meeting, and resolved to give up nothing more, but to sacrifice their dwellings rather than lose the remainder of their precious guns and ammunition.

The committee informed Captain Mowatt of the decision, and besought him for humanity's sake to allow them further time.

"I will give you thirty minutes and no more," replied the cruel and ungrateful man.

9. There were few teams in the place, and most of the household goods still remained in the dwellings or piled up before the doors when the vessels opened their batteries upon the town. The firing was rapid, and the cannon balls, bombs and grape shot poured in a terrible shower upon the defenseless village. No spot was safe from them, and the inhabitants were forced to flee for their lives — many of them saving only what they bore away on their backs. Under cover of the guns, armed parties came from the ships and applied the torch to the buildings; yet the citizens, with devoted courage, followed after them, putting out the fires at the risk of their lives; but in spite of their efforts the flames prevailed. Towards night the bombardment ceased, but the fair and flourishing village of yesterday was riddled with shot and shell, or lay in ashes. St. Paul's church, the new court-house, the town-house, the public library, the fire engine,—

all were gone; and the houseless people gazed from afar on the fading smoke columns that marked the places of their desolated homes.

10. Scattered over the peninsula there were still nearly an hundred houses which had escaped the bombardment; and the owners of these, with such other of the inhabitants as decided to remain, began at once to prepare against any future attack. All the heavy arms they could procure were two six pounders; and before the walls of the battery were built, another vessel came into the harbor and forbade their going on with the work. She carried a heavier armament than all of Mowatt's fleet put together; but the people only pressed their fortifications more vigorously, and began to contrive ways to capture the vessel. As soon as the commander found his threats disregarded, he hoisted sail and left the harbor,—probably thinking that he had a good ship to lose, but nothing to gain.

What fort was dismantled by Capt. Mowatt? How soon after this did the battle of Lexington take place? What troops were immediately sent from Maine? What happened at Bath? What **affair occurred soon after in Falmouth?** Where was the first capture of British vessels made by Americans? Give an account of **the burning of Falmouth.** What happened subsequently when a **vessel of** the enemy threatened the place?

CHAPTER XXIV.

1. **The** expedition against Quebec through Maine, in 1775, was one of **the** most famous, and also one of the most unfortunate events of the Revolution. It was led by Benedict Arnold, who subsequently proved a traitor to his country. His army consisted of ten companies of musketry, from Maine and Massachusetts, and three **companies** of riflemen, from Pennsylvania and Virginia,—altogether about 1,100 men. Several persons connected with this expedition afterward became noted as war leaders and public men; among whom were Daniel Morgan, commander of the riflemen; Aaron Burr, subsequently Vice President, then a youth of twenty; and Henry Dearborn, of Pittston on the Kennebec, who afterwards **became Secretary of War. The plan was to ascend Kennebec River and its chief western tributary to the range of hills which forms the boundary of Maine on the northwest, whence they would soon strike the head waters of the Chaudiere, a river emptying into the St. Lawrence.** The expedition sailed from **New**buryport on the 18th of September; **and, entering** the Kennebec, ascended to Pittston, where two hundred bateaux were in readiness. Dismissing the vessels, the troops entered the bateaux and continued on to Fort Western, in Augusta, where they spent several days in procuring guides and provisions.

2. First of all went a small exploring party; after this followed Morgan with the riflemen, then **Green, Bigelow and Meigs** with the main body of the troops, while Colonel Enos brought up the rear. Arnold staid to see the last boat load depart; then, entering an Indian canoe, he passed one company **after** another, overtaking the riflemen on the third day at Bombazee Rips in Norridgewock. **Here the boats** had all to be

drawn ashore **and carried a** mile **and a** quarter to reach the navigable water above. It was found that the boats were leaky, and that a great part of the provision **was spoiled or** damaged; and seven days elapsed **before repairs were** completed and they again embarked on the river.

After passing Carratunk Falls the stream grew so rapid that the **men** were obliged to wade and push **the** boats more than half the way to the Great Carrying **Place,** twelve miles below the Forks. The carry was fourteen miles long; but three little ponds on the way afforded them as many rests, and a plenty of delicious trout. Then they met Dead River flowing calmly through grand old forests resplendent with all the brilliant hues of autumn. Passing falls and rapids, they at length beheld rising above the woods a lofty mountain already white with snow. Here Arnold encamped for three days, displaying from a tall staff over his tent the Continental flag; while Major Bigelow ascended the mountain in the vain hope of seeing the spires of Quebec. The township in which the camps were pitched is now called Flagstaff Plantation, **and** the mountain bears the name of Bigelow, in commem**oration of** these events.

3. Soon after leaving this point a heavy rain storm **set in.** The water rushed in torrents down the hills, **the river** channel filled with drift wood, and the water **burst into the** valley where the soldiers were encamped **with such** suddenness that they had scarcely time to retreat to the bateaux before the whole plain was covered with water. Worse than all, seven boats were upset, and the stores lost; leaving them only twelve days provisions, with thirty miles more of hills, woods and marshes between them and the head waters of the Chaudiere. Many had become sick from toil and exposure, and were sent back to the division of Colonel Enos, who was now ordered to send the invalids to the settlements, and come on as fast as possible with his

best men, and provisions for fifteen days. He had only three days provisions; and, at a council of his officers, it was decided that the whole division must return or perish.

The rain had changed to snow, and the ponds, marshes and streams became covered with ice; yet the men were often obliged to wade and push the bateaux. Many of the boats were abandoned, for the oxen had been killed for food; and everything had to be carried by the men. On the 27th of October the boats were lifted for the last time from the waters of Maine, and a portage of four miles brought them to a small stream down which they urged the remaining bateaux to Lake Megantic, the chief source of the Chaudiere.

4. The next morning a party of fifty-five men was sent forward through the woods to the French settlements, still seventy miles further, for provisions, while Arnold with thirteen men set off in five bateaux and a canoe. They were without a guide; and no sooner had they left the lake and entered the river than they were obliged to lash their freight to the boats lest it should be thrown overboard by the turbulent current. The roar of the stream increased. Three boats were dashed in pieces upon the rocks, their contents lost, and their crews left struggling in the water.

The main body of the troops followed on as rapidly as they could. In a few days nothing was left except a little flour, which was eaten with water without salt. On coming near the sandy beach of the river some keen-eyed soldier would be seen to dart from the ranks down to the water's edge, closely followed by half a dozen more. They had caught sight of some water plant, supposed to be eatable, and the foremost man dug it up with his fingers and instantly devoured it without washing. A little lean dog belonging to one of the officers disappeared one night, and the next day a few of the soldiers had some thin, greenish fluid which they called bear's broth, though no one had heard that a bear had been killed. Old moose hide breeches were boiled and then broiled on the coals, and eaten. Many men died with hunger and fatigue, frequently four or five minutes after making their last effort and sitting down.

5. Friday, November 3d, was a memorable day to the little army. Weary, despairing, *starving*, few could have kept on much longer, when they were met by some cattle sent back by the advanced party with Arnold. They were saved from starvation; but most of them lived for a bloodier death. After many unnecessary delays Arnold led them against the strong city of Quebec, but the golden moment had passed. The garrison had been reinforced, and hundreds of these brave men, who, for the sake of gaining this important post, had endured the toil and famine of the wilderness, lay down before the fatal hail of the artillery, making the blood-stained snow their winding sheet. The brave Montgomery and his victorious little army, fresh from the capture of Montreal, shared their fate. More than four hundred Americans fell in this attack, while four hundred more were taken captive, and suffered many months of severe imprisonment.

6. By the close of the year 1775, the Continental Congress was fully entered upon its labors of law-making. Post offices were established and put in operation from Maine to Georgia; and during the winter the militia was arranged anew. Massachusetts was formed into four military divisions,—Maine being one by itself. The militia of each county constituted a brigade, which was again sub-divided into regiments and companies. John Frost, of Kittery, was Brigadier General of York county, Samuel Thompson, of Brunswick, commanded the Cumberland militia, and the officer for Lincoln county was Charles Cushing of Pownalborough.

The British cruisers were on our coast, and the militia was at once put in condition to meet the redcoats wherever they might set foot on our shores.

Falmouth was partially rebuilt, having **fortifications** mounting six **cannon**, and she **now** felt **herself** competent with the **aid of** the militia to beat back any force the British might **send** against **her**. But General Washington had driven **the** British army out of Boston and early in **the** summer their vessels mostly **went** southward.

On July 4th, 1776, the Continental Congress declared **the thirteen** United Colonies to be *Free* and *Independent*. In Maine the ministers read the Declaration to their people, **and** the town clerks **entered it at full length** in their records. We had a **country, now,** and were no longer rebellious subjects **of** a foreign **power,** but citizens and sovereigns of Independent States. The question was no longer whether **we** would be able to obtain our rights of Great Britain, but whether we would be a *Nation* **or** a subjugated people. Tories were no longer a political party, but enemies, spies and traitors, and to be treated **as** such, **or in pity** allowed to depart from the **country.** This *Independence* infused *spirit* into the people; and the **citizens of** Maine wanted **to be** doing something **by which it** might be *secured forever*.

7. Therefore in September of this year **an expedition set out** from Machias to **capture** Fort Cumberland on Chignecto Bay in Nova Scotia. The force consisted only of a schooner and a few whale boats, carrying seventy **men.** The commander was Johnathan Eddy, who had formerly lived in the neighborhood of the fort, but had been driven away by the authorities because he **wished that** province to join **the other** colonies. At Chepody Hill, not **far** from the **fort,** Colonel Eddy's men captured fifteen **soldiers with their captain.** Two or three days later a vessel came into the harbor with supplies for the garrison, **and Colonel** Eddy with twenty-five men sallied out afoot over **the** flats during a fog, and **made** her a prize. Many of Eddy's old neighbors joined him, so that he soon had a force of one hundred and fifty men.

At length on a cloudy night the attack was made on the fort. Its embankments were very high, and along the top were placed heavy logs, ready to roll down upon any assailants. The garrison had been reinforced and was expecting the assault; and Colonel Eddy was repulsed with much loss. The result of this expedition was very painful. The enemy pursued the little band, destroyed their camp, and captured their vessels, forcing them to make their retreat through the wilderness. After twenty-five days of toil and suffering the straggling remnant arrived at Machias, hungry and gaunt, with clothing half stripped from their bodies. The houses of such as lived at Chignecto were burned by troops from the fort, and their families left homeless and destitute until the next spring, when, after extreme sufferings, they were brought away by a vessel under a flag of truce.

8. Another patriotic refugee from Nova Scotia, John Allan, had been a member of the General Assembly of the province, but sympathized so openly in the American cause that he was obliged to fly for his life, and had not even time to bring away his family. At the failure of the attack on Fort Cumberland his house was plundered and burned with the rest, and his wife thrown into prison. Congress made him its agent to keep the Indians from joining the British, who were using every means to win them. If they had succeeded, all of Maine east of the Penobscot would probably have now been a part of the British dominions. Colonel Allan spent most of his time with the Passamaquoddy Indians, keeping a government store for the benefit of this and other tribes.

After the Indians had joined with the Americans in the repulse of the vessels at Machias, they were in much dread of the British, and relied greatly on Colonel Allan for counsel and aid in case of an attack upon them. They were also very much attached to him; yet, as he was obliged to leave them frequently for other duties, they feared he might forsake them entirely; and at last they refused to permit his departure unless he left his two boys as security for his return. These boys remained with the tribe two years; and though they must have found much to enjoy, they were many times obliged to live on fish, parched corn, and seal's flesh, and were often ragged, hungry and miserable. Their father did the best he could to keep up their courage and character under these difficult conditions; often writing them such letters as the following:

9. "Be very kind to the Indians, and take particular notice of Nicholas, Francis, Joseph and old Coucou-guash. I send you books, paper, pens and ink, wafers, and some other little things; shall send more in two or three days. Let me entreat you, my dear children, to be careful of your company and manners, be moral, sober and discreet. Duly observe your duty to the Almighty, morning and night. Mind the Sabbath day, not to have either work or play, except necessity compels you. I pray God to bless you, my dear boys."

In 1777, Machias was made a national military station, and supplied with two nine pounders, and garrisoned with three hundred men under Colonel Allan. The British remembered well the previous exploits of the Machias people, and as soon as the admiral heard at New York of this new movement he despatched a naval force to destroy the town and to defend the Nova Scotia coasts against the troublesome people of Maine. In August of this year, and before a garrison was collected together, a sloop, two frigates and a brig anchored in Machias River. Having burned a tide mill and taken a coasting sloop, they sent the brig, the sloop, and some barges laden with soldiers up the west branch to destroy whatever came in their way. They landed at "Indian Brim," where they burned down a few buildings; then, the wind having died away, they towed their brig and sloop up river to a point within a mile and a half from the falls.

10. By this time it was late in the afternoon, and the people had learned the position of the enemy, and gathered for the attack. The barges had come up to within half a mile of the falls, and here the firing commenced upon them from both banks of the river. The men were speedily driven from the barges on board the sloop and brig, which drifting down river, made the guns of the British very uncertain in their aim. Soon the brig ran aground, and such a shower of bullets was poured down on the deck from the banks that the men were obliged to go below to save their lives. At length a breeze sprang up in a favorable quarter, and the vessels succeeded in getting off. Every man in town capable of bearing arms had now found his place somewhere along the river, and watched to get a shot at the invaders. Colonel Allan had brought down his Indians who whooped in their peculiar way from their hiding places, and the white people who were scattered through the woods along the river imitated their yells, until the retreating marines thought the forests full of wild warriors. The British were quite discouraged by this experience from attempting anything more; and a day or two later the squadron left the harbor.

The great event of this year was the surrender of the British army under Burgoyne to General Gates at Saratoga; and the news gave a joyful close to the season's campaign in Maine.

What famous expedition passed up the Kennebec in 1775? What noted men were connected with it? What was the result of this expedition? What was done by Congress at the close of the year? What effect did the declaration of independence have in Maine? What was the result of Johnathan Eddy's expedition against Fort Cumberland? What valuable service did Col. John Allan render to the American cause? Describe the action with the British at Machias? What great victory occurred near the close of the year?

CHAPTER XXV.

1. The Continental currency, which was almost the only money in circulation, had constantly fallen in value, until at this time it took thirty dollars in bills to equal one in specie. Six dollars in currency was the price of a pair of stockings; seven dollars were paid for a pair of common cowhide shoes,—while beef was five and six dollars a pound. In 1779 corn sold for thirty-five dollars per bushel, wheat meal for about seventy-five dollars, molasses at sixteen dollars a gallon, and tea at nineteen dollars a pound. Yet the high price of some of these articles was owing partially to the injury of the crops by drought. Surely these were times when men's courage and strength were tried to the utmost. The pay received by a private soldier was insufficient to keep his family from want; yet the ranks of the army, thinned by battle and disease, must be filled up,—if not by volunteers, then by draft.

2. Early in the year 1778 Hon. John Adams was appointed minister at the French Court. This was an important appointment; for it was hoped that France would be induced to aid us in our arduous struggle. His safe conveyance to that country was entrusted to Commodore Tucker, afterward a citizen of Bremen in this state. He was then in command of the frigate *Boston*, and in February he sailed for France with Mr. Adams on board. He soon found himself pursued by three British ships, which had been on the watch for the minister's departure. It is difficult to escape from two swift vessels, the fugitive being almost sure to be intercepted on one side or the other; but if there is a third to follow up in a direct line it must ordinarily be impossible to avoid an encounter. By uncommon skill in maneuvering Tucker

eluded them for several days. As they entered the Gulf Stream a great storm arose, and the Boston saw its pursuers no more.

3. A few days later they discovered an English ship ahead; and this both the captain and his noble passenger desired to capture. Mr. Adams, having obtained a musket, placed himself among the marines with the determination of taking a part in the fight. Captain Tucker soon caught sight of the minister; and, stepping up to him, placed a hand upon his shoulder, saying sternly, "Mr. Adams, I am commanded by the Continental Congress to deliver you safe in France, and you must go below, sir." Mr. Adams smiled and went down to the cabin.

When within range a shot was fired at the Martha, which was the name of the enemy's vessel, to bring her to. She replied by a discharge of three guns, which cut away some of the rigging; and a piece from the mizzen came down upon the captain's head, felling him to the deck. But he was upon his feet the next moment, and soon had his frigate in position for a raking fire upon the enemy. The marines were at their posts, the great guns were shotted, the matchstocks of the gunners were smoking,—still the order to fire was not given. The men grew impatient, and began to murmur and swear bitterly that so fine a chance should be allowed to pass,—when the commander shouted in that stentorian voice for which he was famous, "Hold on, my men; I wish to save that egg without breaking the shell." They did not have to wait long; for the enemy overheard the order, and took the hint; and his flag came down immediately.

4. It is said that Tucker captured more guns from the enemy than any other naval commander of the Revolution. By his success he amassed considerable property, and resided in a fine mansion on a fashionable street in Boston; but, becoming fatally addicted to strong drink, he lost his standing with government,

his property slipped from his hands, and he was reduced at length to a farm in Bristol, Maine, where in a rough house of three rooms he and his family lived many years.

The ambassador had been safely landed in France; and in the following June, Count d'Estaing reached our shores with a fleet to aid the American cause. This event, with the success of our arms in the battle of Monmouth, lifted the gloomy clouds and gave assurance that Independence would finally be won.

In 1779 Congress divided the whole country into districts, for the purposes of revenue and better administration of national laws; and thus it was that we became the District of Maine,—still a part of Massachusetts, yet having a United States court and the district officers, as we have had ever since.

5. The British commanders now saw that something must be done to check Maine, or she would wrest Nova Scotia from them; so in July, 1779, General McLane with a force of seven or eight vessels and nine hundred men, came to Penobscot and took possession of Castine. The place was undefended; and the larger portion of the fleet soon departed, leaving three sloops of war under Mowatt to assist the troops in holding the position. Steps were immediately taken to dislodge them; and about the middle of July a flotilla reached Townsend (now Boothbay) Harbor, where the land forces awaited them. The fleet was commanded by Commodore Saltonstall, of Connecticut, and had on board a few companies of marines and a company of ordnance under Col. Paul Revere. Brigadier Generals Frost, Thompson and Cushing, of Maine, were there with their militia, ready to embark on the patriotic enterprise. The fleet consisted of the flag ship *Warren*, which was a fine, new Continental frigate of thirty-two guns, together with nine ships, six brigs and three sloops,—the whole carrying three hundred and forty-

four guns. General Lovell, **of Massachusetts, was commander of the land forces, and his associate was** Adjutant General Peleg **Wadsworth, afterward a resident of Maine.**

The British commander at Castine had heard of the expedition several days before its arrival, and had done his **utmost to** prepare for the attack. As soon **as it appeared in** sight he concluded that defense was **impossible,** except he was reinforced; and he sent **at once to** Halifax for aid.

6. Early in the morning of July 28th the vessels were drawn up in a line before the British position on the peninsula, and four hundred men were sent ashore under cover of the fog to commence the attack. The **neck had been separated from** the mainland by a broad, deep **trench, and the sides were so** well defended that the troops could **only be landed on** the northwest, where the shore, **at one** point, **rose** precipitously nearly one hundred feet. As they left the boats the cannon balls from the British ships began to whistle over their heads, and a line of soldiers posted along the heights threw down a brisk fire of musketry into their faces. They immediately divided into three parties,—the center remaining to engage the enemy, **while the other parties** climbed the bank at right and left. **On reaching the top they suddenly** closed in upon the British line, which **hastily** retreated, leaving thirty of their number **killed, wounded and prisoners.** It was **a short but sharp encounter, lasting** only twenty minutes; **but in that** time we lost one hundred men. There was scarcely a more brilliant engagement during the war; and if the action had been followed up by the fleet the place must in a short time have surrendered. A council was now held, in which it was proposed that a surrender should be demanded; but Saltonstall opposed, and it was not done.

7. But General Lovell still pressed his advantage **on shore, reducing the** enemy's outworks and captur-

ing several field pieces. His troops worked all through the nights constructing their zigzag entrenchments,— which were at length advanced within musket shot of the fort, so that in the daytime a soldier seldom dared to put his head above the walls. Meanwhile all that the ships did with their three hundred and forty guns was to cannonade the enemy at intervals from some safe place beyond the reach of his cannon.

A fortnight had now passed since the siege commenced, and Generals Lovell and Wadsworth were preparing to take the place by assault,—when, just before they were ready, a British fleet appeared in the bay. Valor had done all it could, and now prudence dictated a retreat. During the following night the Americans embarked in safety, while Saltonstall made preparations to check the approach of the enemy, arraying his fleet in the form of a crescent. The British fleet consisted of a large man-of-war, a frigate, two ships, two brigs and a sloop, under the command of Sir George Collier. It came steadily on, and, getting within range, poured a broadside upon Saltonstall's vessels.

8. Immediate confusion followed. Most of the masters of the vessels were also their owners; and, interest prevailing over patriotism, they fled without waiting for a second broadside, and some of them without firing a gun. Some of the transports ran ashore near Orphan Island, and were set on fire and abandoned, while others escaped up the Penobscot. Few inhabitants then dwelt along the river, and the scattered troops were forced to take their tedious way through the wilderness to the settlements of the Kennebec, suffering greatly on the journey for lack of provisions; and some who were infirm actually perished in the woods.

A court of inquiry was held at Boston soon after upon the "Penobscot Expedition"; and the General Court adjudged that "Commodore Saltonstall be incompetent ever after to hold a commission in the service of the State, and that Generals Lovell and Wadsworth be honorably acquitted."

9. In August, 1780, two armed vessels of the enemy came up the Kennebec to destroy the shipping, and do whatever other damage they could. On their way they anchored near Bluff Head. During the night they were alarmed by the whistling and crashing of shot over their decks,—the missiles coming from two field pieces on the hill. Though imperfect aim could be taken by the gunners in the darkness, several of the British were killed, and the vessels considerably damaged. As soon as it was light the vessels slipped their cables and went to sea, followed by several boatloads of men from up the river, anxious for battle. This was the enemy's last attempt on the Kennebec.

In the autumn of 1779 Congress had prohibited all exportation from Maine, even to other States; and no timber, live stock, no wool, flax—or goods made of them, no skins, leather, shoes, no kind of food, clothing, or material for ships, could be carried from the province on penalty of forfeiture. Some sales could be made to the government, for which payment was made in the depreciated currency; yet the people of Maine lacked greatly for necessary articles of food and clothing not produced within its limits. The purpose of this embargo was to prevent stores from falling into the hands of the British, and to secure supplies for our own needy forces.

10. The fleet which had driven ours from Castine brought fifteen hundred fresh troops, and the British had now full sway along our entire eastern coast; and many were the outrages committed upon the defenceless inhabitants. They carried off cattle, burned mills and dwellings, and personally abused the people; so that numerous residents in that region abandoned their homes **and sought safety in** the western counties.

The Continental army had drawn so many men from Maine that two or three companies at Machias, a volunteer company in Lincoln, and another in York, were all that remained in service. These were quite insufficient for the defence of any point, and served only to keep the tories in awe.

The next year Maine's quota for the national army was remitted, and six hundred men were taken from the militia for eight months' service at home in the pay of the general government. Three hundred of these were stationed at Falmouth, two hundred at Camden, and one hundred at Machias; while Falmouth also received, in addition to those she had before, two cannon carrying an eighteen pound ball, and five carrying one of four pounds. Though these provisions were insufficient, yet with them the military authorities succeeded in holding the enemy in check, so that the British gained no further advantage in Maine.

11. General Wadsworth, a prudent and able man, had been placed in command of the district of Maine, and made his head quarters at Thomaston. When their eight months of service were out, the six hundred men who had been detached from the militia, retired from active military duty. This left the general with a very small force; but he continued to reside at Thomaston with his family, guarded by only six soldiers. In the middle of a cold February night he was awakened from his sleep by the loud and rapid reports of guns and the crashing of glass in the windows of his room. The British commander at Castine had learned of his undefended situation, and sent a lieutenant with twenty-five soldiers to take him.

On their approach the sentry hailed, "Who's there?" and retreated into the house. Instantly a volley was poured after him, while others fired into the windows. They quickly had possession of the house, excepting one room, which was occupied by the general alone.

Here, with a brace of **pistols, fusee and blunderbuss**, he contended, single handed, against **his** besiegers, driving them away from the windows and door. Then an attack was made at another door, which they broke in. This **time his** blunderbuss missed fire; yet with a **bayonet he still** kept them back. All this time he **was in his night cl**othes; which, as soon as **the door was** opened, rendered him a distinct mark for **a shot,— and a** bullet soon pierced his arm. Longer resistance was useless; and he surrendered himself a prisoner. Presently the lieutenant entered with a candle; and looking at General Wadsworth, said: "Sir, you have defended yourself bravely—done **too** much for one **man.** But we must be in haste. **We will** help **you on with your clothes."** In a few minutes he was on the march with the company toward **Castine**; and his family was left without further harm.

12. In April, Major **Burton, one of his officers,** was captured and confined with him; and they decided to **make** an attempt to escape. With a gimlet obtained of their barber, they bored holes in the pine ceiling of their room, filling the holes with paste made of bread. In three weeks one of the boards was severed, and **ready to** be taken out. At length there **came** a night **favorable to** the attempt, **when** the **rain** and frequent **loud thunder** drowned all **minor sounds.** The board **was removed, and** Major Burton went out first, while **the general,** whose arm was still somewhat lame, found much **difficulty** in lifting himself **through the hole. He finally** succeeded, got into **the entry, and passed out of the door,—then** felt his way along **the outside** of the building directly under the falling **water from** the eaves. He reached the embankment and climbed the pickets just in time to escape the guard. Then by means of blankets he let himself down into the ditch, from whence he crept softly out, and found himself in the open field, wet **to** the skin, but undiscovered and free.

13. Still he had not found the major, whom he supposed was ahead of him; and he made his way northward to a road which had been cut by his direction during the siege of this place two years before. At sunrise he was seven or eight miles from the fort, on the eastern side of the Penobscot; and here he had the pleasure of meeting with Major Burton again, who had all the time been in the rear. They found a boat, and crossed over to the western bank of the river, barely escaping discovery by a barge which came out in pursuit. Three days after they reached the settlements on St. George's River, and were safe.

Since the British had gained a stronghold in Maine the tories of the western counties and even from Massachusetts flocked to their vicinity; and the outrages committed by them upon the patriots of that region were scarcely less atrocious than those of the Indians formerly. Yet Maine, overrun and afflicted as she was, had again to furnish recruits for the national army,—this time five hundred men. Lincoln county, also, raised one hundred and sixty men, and York county one hundred and twenty for their own defence; while the general government, finding it absolutely necessary, offered bounties to privateers, and sent four small vessels and a flotilla of whale boats to cruise along the coast.

14. In the autumn the light dawned of a brighter day. This was the surrender of the army under Lord Cornwallis at Yorktown,—which happened the last of October, 1781. Congress went in solemn procession to church, and returned thanks to Almighty God for crowning our arms with success; and a day was soon after appointed for the thanksgiving of the nation.

The British had so far succeeded in rousing the Canada Indians that in 1781 a party of them killed two men in the town of Gilead; and in 1782 a larger band, roaming through the region, fell upon the infant settlement in Newry, set the buildings on fire, and destroyed all property which they could not carry off. The men of this settlement had gone for a short time to Sudbury-Canada, (now Bethel) where they were followed by the savages, and several of them killed, and others carried away. Among the Indians who had been induced to join the British were two sons of Netallie, a chief who dwelt on an island in Lake Umbagog. Their father was so incensed by their treachery that he drove them from him, and disinherited them forever.

15. At last, on the third day of September, 1783, the treaty of peace was signed at Paris between the agents of the American and British governments. By this act the boundary between Maine and the British Possessions was fixed; being "formed by a line drawn due north from the source of the St. Croix River to the highlands, along said highlands, which divide those waters which empty themselves into the river St. Lawrence, from those that fall into the Atlantic ocean, to the north-eastern-most head of the Connecticut river,"—and "east by a line to be drawn along the middle of the river St. Croix, from its mouth in the Bay of Fundy to its source,"—and "all the islands within twenty leagues of the shore, and the right unmolested to fish on the Grand Banks, and on all other banks of Newfoundland, and generally in every place where the inhabitants of both countries have heretofore used to fish." I have recorded these boundaries and rights literally, because many years later they were partly the occasion of another war.

16. Then the British forces were withdrawn from our borders, the noble armies of the Revolution were disbanded, and we were acknowledged by the governments of Europe to be an independent country, and were thus admitted into the fraternity of nations. In this war Maine had lost a thousand men; and the proportion of the public debt which fell upon our scanty

settlements was larger in proportion to population and property than the debt from the slaveholder's rebellion.

Now once more our people were left free to pursue the noble avocations of peace, and the District of Maine rapidly increased in wealth, population and power.

What was the relative value of government bills and specie in 1778? What citizen of Maine conveyed the American minister to France? At what date was Maine made a district under the general government? Of what place in Maine did the British take possession in 1779? Give an account of the siege of this place by the Americans. What distressing prohibition did Congress make in 1779? Why was the quota of Maine to the national army remitted in 1780? Give an account of what happened to Gen. Wadsworth. What joyous event occurred in 1781? What was done by the Canada Indians in 1781-82? Give the boundaries of Maine as settled by the treaty of Independence.

CHAPTER XXVI.

1. We have now come down to the close of the Revolution—a period when our great grandfathers and great grandmothers were the chief personages upon the stage of action; and as they are so nearly related to us I suppose you would like to know how they looked and what their customs were. You have already learned of their struggles for life and liberty; and I think you will agree with me that they never could have gone through with it all so successfully had they not, like their own fathers and mothers, been possessed of great strength, both of body and mind.

Yet among the wealthier people the period immediately before and after the war was one of "grand" manners and showy dress.

2. Their dwellings were large, but not so elegant and convenient as ours; while carriages for riding were scarcely known in Maine before 1790; but people made up for these deficiencies by personal apparel. The belles had their silks, their laces, their fine linen, high-heeled shoes, hooped petticoats, and long waists. They powdered their hair—which was usually dressed high on the head, and fastened and ornamented with great combs of gold, silver and shell, with the frequent addition of gold and silver skewers and bands. Sometimes they appeared in public in gowns of fancy wool cloth, but often in silks and satins. Calico was little used, not being rich enough for society, and too costly for common wear—at six shillings a yard.

The gentlemen of fashion in the early part of the century generally wore great wigs,—some bushy, others flowing in long curls to the shoulders. Afterward the hair was gathered in a cue or club at the back of the neck, and tied with a ribbon; but about the time of the Revolution monstrous head dresses were discarded by both ladies and gentlemen, and more modest fashions prevailed.

3. The fashionable outside garment was for a long time a scarlet cloak, or one lined with scarlet; but this color went out of style. I suspect that the red coats of the British soldiers made it unpopular. The coats were cut straight in front, having a stiff, upright collar; which, with the pockets and sleeves, were trimmed with gold or silver lace. The shirt had ruffles at the bosom and wrists, and the wristbands extended beyond the coat sleeves, so as to show the ornamental buttons which fastened them. The waistcoat was without a collar, but descended over the hips, and had rounded corners in front. They were often made of silk, had great pocket flaps, and much em-

broidery. Breeches fitting quite tight reached **down to the knee**, where they met the stockings and fastened **with a** buckle. The shoes also were fastened with buckles. In 1790 trowsers descending to the ankle began to be worn, the fashion having been brought in by the French. In the street the head was covered with a napless beaver hat, with a brim genèrally about two feet in diameter, which was drawn up on three sides so as to form three angles, and was worn with a point over each shoulder,—while the other, coming in front, served for a handle to **take** it off by **when making a bow**.

4. **But** those worthy and respectable men who did the work necessary to the sustenance and comfort of life—earning their bread by the sweat of their brows—found themselves most comfortable in their customary loose trowsers of tow cloth in the summer, and woolen cloth, deer or moosehide in the **colder** weather. Their **coats** were of similar material; **while** for shirts, linen **was the** staple **article**. **Wool was rare for a** long time, **because the bears and wolves killed the sheep; but the flax plant grew freely, so that** linen **was plentiful. At the time of the** Revolution the **country women** generally **had** learned to **weave on** the great hand looms; **so** they wove up the coarse tow and **the finer** flax into thick cloths for the wear of men and boys, and into sheets and towels for family use, while they produced a finer cloth woven in colored checks for their own and their daughter's wear on Sundays and social occasions. In some parts of the country, "spinning bees" and "wool breakings" were held for spinning **and carding**. When the work **was** done the men, both young and old, came in; **and the** affair usually closed with simple dances and merry plays.

5. Merrymakings were more numerous than formerly, for settlements increased, and there was no lurking foe to be feared. From a few handfuls of adventurous colonists we had become a numerous and

independent people, able to cope successfully with the nations of Europe. Every Indian tribe was destroyed, or driven off, except the friendly Tarratines. These were secured by government in possession of several large islands in the Penobscot above Bangor, with the right of hunting on all the tributaries of the river above this point. Being now permanently at peace they cultivated the ground more than formerly; and the furs from their winter hunting brought them many of the comforts of civilization. Their manners were still much the same as ever; but their hunting and household implements were such as the white people used, while their dress had undergone a thorough change.

6. They usually wore a woolen cap or bonnet of a conic form, which might be drawn down to cover the ears and the back of the neck. For coats they had a sort of sack or blouse almost as formless as a meal bag, without buttons, being fastened at the waist by a belt. The women wore short sacks, meeting the skirt at the waist, and pinned together in front. Their long stockings of blue woolen overlaid the drawers and covered the knee. Though a supply of shoes was kept at the trading houses, they mostly wore moccasins—doubtless because they were both easier and cheaper. Add to these, bright scarfs, ribbons and plumes, and metallic ornaments of all sorts, and you have a true picture of the Penobscot Indians as they appeared at the beginning of the present century. To-day they have discarded this dress, also; and for the most part appear in the garb of their white neighbors.

7. As soon as peace was concluded with Great Britain, the eyes of many thousands were turned upon Maine; and presently many thousand feet were marching toward her forests, with their property following in ox cart or boat, or, perhaps, carried on their backs. Many were soldiers of the Revolution, fresh from the

disbanded armies; and often their only wealth was a soldier's note or a few **worn** and nearly worthless bills,—the balance of their pay for long and arduous service in their country's cause. But they were rich **in** patriotism and courage, while their industrious habit was shown by the speedy clearing of farms and the rearing of many a comfortable home. It soon began to be seen how small was the reward these noble men had received in comparison with their services; and **the** General Court, a few years after the close of **the** war, offered as a gratuity to every one who had served three years, his choice between twenty dollars in money, and two hundred acres of land on **our** eastern frontier.

8. The government still owned nearly two-thirds of the territory, and a great number of towns were laid out, and many grants made to deserving individuals; while land was sold to soldiers for one dollar an acre. **Yet there were many trespassers, who** both occupied **land** they **had not bought,** and cut **down trees** not their own; and **government** was **forced to** appoint a committee **to** protect the public property. The white pine was the favorite spoil of the lawless lumbermen; and the fine for cutting one of them on government land was one hundred dollars. Perhaps you think this a heavy penalty for a single tree; but it is much less than some of them would be worth for lumber to-day. Sometimes these pines were of such size that when cut down a yoke of full grown oxen could be turned about on the stump. They were **often** found measuring four feet in diameter, and **have been** known to reach six **feet at the butt, and** two hundred and forty feet **in** height. **Their** green tops, towering, like lofty sentinels, far **above** the surrounding forest, raised in the mind of the beholder a feeling **of** grandeur—that was greatly increased when he stood beside the mighty trunk and, gazing upward, saw its **long line shoot** above the shadows of the great woods

into the unbroken light **of heaven.** On the opening of the war for independence one **of** the first flags designed for our national standard bore the figure of **a** pine. **Afterward,** its neighbors of the night—the bright, **twinkling** stars—took its place; but it has its rightful **position on** our State seal, and **we** find **a noble** significance in our popular name of "Pine-tree **State."**

The District of Maine grew so rapidly in population **and** wealth that its separation from Massachusetts and erection into an independent State began to be agitated. The first newspaper published in the District **was started** for the purpose of advocating this project. It was printed in Falmouth, and **was** called "The Falmouth **Gazette."** The first **number was** issued **on New Year's day, 1785.** The **next year Casco** Neck **was set off from Falmouth and incorporated under the name of "Portland."**

9. So far only twelve towns had been laid out east of the Penobscot; and to promote other settlements in this fine region, and to raise money for her treasury, Massachusetts, in 1786, contrived a land lottery. This scheme included fifty townships, each six miles square, **lying** between the Penobscot and **St. Croix rivers.** Against these, 2,720 tickets **were issued at sixty pounds** each; and every ticket entitled the holder to **a prize—the lowest** being a tract of **land** half a mile square. In payment for these tickets government **received the** notes with which the soldiers had been **paid, and all** other public securities; and the lottery **townships, with** those who settled on them, were exempted from taxation for fifteen years. At the time of the drawing, **a** large part of the tickets remained unsold, and these were bought by William Bingham of Philadelphia. Afterward he also purchased most of the prize lots **from** those who had drawn them; so the scheme did not promote settlements **so rapidly as** had been expected. Not long before, **Mr. Bingham had** purchased about one million acres in the counties

of Oxford and Somerset, so that he had now become the owner of above two million acres in Maine,—equal to nearly one hundred townships of six miles square, at a cost to him of twelve and one-half cents per acre. Mr. Bingham afterward removed to England, where he died; but his heirs, up to a late period, owned large tracts in eastern Maine.

In 1790 a census of the inhabitants of Maine was taken by Federal authority, and, to the surprise of everybody, the population was found to reach the number of 96,540. The lottery townships, too, had gained so many inhabitants that they were this year separated from Lincoln county and erected into the two counties of Hancock and Washington.

10. Among the pioneers of Lincoln county none were worthier than the German colonists of Broad Bay; and their virtuous example has never ceased to be a source of strength to our good State. The Scotch and Scotch-Irish, also, had settled at several points—some on the Kennebec at Bath, others in Kennebec county on the east of the river, and others still in Old York. No doubt many of my readers know of localities which bear to this day the name of "Scotland," "Ireland," "Scotland Parish"; thus telling the nationality of their original settlers. In these the names peculiar to those people are still found numerous; and, nearly always, they mark a moral, industrious and thrifty community.

11. In 1790 the general government divided Maine into nine commercial districts, and appointed a collector and other custom-house officers for each. At the adoption of the Federal constitution, Maine, as a part of Massachusetts, became entitled to one representative in Congress; but in 1794 a new apportionment gave her three.

In 1793 Governor John Hancock died. He was president of the convention which framed the Declaration of Independence; and my young friends will recollect his name in clear, bold hand as the first signature to that noble instrument. He was the first governor of the old commonwealth—including the District of Maine—after we became a nation, and was elected to that office twelve successive years, with the exception of two years only, when Governor James Bowdoin filled the chair.

It was from the latter gentleman that Bowdoin College received its name. This college was chartered in 1794, but its first class was not entered until 1802. James Bowdoin, son of the governor, was its great benefactor, presenting it with both money and land, and also with books, paintings and minerals, gathered during his residence and travels in Europe.

> What were some of the fashions in dress at the Revolutionary period? What had become of the Indians? What can you say of the soldiers who at this time settled in Maine? What wonderful natural product was found in Maine? When and for what purpose was the first newspaper issued in Maine? What was done in regard to lands between the Penobscot and St. Croix? What people besides the English settled in Maine?

CHAPTER XXVII.

1. The Muscongus Patent had fallen so much into the possession of the Waldo family that it had now for a long time been known as the "Waldo Patent"; finally Henry Knox, who married a granddaughter of General Waldo, by inheritance and purchase obtained from it a large estate. General Knox had been the chief of artillery in the Continental army, and was the intimate

friend of General Washington. When the battle of Lexington took place Henry Knox was a bookseller in Boston. He was already known to the British authorities as an active rebel, and it became dangerous for him to remain longer in the city; therefore he and his accomplished young wife fled together, with his sword hidden in her petticoat. Mrs. Knox was the daughter of the secretary of the Commonwealth; and when she married this "bookseller" her friends thought her social prospects were ruined. They made a great mistake; all through the first presidency she was in the first rank of social position, and many of her old acquaintances felt it an honor to enjoy the friendship of Lucy Knox.

GENERAL HENRY KNOX.

2. Young Knox was present as a volunteer at the battle of Bunker Hill, and fought so gallantly that he was soon after made a lieutenant colonel of engineers. In the autumn he raised an artillery company; and when, in November, 1775, the patriots besieged the British army in Boston, he brought mortars, howitzers,

cannon and ammunition all the way from Ticonderoga and Crown Point on ox-sleds. He **was next** made Brigadier General **of** artillery, and held that position until the su**rrender of** Cornwallis at Yorktown; when, for **meritorious service,** he was made a Major General; **and when the** British marched out of **New York** it **was he who took** possession. General Knox **was** twice **appointed** Secretary of War; but in 1794 he resigned **that** office and took up his residence in Thomaston on **the** ancestral estate of his **wife.** He built a fine house **in** a commanding position near the banks of St. George's **River**, where he maintained the hospitality suitable **to** his rank and wealth **until his death in** 1806.

3. The **Pemaquid** Patent had been divided into the **Drowne, Browne and** Tappan rig**hts; the** Plymouth, or Kennebec **Patent, had** been sold **to the** "Fifty Associates," **for whom Dr.** Sylvester Gardiner was chief manager; **the** Pejepscot Purchase had passed into the hands of Richard Wharton, and thence become distributed to many persons. On all of these were settlers who had cleared land and built houses, without either purchase or license. They were called squatters; **and the** proprietors of the lands were determined **to drive them** off, unless they **would pay a** suitable **price for their** enclosures. There **were many** also whose farms had been bought and **paid for** by their fathers, or **grandfathers;** and these, too, by the decision of the **courts, had no** rights in the land upon which they had **been born. Some** proprietors had **sold land** outside of **their tracts, while** settlers who had purchased of real proprietors, not knowing the exact boundaries, had located where they had not bought; and the courts of Kennebec and Penobscot echoed for years with the names of these old grants and rival claimants. Therefore in 1808 a law was made called the "Betterment Act," for the relief of these persons. It provided for an appraisal of the land as it was in a state of nature, and also of its improvement by cultivation, with the

value of the fences and buildings; the proprietor then had his choice—either to sell the land to the tenant at the price appraised, or pay him the price set upon his improvements; otherwise he must lose the land.

4. Many of the settlers whose rights were disputed formed companies to defend themselves in their lands and houses; and whenever proprietors, or their surveyors, came into these neighborhoods they were haunted by bands of armed men, and warned to depart. Many times it looked as if there would again be war in the District of Maine,—a war of tenants against proprietors; but in one instance only was life actually taken.

In September, 1809, as four men were engaged in running land in the town of Malta (now Windsor) they were assailed by nine men disguised as Indians. They wore peaked caps of parti-colored cloth, and had a covering over their faces pierced with holes for the mouth and eyes. Some wore blankets also. Two or three carried long staves with pieces of scythes fastened upon the end, but the others were armed with guns and pistols. At the word of their leader, three guns were fired at Paul Chadwick, one of the surveying party, who instantly fell, mortally wounded. The surveyor and one assistant immediately fled; but the "Indians" made no attempt to pursue them. The dying man, was soon removed by his companions to a house in the vicinity. Some of the gang had been recognized by Chadwick; and when the sheriff arrived they were found to have fled to the woods, where they remained concealed. At last by their friends' advice, they gave themselves up to the officers of the law, and were placed in the jail at Augusta to await their trial.

5. As the time of court sessions approached, the friends of the prisoners began to fear for their fate, and to regret that they had advised them to surrender. Rumors of rescue began to reach the officers, and the prison was strongly guarded and a strict watch kept. An intense interest prevailed throughout the commu-

nity; for the land proprietors **were** anxious to see whether their rights could be sustained, while the prisoners had the sympathy of all settlers on doubtful claims. Next, it **was** announced that the woods between Augusta and Malta were full of armed men dressed as Indians, who only waited a favorable moment to burn the county building and the houses of the land proprietors; and such was the known state of feeling among the squatters that the rumor was readily believed. A cannon from the old fort was mounted on cartwheels, loaded with musket balls and set at the west end of the bridge, ready to sweep down the rioters whenever they should attempt to cross the river. Sentinels **were** posted, the **patrol was** enlarged, and excited citizens kept anxious **watch** about **their** dwellings. Still the **expected attack did not come.**

6. The **court sat on** the third of October. At midnight the guard stationed east of the river perceived a body of armed men approaching from the hill. When within about thirty rods of the bridge they halted, and **sent one** of their number forward. The spy came so near the post of the sentinels that he **was caught almost** before he was aware of their presence. **Three of** the guard were hastening **away** with him, when some **twenty or** thirty **of the insurgents** rushed forward, beat off the sentinels, and rescued their comrade. **Major Weeks,** who had just come to learn what was the **matter,** was made a prisoner **and** hurried away to the **woods.** In a few minutes the city was in wild commotion. **Guns** were fired, bells were rung, and the streets were thronged with excited people. The Augusta light infantry company reached the scene of conflict, but the foe had disappeared. Before daylight two other companies had been ordered out; but the insurgents **were not** to be found.

7. In the few days following, companies came in one after the other from Hallowell, Gardiner, Winthrop, Fayette**,** Readfield, Vassalboro and Sidney. Perhaps

my readers will think this was a great and unnecessary array to oppose to three or four score half armed squatters; but you know that a very few men can set a city on fire—and the authorities wished to protect property from the flames as well as prevent a rescue of the prisoners. However, only one or two companies were retained in the city, the others returning home for the time, but alternating with each other until the trial was concluded.

The indictment was for murder; but only seven of the nine men in the party who killed Chadwick were included, since his death resulted from gunshot wounds—and two of them had no guns. The trial commenced on the sixteenth of November, and consumed eight days in the examination of witnesses and in the argument of the counsel. The charge of Judge Parker to the jury presents so many thoughts important to be remembered by all who live under a free government, that I insert a part of it for the benefit of boys who will soon be my fellow citizens.

8. "In this free and happy country, where every man's claims are to be decided by his neighbors and peers, men of like passions and like interests with himself, and under laws of his own making, can there be any excuse for resorting to violence? Do not the most abject and miserable find countenance, support and encouragement in the maintenance of their rights, when they claim it under the laws? Have not the legislature done everything within their constitutional power to aid those who are supposed to have stronger claims upon humanity than upon strict justice? Why then do we hear of our citizens assuming the garb of savages, and perpetrating acts at which even savages would tremble? To what will all this lead? If men of similar interests may combine and, by menaces and violence, deprive their antagonists of the evidence essential to the just determination of their disputes— or if men may with impunity oppose the laws—such

system must go to the destruction of every man's comfort, security and happiness, as well as the constitution and laws under which we live. There have also been menaces that **the courts** of justice will be stopped by **violence; and it is** notorious that assemblies of **men have appeared for the** avowed object **of** rescuing **the prisoners before trial.** There is reason likewise **to apprehend,** in case of a conviction of the **prisoners, that there** will be **similar** attempts to prevent the execution of the law. But have not the prisoners had a fair, patient and impartial trial? **It** has occupied **an** unprecedented portion of **time.** Every indulgence to which **they are** lawfully entitled has been cheerfully **allowed them. They** have had the **best talents and the** best **efforts in their defense. If** they **are** not proved **to be guilty, though themselves** may know **that they are not innocent,** they will still be acquitted, and allowed to return to their families and friends. If they are convicted the law must have its course. Will this government, abounding in loyal citizens, yield to **the violence of a few** deluded men, and tamely see **its** authority defied and its prisons violated without **stretching forth** an arm to prevent its overthrow? **Should its powers** be exerted, what must be **the destiny of these** wretched, mistaken **men?** What, **but either to be killed in** battle, executed on **the** gallows, or to fly **from a land** of freedom and security, to seek a miserable **shelter in** some foreign country. Their habitations will become desolate, and they will be fugitives on the **face of the earth."**

9. The evidence had not shown by which of these seven men the three guns had been fired, so that it was still doubtful whose act had caused his death. The jury, therefore, gave to all the benefit of this **doubt;** and, after deliberating **two days, they brought in a** verdict of "Not Guilty."

Yet the trial had a good effect on **the community, and on the** prisoners themselves — even their **leader** professing with tears his penitence and shame; and both proprietors and tenants became more disposed to peaceable settlement.

What noted men became owners in the Muscongus patent? **What services** were rendered in the revolution by Major General Knox? What can you say in regard to other patents? What law was made to enable the squatters and proprietors to make a settlement? What happened in 1809 in the town of Malta? When the murderers were about to be tried what occurred at Augusta? Did this **affair show** that anything is **to be gained by mob violence?**

CHAPTER XXVIII.

1. Hardly had the excitement from the Malta "Indians" ceased, when fears of another war with Great Britain began to agitate our people. Napoleon Bonaparte was now in the full tide of his victories, and England had joined the alliance against him. The United States had early issued a proclamation of neutrality; but both England and France committed many outrages upon our unprotected merchantmen. Then the English claimed the right to search our vessels for seamen, and many were impressed into their service on the claim that they were British subjects. Our government often protested against these outrages, but it did no good; for they knew our navy to be very small, and supposed that our vessels were no match for theirs. At length they became so bold and overbearing as to search our **armed** vessels; and such as refused to allow it were fired upon. The British

sloop of war, Little Belt, for some offense of this nature, fired upon the American ship, President; and the President fired back, giving the Little Belt such a drubbing that she sailed off as fast as she could to Halifax and complained of the outrage!

2. Over six thousand of our seamen had been impressed and were held to service in the British navy. In all British ports and on the seas our ships were detained by search and seizure, and were not free from molestation even in our own harbors; therefore in April, 1812, an embargo* was laid for ninety days on all vessels in our ports. A treaty had been made with France—that country being now at war with England—by which the edicts of Bonaparte were modified in favor of American shipping; but England gave no attention to our protests, and still persisted in her outrageous proceedings; therefore, in June, war was declared to exist between Great Britain and the United States.

The population of Maine was now over two hundred and twenty-eight thousand, while her exports were above eight hundred thousand dollars in yearly value, and she had shipping afloat amounting to one hundred and fifty thousand tons. With such an amount of exports and shipping, of course the embargo told very severely on our interests; and there were many who opposed the war, believing it to have been declared more to aid the French than because it was a necessity for the country.

3. General Henry Dearbon, formerly of Pittston, in this State, was made commander in chief of the national forces, which were now stationed along the northern frontier from Lake Champlain to Lake Michigan. In August, General Hull cowardly surrendered Detroit, while other divisions of the army did nothing this year to redeem its honor; but on the sea our little navy achieved several brilliant victories. Yet neither the army nor the navy had been idle since the Revo-

* See close of chapter.

lution; the army having **fought successfully with the Indians** from Florida **to the great** lakes, **while our navy had reduced** the Barbary **States to terms.** In the latter service Commodore Preble, a native of Portland, bore an honorable part. The first noted achievement of this officer **was** during the occupancy of Castine by the British **in the Revolution.** Being then first lieutenant of the sloop of war, Winthrop, he with a few men boarded a British vessel in the harbor of Castine and brought her off under an **incessant fire** from the **battery** and troops. **In 1803 he was placed** in **command of** the famous frigate, **Constitution, and sent with a** squadron **of seven vessels to obtain the release of** Americans **held in** slavery **by** the Barbary **States,** and to protect **our** commerce against their **piratical navies.** He had brought Morocco to terms and was proceeding against other States when he was relieved by Commodore Barron, **his** senior, and returned home on account of ill health. Congress recognized the value of his services on the African coast, and voted him the thanks of the nation, and ordered him an elegant medal commemorative of the actions in which he had won distinction. He died in 1807 at the early age of forty-five, and was buried with military honors in his native city.

4. During the summer of 1813 the brig Enterprise **was** stationed on the eastern coast, where she was the **terror of** the British privateers fitted out in the provinces **to** prey upon **our** commerce. She carried sixteen guns **and one** hundred and two men, and was at this time **under the** command **of** Captain William Burrows. **On the 4th** of September the Enterprise **sailed from Portland in search** of British cruisers, which had been reported near Monhegan. On the 5th she discovered **in a harbor near** Pemaquid, **a large vessel just getting underway.** She proved **to be** the Boxer, a British brig of eighteen guns, carrying one hundred **and** four men, and commanded by Captain Samuel

Blyth. She had been sent out especially to capture or destroy the Enterprise. On observing the Enterprise the Boxer displayed four ensigns, and fired several guns to call her boats from the shore; then, spreading her sails, she bore gallantly down toward the vessel.

5. Captain Burrows cleared his ship for action, but ran a few miles southward to secure ample sea-room for the impending conflict; then he shortened sail and turned upon his foe. They met off Seguin Island, at the mouth of the Kennebec. At twenty minutes past three the vessels were within half a pistol shot of each other, when they opened fire at almost the same moment. In the course of the action the Enterprise ran across the bows of the Boxer, whence she delivered such a destructive fire that at four o'clock the officer in command shouted a surrender through his trumpet; for the flag had been nailed to the mast. Captain Blyth was dead, being cut nearly in two by an 18 pound ball; forty-six of his men were killed, and twelve more wounded. Captain Burrows was mortally wounded early in the battle, while assisting to run out a carronade; but he refused to be carried below until the sword of the British commander was placed in his hand. None on board the Enterprise were killed, and of the fourteen wounded, only Captain Burrows and Midshipman Waters died of their wounds. Lieutenant M'Call succeeded to the command of the Enterprise; and the next morning he took both vessels into Portland Harbor.

Captain Burrows died eight hours after the fight; and the two brave commanders, foes no longer, were buried side by side in the old cemetery beside the sea. Longfellow, in the poem called "My Lost Youth," wrote of this scene,—

> "I remember the sea-fight far away,
> How it thundered o'er the tide;
> And the dead captains as they lay
> In their graves o'erlooking the tranquil bay,
> Where they in battle died."

6. **A few days later** the brilliant **victory of Commodore Perry over the** British fleet **on Lake Erie,** filled **the whole country** with rejoicing. **The** next year our naval successes continued, while **the** victories **of** Chippewa **and Bridgewater,** in Canada, covered our armies with glory. **But in** August the British entered Chesapeake Bay in great force; and, penetrating to Washington, they burned the capitol, the president's house, and the public offices.

The enemy's cruisers **were** now so numerous **on our** coast that **no** vessel **thought of** making a foreign **voyage, and** nothing was **done on the water** except a **little** coasting **and** fishing. **As a result,** all important articles became very high. **Yet there** was **an** advantage in this; **for it** stimulated native production so much that this year some thirty companies were incorporated **in** Massachusetts and Maine for the manufacture of **cotton,** woolen, **glass** and metal.

7. **On the eleventh of July, 1814, was made the first attack of the war on the soil of Maine.** On that day a **British fleet swept over the** waters **of** Passamaquoddy **Bay and came to anchor** off **Fort Sullivan,** at Eastport. This **fortification was the sole defense of** the place. **It** mounted **but six** guns, **and** was manned by two companies of soldiers under the command of Major Perley Putnam. The armament of the enemy **was** under the command of Sir Thomas Hardy. It consisted of his flag-ship, Ramilies of seventy-four guns, the sloop Martin, the brig Boxer, the schooner Bream, the bomb-ship Terror, and several transports with troops **under** Colonel Thomas Pilkington. A message **was** speedily **sent to the fort** demanding its instant surrender, **and allowing but five** minutes for consideration. **To the brave Putnam this time** was more than sufficient; **and the** messenger bore back **the** reply,—"The fort will be defended against any force whatever."

8. The armed ships were now put in a position for attack, while at a little distance below the village the

transports landed upwards of one thousand men, with fifty or sixty pieces of artillery. The inhabitants were intensely alarmed for their property and families; and they besought Major Putnam that he would not expose the town to destruction by a hopeless defense. In deference to their wishes Putnam surrendered the fort, with the condition that his officers should be released on parole, and that the property and persons of the inhabitants should be secure.

On taking possession of the place the British found in the custom-house nine thousand dollars in United States treasury notes, which only lacked the signature of the collector to become valid. Promises, threats and menaces were all brought to bear on that officer to induce him to sign the notes—and thus rob his government of so many thousands for the benefit of the British; but the noble man persevered in his refusal to perform the traitorous act, declaring that "Death itself would be no compulsion."

9. A proclamation was issued announcing that the only intention of the British government in the present expedition was to take possession of the islands of Passamaquoddy Bay, which belonged to it by the treaty of 1783; and that the inhabitants of the mainland would not be harmed, unless their conduct should provoke severities. Having established a custom-house of their own, the British now issued another proclamation, commanding the citizens to appear and take the oath of allegiance to his Britanic Majesty, or depart from the islands within seven days. About two-thirds of the inhabitants submitted; and the commander announced that the crown now had its due. New batteries were erected, and between forty and fifty cannon mounted, and the place was garrisoned with about eight hundred troops; then the squadron departed southward, spreading alarm along all the coast. A strong party of British soon after marched against Robbinston, a few miles up the bay on the

mainland. This place was garrisoned by only twenty-five men, under Lieutenant Manning; who, knowing his inability to withstand a siege, destroyed such property as could not be removed, and retired to Machias.

10. A part of the vessels which had acted against Eastport continued to cruise off our coast; and one of them, the Bream, a schooner carrying eight guns, greatly harassed Bristol and the neighboring towns. At last the citizens met to consider what could be done to rid themselves of this troublesome craft; and Commodore Tucker was sent for to take lead in the business. The old hero was living upon his farm a few miles off, and at once answered the request of his townsmen by his presence. A wood schooner was procured and armed with an old swivel; and forty-five volunteers were quickly on board, armed with muskets, bayonets, and scythe points bound on poles for boarding pikes. After cruising along the coast for several days, they discovered an armed vessel in, or near, Muscongus Bay. As the vessels approached each other the stranger was found to be the schooner Crown, a British privateer of six guns. Tucker kept most of his men below, so that the enemy should not detect his purpose and fire too soon; but when a shot came tearing through the sails the men sprang upon deck. The commander formed them into platoons, directing them, when the order was given, to fire and kneel, while another row in the rear fired over their heads. The enemy's guns all this time kept banging away, the sails of the sloop were riddled beyond repair,—and not a gun on board of her had yet been fired. But the commodore had now got his favorite position, and in a voice of thunder uttered the word, "Fire!" Volley after volley followed from the successive platoons; the crew of the privateer rushed below, and every gun was silenced. The captain alone remained on deck, lying beside the rudder to steer. One of Tucker's men caught sight of his head through

a port hole, and sent a bullet so close as to knock off his hat. The Americans now prepared to board; and a stalwart young fellow six feet and six inches in height was stationed at the bows with a kedge anchor lifted over his back ready to throw on board the enemy for a grapple. The vessels neared each other. "Commodore, shall I heave?" shouted the young giant with the anchor. The British captain waited no longer, but cried out for quarter. The prize was found to be full of provisions which had been sent to supply the Rattler, a seventy-four gun ship cruising somewhere on the coast. The crew, consisting of twenty-five persons, were placed in the jail at Wiscasset; while the provisions were distributed among the suffering families along the coast.

*The government had, early in 1808, laid an embargo upon all shipping of American ownership in our ports, thus cutting off the coast trade as well as foreign commerce. It continued fourteen months, depressing business to the lowest point in Maine. In March, 1809, the embargo act was rendered nugatory by another called the "non-intercourse act," which prohibited commerce with France and Great Britain only; affording at once great relief to business. On the 2d of November this, also, ceased to have effect against France; that power having rescinded her obnoxious edicts against the United States.

What causes brought on the war of 1812? What citizen of Maine was made commander-in-chief of the national armies? What can you say of Commodore Preble? Give an account of the battle of the Enterprise and Boxer. What other brilliant victory happened soon after? What effect did the destruction of our commerce have upon manufactures? When and where was the first attack made on the soil of Maine? What sea-fight occurred near Muscongus Bay.

CHAPTER XXIX.

1. The pleasant town of Castine on Penobscot Bay has had a varied experience for a place whose history is not so old by many years as several others in New England. Six different attacks upon it by armed enemies have already been recorded in these pages; while it has been held by five different nations. We must, of course, reckon the Indians as the first nation; after whom it was held by the French, Dutch, English and Americans. I will now tell you of its seventh and last experience of the miseries of war.

In the year 1814 the village of Castine consisted of a few dozen dwellings and stores, a small church, a custom house, and, possibly, a court house—for it was then the shire town of Hancock county. Its only defense was a small fortification on the peninsula in such position as to command the channel of its harbor. This was an earth-work in the form of a half moon, armed with four 24 pounders and two field-pieces, and garrisoned by about forty men, under Lieutenant Lewis.

On September 1st, the garrison and inhabitants were alarmed by the appearance of a British fleet in the bay, bearing toward their harbor. About sunrise a small schooner ran up near the peninsula, and sent to the garrison a summons of surrender. Lewis saw that resistance would be useless; so he gave the schooner a volley from his cannon, then spiked them, blew up the redoubt, and departed with his men up the river. So the British took possession of the place without further resistance, and with it gained the control of the Penobscot.

2. The armament was under **the chief** command of Sir John Sherbrook, **and consisted of the** 74 gun ships Dragon, Spenser and Bulwark, the frigates Bacchante and Tenedos, **the sloops** Sylph and Peruvian, **the** schooner **Pictu,** a large tender, and ten transports. On board **these were about** four thousand **troops, under the command of General** Gerard Gosselin.

On the afternoon of the same day, having landed the **larger portion of** the troops, General Gosselin **with two** vessels and six hundred men crossed **the** bay **and took** possession of Belfast; while Captain Robert **Barrie in** the Dragon accompanied by the Sylph and Peruvian, with a small schooner as **tender,** and having **on** board about seven hundred troops, ascended the river **to** Marsh Bay, where they remained at anchor during the **night.** In **the** morning **five or six** hundred troops **were landed to take possession of** Frankfort, **whence** they **were to** complete **the journey on** foot on account of unfavorable winds. The Dragon remained that night at her anchorage, but the smaller vessels proceeded on their way.

3. Up the river, at Hampden, lay the United States **corvette** John Adams, commanded by Captain **Charles Morris.** The Adams had within three **months captured of the enemy a ship, two brigs and a** schooner, **and was now undergoing** repairs; **and of course** the **British were very** desirous of destroying such a troublesome foe. News of the enemy's arrival flew speedily **up the river;** and on the afternoon of the 1st, General **Blake of** Brewer, commander of the militia, had ordered out his division, and at night was in Hampden to make preparations of defense. During the next day about five hundred militia had collected, who were soon joined by Lieutenant Lewis and his garrison from Castine. General Blake with his officers, Captain Morris, **and the** leading citizens **of** Hampden held a council **of war;** but there **were** such differences of opinion that **no plan of defense was adopted.** Meantime the enemy

had continued on his course, and on the evening of the 2d came to anchor at Bald Hill Cove, nearly two miles below Hampden, where a junction was formed with the force which had marched up the river.

4. The militia continued under arms all night; but it was nearly eight o'clock the next morning before the British came in view. General Blake had arranged his little army with the right wing near the meeting house, the line stretching off toward the hill near the river. An 18 pound carronade had been brought from the Adams, and with two field pieces, placed in the highway near the meeting house—a position commanding the approach from the south. Yet, owing to a diversity of counsel, no breastworks or other defense had been erected. The disabled Adams lay at Crosby's wharf at the mouth of Soadabscook Creek. Captain Morris had hoisted the cannon from her, and formed a battery of fourteen guns upon the wharf, and another of nine 18 pounders upon a hill fifty rods below, whence they would rake effectually any craft which might approach.

5. The morning was very misty, but between seven and eight o'clock the skirmishers sent out by General Blake to watch and harass the enemy, reported him as crossing the stream that divides Hampden corners from Hampden. The main body was preceded by a company of sharpshooters, while on the flanks were detachments of marines and sailors with a six-pound cannon, a 6 1-2 inch howitzer and a rocket apparatus. In front of the line of militia the fog was still so thick that the enemy could not be seen, but the field pieces blazed away with good effect; and the enemy suddenly began to advance at "double-quick," firing volleys in rapid succession. The militia discharged a few rounds in return; but, several having fallen near the center, a panic siezed them, and they broke and fled in every direction, leaving the mortified officers alone on the field.

6. Meantime the enemy's vessels, preceded by barges full of soldiers moved up **the stream to** support the troops, until they **were** checked by the fire from Morrises batteries. The retreat of the militia left this position **unsupported**; and capture could now be avoided **only by immediate** retreat. Therefore, spiking his guns **and setting** his vessel on fire, Captain Morris and his **men forded the** stream, and took the road to Bangor; from thence, **a few** hours later, he **departed through the** wilderness to the Kennebec.

Within an hour after the **attack** the town **was in the hands of the** enemy, **and the** soldiers engaged **in pillage.** A large number **of the citizens were** placed in close **confinement, and a bond with the** penal **sum of** twelve thousand **dollars was exacted from the town for the delivery of certain unfinished vessels at Castine the next month. When the citizens remonstrated** with Captain Barrie, **the commander of** the expedition, he answered them, "My **business** is to sink, burn and destroy. Your town is taken by storm, and by the rules of war we ought both to lay your village in ashes and put its inhabitants to the sword. But I will spare **your** lives, though I mean to burn your houses." Probably he would have burned them the next **day,** had **not a messenger,** who had been sent to **General Sherbrook at Castine,** returned **with the order to spare if possible.**

7. After a brief delay **the vessels and** troops set out for Bangor. It was about noon **when** the vessels **came to** anchor at the mouth of the Kenduskeag, throwing **a few** rockets over the town as a signal to the troops, which had marched **up** the shore. Flags of truce were sent to meet the **enemy**, requesting the security to life and property which is customary when no resistance is made. This they agreed to give on condition of quarters and provision for the forces. Therefore the courthouse, two school-houses, several dwellings and other buildings were placed at their disposal; cattle were but-

chered for them, pork and vegetables provided, bread was supplied from the bakery, and plenty of liquor furnished. A quantity of merchandise in the custom house, the money in the post office, and all the arms and ammunition they could find, were seized; while nearly all the citizens capable of bearing arms were forced to sign themselves prisoners of war. But these were released on parole, with the stipulation that they should not do military service against his Britannic Majesty until the war was over, unless exchanged.

8. Yet in violation both of the rules of war and their own agreement, the soldiers and marines were permitted to pillage unrebuked. Twelve stores were emptied of most of their contents, and offices and dwellings forsaken by their owners were searched for valuables. Towards night the enemy threatened to burn several vessels which were on the stocks, and the oppressed inhabitants were quite in despair; for, as the wind then was, the flames would have swept the village. Therefore, to save their homes, the selectmen were forced to give a bond for thirty thousand dollars, or the delivery of the unfinished vessels at Castine by the end of October. That night was to the inhabitants a period of fearful suspense; for they knew not what cruelty might next be attempted. However, the British withdrew on the following day without any worse acts than supplying themselves with horses, and taking off vessels and goods to the value of about twenty-three thousand dollars. Some of the vessels ran aground in going down the river, and were at night abandoned and set on fire—their flames lighting up the shores for several miles.

9. In passing Hampden the enemy again engaged in pillage; but the imprisoned citizens were mostly set at liberty. Captain Morrises guns were thrown into the river, and the enemy departed; having secured two merchant vessels with valuable cargoes and other property to the amount of forty-four thousand dollars.

The people on the Kennebec were greatly alarmed by the ravages on the neighboring river, and prepared to give the British a warm reception, should their towns receive a visit. Major General King ordered out the militia; and Wiscasset, which was appointed as the rendezvous, was soon full of soldiers. One zealous detachment even marched over to the Penobscot to harass the enemy's vessels as they returned. But the British discovered them, and bound at prominent points on the decks several citizens from the towns above, so that none dared fire for fear of wounding their countrymen; and the ships passed by unharmed, while the militia-men marched angrily back to camp.

10. Proclamations were now issued by the enemy proclaiming the country between Penobscot River and Passamaquoddy Bay to be a province of Great Britain, and promising protection to the citizens if they would take the oath of allegiance and be faithful subjects of the king. I am happy to know that very few of the inhabitants would make any such agreement. General Gosselin was instituted governor of the new province; and the larger portion of the enemy's force now set out on other enterprises.

The first destination of the squadron proved to be Machias. There was here a fort mounting ten 24 pounders, and garrisoned at this time by about one hundred men, including several of the militia, and the garrison which had a short time before escaped from Robbinston. After landing the troops at Bucks' Harbor, the vessels ascended the river and opened a heavy fire on the fort, covering the advance of the land force, which was to make an attack in the rear. Finding they were likely to be surrounded, the garrison destroyed the guns, set the barracks on fire, and evacuated the fort.

11. A few days later a party of the enemy were sent to Frankfort to secure whatever arms and merchandise they could find. Before they got away, the

garrison from Machias reached the place and captured the whole of them.

There ensued a great deal of smuggling between the American and British lines, which were divided by the Penobscot, now under control of the enemy. The British wanted cattle and provision of all kinds for the troops, and our oak, pine and lumber to build vessels on the Bay of Fundy, or to transport across the sea; while our people needed the clothing, sugar, molasses and utensils which merchantmen brought into Castine. Our custom-house officers watched the river as well as they could, yet great quantities of goods were brought across, particularly in the winter when the river was frozen; and many found their way even as far as Massachusetts. The British did not care how much the American government lost on imports; so they took a five per cent toll on the goods, and let smuggling go on. Neutral vessels were constantly in the river, particularly the Swedish; but these honorably paid their dues at the custom-house. Such was the extent of trade on the river at this time that one hundred and fifty thousand dollars were said to have been secured at Hampden for duties in five weeks.

12. On December 24th, 1814, a treaty of peace between Great Britain and the United States was signed at Ghent; but before the news had reached this country General Jackson had won his famous victory at New Orleans. After this there were no further depredations in Maine, and most of the points they had held were soon deserted by the enemy—Castine being retained till the last.

During its occupation by the British, Castine was the center of considerable business; of which, however, the larger part fell into British or Tory hands. It was also a place of much gayety and amusement; for, beside the balls, a theatre was maintained through the winter by the officers—many of whom were men of culture and courtesy. The British evacuated the city in April, having **held** possession **for eight months** —during which time **the** inhabitants **had suffered much inconvenience and** oppression; and the restoration of their liberty **and property was** celebrated with **thanksgiving and festivity.**

How many nations have held possession **of** Castine? **By whom was it captured in 1814? What** successful war vessel lay **at Hampden? About** how many troops **were** in **the** engagement at **this place? What** amount of spoil did the British obtain? What was **done** at Bangor? What was done on the Kennebec? What territory did the British claim? What happened at Machias? What can you state **of** commerce on the Penobscot at this period? **What treaty was** signed just before Jackson's victory at **New Orleans?**

CHAPTER XXX.

1. **When the war was over there was soon found to be a great** increase of **profanity,** Sabbath-breaking, **and intemperance.** Thoughtful **people** were shocked **at its extent, and the** safety and **comfort** of the community were seriously diminished. **It was** chiefly the **dismissal of the militia from active service** in the District, **and** the **return of the** soldiers **from the national army,** which had **produced this** dangerous **and disagreeable** condition **of morals; for** men are often **made** dissolute by the **idle life of** camps, especially **when** discipline is loose **and** intoxicating liquors freely dispensed.

This state of society stimulated the religious associations to more earnest effort for the good of souls;

societies were formed to distribute the Holy Scriptures, and Sunday Schools were established for instructing the children of ignorant, careless, or vicious parents, in the important truths of the Bible. On the part of the government, the General Court made a new law against the profanation of the Sabbath, and appointed a great number of tythingmen to enforce the law and secure a decent behaviour on that sacred day.

2. Other misfortunes came with the close of the war. Manufacturing being at that time done much cheaper in England than America, our stores soon became stocked with British goods; and many of our factories, being unable to sell their products, were obliged to stop—by which many people were thrown out of employment and much capital lost. People became restless, and many thought any other business or any other State was better than their own.

Some of our citizens had already invested money in lands in Ohio, and liked there so well that they wished their friends to join them. The winter of 1816-17 was unusually cold, the spring was backward—and the season was so unproductive that this year was long after familiarly known as "eighteen hundred and starve to death". All classes, particularly farmers and mechanics, became much discouraged. Then the friends of the Ohio people who had lands to sell told attractive stories of the mild climate and rich soils of Ohio and Kentucky; and the "Ohio fever" set in with violence. It is believed that from ten to fifteen thousand people emigrated from Maine to those States—many selling their property at a great loss. But the very next year some of the emigrants returned with the other side of the story; and it is reckoned that after this the number that emigrated scarcely equalled those who returned. The tide of business, also, had turned; and in a few years the State again became prosperous.

HISTORY OF MAINE.

1819

3. Maine possessed many attractions in its soil, mill sites, forests and fisheries; accordingly we find that in 1820, the year of the separation, it had nine counties, and two hundred and thirty-six towns; while its population was 298,335—an increase of nearly 70,000 within the last ten years. Business was flourishing; and with such a population and so many towns and counties, it is not strange that the District aspired to become a State. This measure had been agitated as early as 1785; and several conventions had been held in its interest—one at Brunswick in 1816 fell but little short of accomplishing its object. In 1819, instead of one newspaper, as at the first attempt, there were six, three of which favored separation from Massachusetts, while the other three opposed. At last seventy towns joined in a petition to the General Court; and, this time, a bill favoring the measure was passed by a handsome majority. Its conditions were that all the public lands and buildings in Maine, except such as were the property of the United States, should be equally divided between the proposed State and Massachusetts. Maine was also to have her proportion of the military stock, and one-third of all moneys which might be reimbursed by the general government for war expenses.

4. On the fourth Monday in July, 1819, the citizens of the District of Maine voted on this question:— "Is it expedient that the District shall become a separate and independent State, upon the terms and conditions provided in an act relating to the separation of the District of Maine from Massachusetts proper, and forming the same into a separate and independent State?" On counting the votes, above two-thirds were found to be in favor of separation; therefore delegates from the towns met at the court-house in Portland, and adopted a constitution; appointing the first Monday in December as the day for the towns to vote for or against the constitution. On the first

Wednesday of January, 1820, the delegates again met; and, finding the constitution to have been adopted, made application to Congress for admission into the Union.

5. But now an unexpected obstacle came in the way of our independence. This obstacle was slavery—but not slavery in Maine. The territory of Missouri had applied for admittance at the same time; and, having many slaves, she wished to get in without any conditions against slavery. So the supporters of that institution, with characteristic craftiness, coupled the Territory and the District, and brought them before Congress in the same bill, that each might share the other's fate. Many weeks passed, but still this clog upon Maine held her back, so that she could not take her place in the sisterhood of States. The act severing the connection of the District from Massachusetts was to go into effect on the fifteenth of March; after which time, unless admitted previously, Maine would be simply a territory. The first of March had come, and still the slave power clung to her in close embrace. At length the friends of the District succeeded in divorcing the two applicants; and on the third of March the District became the twenty-second State of the Union.

6. The election for State officers was held for the first time on the first Monday of April, 1820; and on the last Wednesday of May the new senators and representatives met at Portland. On counting the votes for governor it was found that General William King of Bath was elected without opposition.

Mr. King was born in Scarborough in 1768. Not having been favored with a liberal education, on reaching the years of manhood he engaged in a saw mill in Topsham. Being prosperous he was able a few years later in connection with his brother-in-law to open a store in the same town. He afterward removed to Bath, where he resided until his death. He was the most prominent

GOVERNOR WILLIAM KING.

of our citizens in bringing about the separation of the District from Massachusetts; and, as we have already seen, was thought altogether the most suitable person for governor. Indeed, he has since often been spoken of as "the first and best of our governors." In 1821, before the close of his first term, he resigned the office; having been appointed one of the commissioners of the general government on the Spanish claims; and the president of the Senate, William D. Williamson, afterward the author of a valuable history of the State, became acting governor for the remainder of the term.

7. Among the first acts of the first session of the Legislature, was the adoption of a State seal. The moose and the mast pine, those princes of the forest, were chosen for the central figures of the design. At one side was an anchor, on the other a scythe, emblematic of the occupations of our people; while above was the North Star, signifying the place of Maine in the constellation of States. These, with the motto,

Dirigo (I lead), and two figures representing a farmer and a sailor, form the seal now in use by our State government. There was also an act for the improvement of public schools, another for the incorporation of religious societies, and one for the regulation of lotteries; for the latter had already been found to work much harm. A charter was also granted for a second college in Maine, to be called Waterville College—now changed to Colby University. It had first been started in 1813, under the name of "Maine Literary and Theological School". The General Court of Massachusetts quite unwillingly gave it a township (now the towns of Alton and Argyle) on the west side of the Penobscot River, fifteen miles above Bangor; enacting that the institution should be located within the township. This seemed very unfair; for it was even beyond the limits of the common school—where bears and wolves were much plentier than boys and girls. It was a Baptist institution; and one of its presidents has well compared it, during that struggling period, to "the voice of one crying in the wilderness."

8. The Congregationalists and Baptists now had each a literary institution and theological school; and in the year 1825 the Methodists established at Readfield a classical and theological school, under the name of "Maine Wesleyan Seminary". A theological seminary of the Congregationalists had been established in Bangor in 1814, under the name of "Maine Charity School"; and this is still the only exclusively theological school in the State.

At the time of the separation there were already nine religious denominations in Maine—the Roman Catholics, Episcopalians, Presbyterians, Congregationalists, Baptists, Methodists, Friends, Universalists, and Shakers. The sound of the church bell was as yet heard in but two or three towns; while organs in religious worship, and pianos at home had not ceased to be wonders in the **largest cities of the** land. Yet we had at this time **within** our own borders, twelve missionary and **education** societies, **nine** Bible societies, nine charitable societies, a Grand Chapter of Masons, **four Arch Chapters** and thirty-three Lodges. The first **Masonic Lodge in** Maine was instituted in Portland in the year **1769;** and the Grand Lodge of **Maine was** established **at the same** place **during the first session** of our State Legislature.

9. There were also in **the State at** this time 1,768 mechanical workshops, a **great** number of shipyards, **248** tanneries, 85 potash works, **524** gristmills, **746** sawmills, **210** carding machines, 149 fulling mills, and 17 spinning machines. Passing **from the trades to** cattle, we find **that** Maine had **17,849 horses, 48,224** horned cattle, **and 66,639 swine.**

When **one has a horse** now-a-days he has **usually a** carriage of two or **four wheels, either open or covered, for** pleasure riding; but some may **be** surprised to learn that before the Revolution there was not a four-wheeled passenger carriage in Maine. Two-wheeled chaises came into use in Portland in 1760, but they **were** kept by their owners like the Sunday **dress, to be** displayed only on gala-days. The first **four-wheeled carriage ever** seen in Augusta **was built about** the **year 1800;** while in 1798 **two two-wheeled** chaises **were the first** and only pleasure vehicles in that town.

10. **Men** and women made their journeys on horse**back; and** pillions for ladies' seats, and horse-blocks **to aid them in** mounting, were very common objects. **On a** Sunday morning the road to church must have presented a lively scene, with the groups and scattered files of foot people among the prancing steeds, bestrode by husband, father **or brother,** while about his **waist** twined the arm of **fair maiden or** stately **dame,** who sat **on** the pillion behind him. The people of that day minded little the few **miles between** them and **the meeting or** the market; and there are ladies still living

who could tell wonder-waking stories of their exploits of travel. It was thought a great enterprise when, in 1787, a coach was put upon the line between Portland and Portsmouth, for conveying the mails and for the accommodation of travelers. In 1806 the line was extended to Augusta, and in 1810 to Farmington. The western stage in the latter year started from Augusta early enough in the morning for the passengers to breakfast at Brunswick, dine at Freeport, and lodge at Portland. The next day their breakfast was taken at Kennebunk, dinner at Portsmouth, and their lodging at Newburyport. At two o'clock in the morning they started again; reaching Salem at daylight, and getting into Boston before noon. Mail routes and stages were from this time rapidly extended over the State; and with them country taverns multiplied and flourished exceedingly.

11. In July, 1823, a great event happened at Portland; nothing less than the arrival in the harbor of the first steamboat ever brought to Maine. This was the Patent, a vessel of about one hundred tons burthen, owned by Captain Seward Porter, of Portland, who had bought her in New York to run as a passenger boat between Portland and Boston. Captain Porter had in 1822 placed an old engine in a flat bottom boat, which he ran to North Yarmouth and the islands of Casco Bay. This he named "Kennebec," but the people called it the "Horned Hog." In August, 1823, the "Kennebec Steam Navigation Company" was formed. This company bought the Patent, and also built at Bath a little vessel called the Waterville, which commenced running on the river in April, 1824. The next year the Maine, of about one hundred and five tons, was fitted out at Bath by the same company. It ran between Bath and Eastport, calling at Belfast and Castine. The steamer Eagle, a British boat, was running between Eastport and St. John; thus completing a coast line of steamers from the Bay

of Fundy to the Gulf of Mexico. In 1825 the Waterville had the honor of conveying the nation's guest, the noble Lafayette, who at that time made a brief visit to Augusta. These boats in the course of a few years were succeeded by various others, built at home or purchased abroad; and among the latter, in 1833, came the Chancellor Livingston, built under the direction of Robert Fulton, the father of steam navigation.

What caused a depression in business soon after the close of the war? Whither did many of the people of Maine emigrate? What was the population of Maine in 1820? For what did our people vote in 1819? What delayed the admission of Maine into the Union? When did the admission take place? Who was elected first governor? What college was chartered by the first legislature? State what religious societies and other organizations existed in Maine at this time. At what date were mail coaches first used in this State? What happened in Portland in 1823? What distinguished foreigner visited Maine in 1825?

CHAPTER XXXI.

1. Albion K. Parris, elected second governor of Maine, took his seat at the opening of the year 1822. He was a native of Hebron, in this State, where he worked on his father's farm until he was fourteen years of age. A year later he entered Harvard College, and graduated in due course. In 1809 he was admitted to the bar, commencing practice at Paris, in Oxford county. At the age of twenty-eight he was elected Representative in Congress, at thirty he was appointed judge of the United States District Court, and was but thirty-three years old when he became governor; and he held the office for five consecutive years. The attainment of such high honors at so early an age is unusual. In looking for the cause of his popularity we find that he was without brilliant talents; and that the secret of his success lay in his industry and close attention to the duties of every office confided to him—in his promptness, fidelity, sagacity, and his uniformly courteous manners.

2. Governor Parris was, in 1827, succeeded by Enoch Lincoln; who had also been his successor in legal practice at Paris, and as representative in Congress. Mr. Lincoln was a popular and upright chief magistrate; and his messages and other communications were noted for their suggestiveness, point, brevity and good taste. He died near the close of his third term, being the only one of our governors who has died in that office.

In the term of his successor, Jonathan G. Hunton, of Readfield, was opened the only considerable canal in the State, by which Sebago pond was connected with Casco Bay. In 1831 Samuel E. Smith, of Wiscasset, assumed the gubernatorial chair, to which he was annually re-elected until 1834.

3. The matter of our northern boundary had attracted the attention of the State government very soon after the separation; and, during the term of Governor Lincoln, Maine took the stand which she afterward maintained upon the question. The United States and Great Britain, being unable to agree as to the location of the boundary line described in the treaty of 1783, at length referred the matter to the king of the Netherlands; who, in 1831, rendered his award. But instead of determining what, by a fair construction of the treaty, was the true boundary line—which was the question submitted—he declared that the line ought to extend north from the source of the St. Croix river, to the middle of the channel of the St. John's, thence to the St. Francis, at the extreme north, and through the middle of that river to the source of its southwest branch. This was a singular departure from the plain language of the treaty, which as my readers will have observed, placed the line upon a ridge of highlands—not in the bed of a river; and the decision of the umpire, of course, made the people of Maine very indignant. Yet this boundary certainly had the advantage of being more definite than that of the treaty. Then followed a lengthy correspondence upon the question between Governor Smith and the authorities at Washington; and the latter, being desirous of accepting the award, offered to reimburse the State by money or land equivalent to the territory lost. But the Madawaska settlements had at this time a representative in the legislature; and Maine took the ground that she could not in honor relegate her inhabitants to Great Britain; therefore the award was repudiated.

4. Another event of importance during Governor Smith's term was the removal of the seat of government from Portland to Augusta. The legislature held

its first session in the State House in 1832. The building and furniture had cost a little more than $125,000; about half of which was paid by the proceeds from the sale of ten townships of land. The architect was Charles Bulfinch of Boston; and the external design was a reduced plan of St. Peter's Church, at Rome. Few who approach the capitol fail to perceive its elegance; and, although not faultless, it is certainly a noble specimen of architecture. Constructed of the beautiful granite of the neighborhood, its massive foundation seems but a part of the fine eminence upon which it rests; and the great Doric pillars of the front, each a solid shaft of the same fair stone, can hardly fail to give an impression of grandeur.

In 1834, Robert P. Dunlap of Brunswick succeeded to the chief magistracy; and, by re-elections, held that position for four years. The chief measures for the benefit of the State during his term were the foundation of an asylum for the insane, and our first scientific survey.

5. In the month of June, 1837, an officer of Maine, while taking a census of the Madawaska settlements, was arrested by order of the governor of New Brunswick, and conveyed to Fredericton on a charge of exciting sedition. These settlements were on the St. John's river, at the extreme north-eastern part of the State, and within the limits of the treaty of 1783—by which Great Britain acknowledged our independence. The officer had acted with entire propriety; and the British authorities simply meant to show that Maine would no longer be permitted to exercise authority in this region. The claim of that government extended southward nearly to the forty-sixth parallel of latitude; which, if allowed, would rob Maine of about one-third of her territory. Governor Dunlap immediately issued a general order declaring the State to be invaded by a foreign power, and notifying the militia to hold themselves in readiness for military service. But as no

other act of hostility occurred, and the officer was released on parole, further hostile acts were, for the present, averted. Some attempts at revolt against British rule had already occurred in Lower Canada, and all through the season independent bands composed of Americans and outlawed Canadians hung about the great lakes; and in some disturbances at Navy Island in Niagara River, the American steamer Caroline was burned by the British, and a number of persons killed, among whom was one or more American citizens. This also occasioned some altercation between the governments; and there was good reason to apprehend another war from the boundary disputes and these repeated breaches of the peace. In the autumn of this year, therefore, the national government completed the military road in north-eastern Maine, making a continuous line from Bangor to the Madawaska settlements, in readiness for possible events.

6. In the term of Governor Dunlap also occurred the first conflict of Maine with the slave power. It was caused by the escape of two slaves from the State of Georgia in a Maine vessel. The governor of that State sent a requisition upon the executive of Maine for the master of the vessel; but, as it appeared that the negroes had concealed themselves on board unknown to the captain, Governor Dunlap refused the requisition. In 1838 Edward Kent of Bangor succeeded Mr. Dunlap as governor. He, also, refused to yield up the shipmaster; therefore Georgia, in retaliation, put all Maine vessels visiting her ports under peculiar restrictions, contrary to the constitution of the United States.

Another event connected with national politics in which Maine was deeply concerned, also occurred in the term of Governor Kent. This was the death of our representative in Congress from the Lincoln district, Hon. Jonathan Cilley, in a duel with Mr. Graves, a member of the House of Representatives from Kentucky. There was no personal enmity between the two men; but some words used by Mr. Cilley in debate reflected upon the editor of a New York political journal, a friend of Mr. Graves, who espoused his cause. Mr. Cilley reluctantly accepted his challenge; and they fought with rifles at a distance of seventy yards. Three times the men had fired at each other without effect, when Cilley's friends endeavored to reconcile the combatants; but the seconds of Graves repulsed all efforts for a bloodless settlement, and the conflict was resumed. Cilley fell at the next fire, and expired instantly.

7. This duel was remembered in Maine with much bitterness. The principal blame fell upon the political friends of Graves; but the latter soon retired from Congress, and years after was reported to be still a very unhappy man.

In home affairs this year the events of note were the formation of Franklin and Piscataquis counties, and the completion of the first scientific survey, begun in 1836. A large portion of the work in the Aroostook region was done in the first year by Dr. Ezekiel Holmes, under the direction of the governor, with special reference to the boundary claims. Dr. Holmes was a great benefactor of the agricultural interests of the State, in the promotion of which he had already made his influence felt. The survey in other parts was in charge of Dr. Charles T. Jackson of Massachusetts; who, with his assistants, visited nearly every river and mountain in the State. Attention was thus called to our valuable mines of ore and quarries of limestone and slate; and a cabinet of 1600 mineral and geological specimens was collected, which is now to be seen in the State House at Augusta.

What important question began to occupy the attention of Maine soon after the separation? To whom was this question referred for decision? **Was** the award **accepted** or rejected? **In what** year was the seat of **government removed to** Augusta? Where are the Madawaska **settlements?** How far south did the British claim possession **of Maine?** What disturbances happened in 1837? What difficulty **occurred** between Maine and Georgia? What congressman **from this State fell in a** duel? In what year did the first scientific **survey of Maine begin?**

CHAPTER XXXII.

1. In 1839 Mr. Kent was succeeded as governor by John Fairfield, of Saco. Scarcely had the **latter** taken his seat when hostilities began in Aroostook between intruders from the British Provinces and the **civil** authorities of Maine. Early in February **a deputy** of the land agent reported to the governor **that a large** number of lumbermen from New **Brunswick** were **engaged in** robbing the disputed **territory of its best timber; whereupon Sheriff** Strickland, of **Penobscot county, was** ordered **to aid Land Agent** McIntire **in dislodging the trespassers. With a posse of** about **two hundred men the officers proceeded** to the **Aroostook for this** purpose. The trespassers, having got **news of this movement,** supplied themselves with arms from **the Province** arsenal at Woodstock, and **prepared** to maintain their ground. There were **near three** hundred of them; but when they found the sheriff had a six pound cannon, they concluded to retire. **The** land agent followed them **down the** river, capturing **about** twenty men, who had **been at work** further up **the stream.** The **posse encamped for the night on the Aroostook** River **at the mouth of the Little Mada-**

waska, while Land Agent McIntire, with four companions, repaired to a house about four miles down the river, under an appointment to meet Mr. McLaughlin, the warden of the British in the disputed territory. The trespassers somehow learned the situation of the land agent; and during the night about forty of them made a descent upon his lodgings, and made him and his company prisoners. They were taken on an ox-sled to Woodstock, where they were turned over to the civil authorities, who conveyed them to Fredericton jail. Early the next morning the sheriff's force learned of this capture, and at once retired to Number Ten, where they fortified themselves in expectation of an attack. But the sheriff himself started for Augusta as fast as relays of galloping horses would carry him. He reached Bangor the next day, having accomplished within the time the surprising distance of above one hundred and twenty miles.

2. Governor Harvey of New Brunswick now issued a proclamation ordering the arms which had been illegally taken from the arsenal to be restored; and declaring that hostile invasion would be repelled by the civil authority. He also ordered a draft from the militia for immediate service. When the news of these events reached Augusta, the people began to see that the matter was growing serious, though at first it had been made a subject of ridicule; and on Sunday a company of fifty volunteers set out from that place for the scene of conflict. A messenger was sent by the governor to Washington; and 1,000 men of the Eastern Division of the militia were ordered out. That night a message was received from Governor Harvey demanding the recall of the State forces from the Aroostook, and announcing that he was instructed by his government to hold exclusive jurisdiction over the territory in dispute, and that he should do so by military force. On Monday these facts were laid before the legislature, which immediately passed a resolve to

protect the public lands, and appropriated $800,000 to carry it into effect. The next day the governor ordered a draft of 10,000 men from the militia, to be held in immediate readiness for service.

3. Meanwhile New Brunswick was marshalling her forces, and our own were sent forward as rapidly as possible. Our chief towns were filled with the sounds of war from the passage of troops, or the repair of decayed defenses. Early in March the national house of representatives passed a bill justifying the action of Maine in repelling the invasion of her soil. They also authorized the president, in case the governor of New Brunswick proceeded to carry out his threat of maintaining exclusive jurisdiction, to raise 50,000 volunteers for a term of six months—appropriating $10,000,000 to defray the expense. On the 6th of March General Scott with his staff arrived at Augusta, announcing that he was "specially charged with maintaining the peace and safety of the entire northern and eastern frontiers."

Our troops were now well on their way toward the Aroostook. The sheriff's force, having been increased by volunteers from Bangor and other towns to the number of about 600, again moved down the river. They captured a number of ox-teams, their drivers, and McLaughlin, the British land warden; but so little opposition was discovered that it was concluded that, for the present, the British had abandoned the river.

4. Immediately on his arrival General Scott opened negotiations with Sir John Harvey of New Brunswick, and Governor Fairfield of Maine; and presently the former gentleman was led to declare that, under expectation of the peaceful settlement of the question between the two nations, it was not his intention, without renewed instructions, to take military possession of the territory, or seek to expel therefrom the civil posse or the troops of Maine; while Governor

Fairfield was, in turn, invited to declare that he should not, without renewed instructions from the legislature, **attempt by** armed force to disturb the Province in its **possession of** the Madawaska settlements, or to interrupt **the** usual communication between New Brunswick and Canada; and that the troops should be withdrawn, leaving only a civil posse to protect the timber from further depredations. Presently **the** prisoners on both sides were set at liberty; and in **a few weeks** the troops **were** dismissed and returned **to their homes** rejoicing. Thus ended the bloodless Aroostook **war**. The promptness with which **our forces were** put upon the ground gave us **an advantage in** the situation, which, no doubt, had much influence in the negotiation **by which the** peaceful arrangement of **the** difficulty **was** so easily brought about. General Scott soon departed; and for a long **time** after the good people of Maine humorously styled him the "Great Pacificator."

The Aroostook region, being **now freed from invaders, was in** March erected into **a county, having been previously included in Penobscot and Washington.**

5. Two years passed away, and still the **boundary** of the State **remained unsettled, though** the **question** continued to be discussed by the two governments. On the accession of William Henry Harrison to the presidency, in 1841, Daniel Webster became his Secretary **of State.** The boundary question and its connected **disturbances** had now come to **a** crisis; and the new secretary **took hold of** the question with **vigor.** A month after his inauguration President **Harrison** died, **and was succeeded by the Vice-President, John** Tyler. Yet it was thought of so much importance that the matter **should be** brought **to a conclusion** by Mr. Webster that, though differing **in** politics with Mr. Tyler, he still continued to fill the office of secretary.

In the spring of 1842 arrived the new minister from England, Lord Ashburton, accredited with powers to form **a** new treaty in settlement of the boundary difficulties. An extra session of the legislature of **Maine** was called on the **18th** of May, for **the** purpose of choosing **commissioners to** confer with Lord Ashburton and **Secretary Webster** upon this subject. On the **22d of July the** commissioners sent **in** their **adhesion to the line agreed** upon between **the** Minister and **Secretary. As in the** award **of the king** of the Netherlands, **this line extended** north **from the source of the** St. Croix **River to the** St. John's, **and along the** middle of this river to **the** St. Francis at **the extreme** north, and through **the** middle of that river **to the source** of its southwest **branch.** From this point, instead of following the highlands which divide the waters falling **into** the St. Lawrence from those emptying into **the Atlantic ocean, it went in a straight** line southwesterly, **with but one angle, to the southwestern** branch **of** the **River St.** John, **whence it continued in** an irregular **line between the** waters, as in **the former treaty.** We were also secured in the free navigation of the St. John's throughout its length.

6. By the change in the boundary we lost a **considerable** tract; a large portion of this, however, **was of** little value to us either from its position **or the** quality of its soil. The inhabitants **on the north of the St. John's had for some years ceased to send any representative to the** legislature **of** Maine; consequently **our** government felt little hesitation in yielding these settlers to the government of their choice. For the territory surrendered from Maine, the United States **received** tracts of much greater value to **the** nation on Lakes Champlain and Superior. To recompense Maine for this loss of territory, she received from the general government $150,000; Massachusetts also receiving the like sum, as she was still the owner, by agreement at the separation, of one half the public lands in Maine. Maine also received $200,000 **to** reimburse her expenses **in the** boundary disturbances. This **treaty** was ratified by the Senate of the United

States on the 20th of August, 1842, and the exact limits of Maine were thereby definitely and finally settled.

7. In 1841 Edward Kent again occupied the gubernatorial chair; but in 1842 he was for the second time succeeded by Governor Fairfield, who, therefore, has the honor of having guided Maine through the most critical period of her history.

With these events closes the formative period of our State: all disputed questions between her and other States were put to rest; the form of her political organization had been decided; and she was now free to pursue plans for the development of the wealth contained in her soil, the utilization of her immense water power, and the extension of her commerce.

8. Within half a dozen years preceding 1842 we may note also the first stirrings of those important movements whose beneficial character has since been realized in our State and nation. During the term of Governor Dunlap the subject of humane institutions was urged, especially the establishment of an insane asylum; in 1836 our first scientific survey was begun, and our first railroad charter granted. In 1837 occurred our only special conflict with slavery; while in 1841 was commenced that energetic and beneficent movement against the use of intoxicating liquors, which at length culminated in the prohibitory laws.

What disturbances occurred in Aroostook in 1839? What message did Sir John Harvey send to the governor of Maine? What captures were made by each party? What was the action of Congress on this matter? What was the mission of General Scott? What was its result? By what treaty and in what year was our boundary finally settled? Give the boundaries as defined by this treaty. What compensations did Maine receive? Who was governor of Maine at the time of the disturbances and of the treaty? Of what period in our history do these events mark the close?

CHAPTER XXXIII.

1. The abuse of alcoholic liquors had at this time become so great that its effects were everywhere traceable in ruinous dwellings and neglected farms, in coarse manners, and in the prevalence of vice in all classes of society and in all the states of the American Union. The pressing need of reform in drinking customs had, in 1813, induced the formation of the Massachusetts Society for the Suppression of Intemperance, in which Maine participated. This led to the formation in Boston in 1826, of the American Temperance Society, in whose platform of principles *distilled* liquors were prohibited. In 1833 the Massachusetts Society adopted a new constitution, with a pledge of total abstinence.

2. In May of the same year the first National Temperance Convention assembled in Philadelphia, being composed of 400 delegates from twenty-one States. This convention took no stronger ground than to declare that "the *traffic* in ardent spirits as a drink, and the *use* of it as such, are morally wrong, and ought to be abandoned throughout the world." At this convention the United States Temperance Union was formed, having for its object the diffusion of knowledge and the exertion of moral influence for the extension of temperance principles.

There had been laws *regulating* the sale of intoxicating liquors in Maine, as in other parts, from the first establishment of civil government; but the declaration of the National Convention pointed to a *restriction* of the traffic, which finally took the form of prohibiting absolutely the sale of intoxicating liquors for the common purposes of drink.

3. The first extensive reform of intemperate persons in Maine began with the introduction of the Washingtonian temperance societies. The leading principle of the Washingtonians was total abstinence from all that could intoxicate; and their method was to convert the drunkard and drunkard-maker by moral suasion. Their first organization was formed in Baltimore in 1840. The famous temperance lecturer, John H. W. Hawkins, was associated with it from the start, and the still more famous John B. Gough became identified with the movement a few months later. At the first anniversary of this society more than one thousand reformed drunkards marched in procession; and its results in all parts of New England were very great.

4. But there were so many who were determined to indulge their appetites for strong drink, and so many who found profit in the traffic, that only a comparatively small number could be rescued from the degrading bondage. Therefore it became evident that the traffic must be restrained by law, in order to diminish the use of intoxicants and to remove temptation from the way of the weak. In most of the northern States efforts were make to awaken the minds of the people to the evils of strong drink, and to regulate its sale.

In Maine, temperance tracts were distributed, and there was no town hall, country church, nor district school house, where the people were not called together to consider this subject. Several of the States adopted license laws, but prohibitory laws were not thought practicable except in Maine. There was also an honest scruple in the minds of many personally temperate people in regard to interference with the liberty of the individual in the use of beverages.

5. Petitions for the enactment of a prohibitory law in Maine were refused by the Legislatures of 1844 and 1845; but in 1846 a law was enacted which pro-

hibited the sale of alcoholic liquors absolutely, except for medicinal and mechanical purposes. It was the first law in Maine, or elsewhere, that made the sale of liquor as a beverage illegal. This was a long step forward; but the penalties imposed were so slight that the law was practically useless,—except that it called public attention to the evils of the traffic, leading to renewed effort and better laws.

The cause of temperance was growing. In the following year the Supreme Court of the United States decided, without a dissenting voice, that prohibition laws were not inconsistent with the Constitution of the United States, nor with any act of Congress.

6. Meanwhile the people were becoming more and more enlightened in regard to the tendency of strong drink to destroy prosperity and degrade men and women, so that really good society might nowhere be found. The progress of the arts and sciences were holding out to mankind new and wonderful means of a superior condition of life, in the machinery for the manufacture of every conceivable article, and in the application of the steam engine to transport men and merchandise with great rapidity and small cost over sea and land, so that there came to be many new and profitable occupations for such persons as were qualified to engage in them. But the nice machinery could not be run by a person in any degree affected by intoxicants. Passengers would not trust themselves on railroads and steamboats if their lives were to be endangered by tipsy employés; so that the material forces of civilization, as well as moral and intellectual ones, were urging to sobriety and the banishment of the dangerous alcoholic drinks.

7. In 1842 the organization called "Sons of Temperance" was organized in New York city, and its divisions were speedily extended into Maine. Unlike the Washingtonian societies, its membership was

formed chiefly of temperate people of good reputation. It was largely social in its character, but secret in its proceedings. The society proved very effective in cultivating a sound sentiment in the community in regard to beverages, and greatly aided in bringing about the adoption of more stringent laws relating to the liquor traffic. Nor was this the only association which contributed to the cause of prohibition. Others were the Independent Order of Rechabites, organized in 1842; the Cadets of Temperance, in 1845; the Temperance Watchmen, originating in Durham, Maine, in 1849; with the later organizations of Good Templars, the Juvenile Templars, Band of Hope, and the Loyal Temperance Legion.

8. The Legislature of 1851 was composed largely of temperance men; and on the last day of the session it enacted the first prohibitory law that has proved effective. The governor in that year was Dr. John Hubbard, of Hallowell, a Democrat, but who, as a physician, had accurate knowledge of the injury wrought by strong drinks; and he signed the new law the very day it came to him. This was the famous "Maine Law." It was framed chiefly by Neal Dow, since so well known in America and England as the advocate of prohibition; who also, in 1844, had circulated at his own expense the first petitions for prohibition.

9. Up to the close of that day the dealers were selling their liquors freely, and had their usual large stocks on hand; the next morning all sales were unlawful, and their liquors were liable to be confiscated and destroyed; but the authorities very properly allowed them a reasonable time for their removal. Very soon, in the cities where large quantities were kept, long processions of drays, full of barrels and casks of the mischievous spirits, were to be seen on their way to railroad stations and steamboat landings, going off to afflict communities in other States.

Governor Hubbard, who had signed the prohibitory law, was re-nominated by his party, but a large number refused to support him, and nominated an anti-Maine Law candidate. From this action it resulted that none of the several candidates voted for received a majority, and the election therefore devolved upon the Legislature; and William G. Crosby, a Whig, was chosen.

10. The law was amended, in order to make it more effective and acceptable, in 1853, and again in 1855. In the spring of the latter year a city agency for the sale of liquors for medicinal and mechanical purposes was established in Portland. The Mayor, in that year, was Neal Dow, who had himself taken care to purchase suitable liquors for this purpose, and they had been stored in City Hall, in which place the agency was to be opened.

The statement was thereupon circulated that Mr. Dow had, in violation of the State law, engaged in the liquor business himself. The police had been searching stores and dwellings for liquors kept for illegal sale, and the Marshal was called upon to seize and destroy "Mayor Dow's rum," as well as that of others. The Mayor called a meeting of the Aldermen in order to transfer the liquors to the city, as had been intended; but while they were in session, the Marshal, armed with a warrant from the Police Court, seized the whole stock.

11. A crowd had collected about the depository of the liquors in old City Hall, in Market Square, which, in the evening, greatly increased, and manifested a purpose to destroy or get away with the liquors. No doubt some believed Mr. Dow had, by means of the law, secured a monopoly in liquor selling, and was about to engage in it for his own profit; but most knew the truth, and were moved merely by malice against the prohibitory law, and were glad of an opportunity to avenge themselves upon its author.

The crowd still continued to increase, grew violent, and stones and brickbats were thrown at the doors of the City building. Soon after ten o'clock Mayor Dow, accompanied by a portion of the Rifle Guards, appeared upon the scene and ordered the crowd to disperse. They did not obey, but on the contrary, became more violent, and the Mayor gave the order, "First platoon, fire," but the order was not obeyed; and the Mayor, escorted by a part of the company, left the scene. After the Guards had retired the riotous demonstrations increased. The police fired blank cartridges into the crowd, hoping to frighten them away, but without success. About eleven o'clock the Mayor, with a portion of the Rifle Guards, under Captain Roberts, returned to City Hall. The doors of the liquor store were flung open, and firing began upon the crowd. A sailor was killed and ten or twelve persons wounded. At this the mob dispersed.

12. The Mayor was severely censured for ordering the fire, and was tried on a charge of having liquors in his keeping. The legal proceedings were long continued, and it finally became evident that the whole movement proceeded from the hostility of those who hated the law; and the persecuted magistrate was acquitted.

At the election in the autumn following the liquor agency riot in Portland, the vote for the Maine Law candidate for Governor showed increased favor to the cause, but a plurality of votes defeated him; while a majority of the members of the Legislature proved to be against prohibition; and Samuel Wells of Portland, who had been the Democratic candidate, was elected Governor. In the following session the prohibitory law was repealed and a stringent license law substituted. Then followed nearly two years when liquors were freely sold wherever there were found sufficient patrons to pay the annual license fee. There quickly followed a large increase of poverty, crime and public disorder.

13. In 1856 the members elected to the legislature were almost unanimously anti-slavery men, yet the license candidate for governor was defeated by an adverse majority of 20,000 votes. Slavery rather than temperance was the issue that year, but in the next year the increased drunkenness brought the question of prohibition or license into prominence. The legislature elected in 1857, therefore, contained many ardent temperance men, and in March, 1858, the Maine law, much improved, was enacted to go into effect on July 15th, 1858, with a provision that it should be submitted to the people the month previous. The new law was approved by a large majority. Prohibition now became the settled policy of the State, and while neither of the national parties gave hearty support to the strict execution of the law, neither has since ventured to set itself plainly in opposition. At length, after more than thirty years' experience of the benefits of the prohibitory policy to the moral and material interests of the State, a constitutional amendment embodying the principle of prohibition, was, in September, 1884, submitted to the people, and they chose to put it in the constitution beyond the reach of repeal or change, at any one election, by a vote of nearly three to one,—a majority twice larger than any party or any proposition ever before obtained in Maine.

14. The constitution of the State now prohibits forever the manufacture of intoxicating liquors, and their sale, except for medicinal or mechanical purposes and the arts. The amendment went into effect on the first Wednesday of January, 1885.

The share of Maine in the national drink bill, if she filled her proportion, would be about thirteen millions of dollars, but it is believed that one million will far more than pay for all the liquor smuggled into the State, or sold in violation of the law. So it will be seen that there is an annual saving by prohibition of about twelve millions of dollars directly, with an indirect saving in money and material, nearly, or quite as large. It is this saving and the resulting sobriety which renders Maine so prosperous, her people so intelligent, and her communities so happy, compared with places where the sale of liquor is unrestrained.

15. While there had been Temperance parties in Maine in 1853, 1869, and from 1880 to 1884, their organization had only served to stimulate other parties to enact and execute prohibitory laws. When the first prohibitory law was enacted the government was Democratic, and had been so for many years. In 1857, when the prohibitory law was replaced upon the statute book, the Legislature was largely Republican, and so, also, was the Legislature of 1883, which framed the Prohibition amendment and submitted it to the people.

The reader of this history has found mention of many political parties, and some statement of their principles is necessary to an understanding of the influences which shaped public affairs.

16. The present Republican party was formed in Maine early in 1856, a little in advance of its organization in other States. The first three governors of the State also belonged to a Republican party, but it was another one, having different principles, for the conditions of the two periods were different. The Republican party of 1820 took its rise at the period when the constitution of the United States was formed. Those who favored placing large powers in the national government, were called Federalists, while those who thought that the States should be nearly independent of national control, were called Anti-Federalists, and then Republicans. Of the first, were Washington and the elder Adams, while the opposition was under the lead of Jefferson and Madison. During the French Revolution the Federal

party sympathized with **England, while the Republicans** favored the French.

17. In the political excitements of that period the Republicans were stigmatized by their opponents as **democrats. The** name, though given as a reproach, **was adopted; and** the party of Jefferson and Jackson **called itself** Democratic-Republican, but its **members soon came to** be called Democrats, and their **organization** has ever since been the Democratic party. Following the second war with England, the Federalist party came into a minority, **and** the name grew unpopular, and it adopted the designation of National Republicans.

18 In Maine, **in 1830,** therefore, these **were the names of the** two **parties in** the field. **Governor Hunton was the nominee of** the latter party, **and** the successful **candidate. In 1831** the Democratic-Republicans had **their turn,** electing Samuel E. Smith as governor. By 1834 the last word of the name was dropped, and Governor Dunlap was elected as a "Democrat" simply; and the National Republicans shortened the name of their party and vindicated their patriotism by adopting the name of Whigs, **which** had **been** the designation of **the party of Independence at the** period **of the Revolution.** These **continued to be the names of parties in** Maine until **1852, when the Anti-Maine Law party was** formed. **This drew** so many votes **from the Democratic party that its** candidate for governor was defeated. Thus **far** Edward Kent was the only Whig elected gov**ernor in** Maine, while the Democratic party had Governors Dunlap and Fairfield, Hugh J. Anderson, of Belfast (1844-1846), John W. Dana, of Fryeburg (1847), and **John** Hubbard, **of** Hallowell (1850-1852).

19. In consequence **of the formation of the new party, there was** formed in **1852 the Maine Law party,** to antagonize it; having for **its candidate, in the fol-**

lowing year, **Anson P. Morrill, of** Readfield. But William G. Crosby, **the candidate of** the Whigs, was elected governor, **also** obtaining the office in the following year **by the** choice of the Legislature. In 1854 Anson P. Morrill **was** the candidate of the Maine Law party and of the new " Know Nothing " or American party, and was elected by the Legislature ; no candidate having received a majority of **the** popular vote.

20. In the years since 1841, when the Liberty **or** Abolition party first appeared **in Maine,** the anti-**slavery** sentiment had been growing. **In 1848 the party** threw upwards of 12,000 **votes.** About this **time** the Free Soil party was formed, having a principle that gave it a national and a more popular character. It attained to considerable magnitude in the Middle States, and the Abolition party became merged in this: George F. Talbot being its first gubernatorial candidate in Maine, in 1849. It threw a **variable number of votes** until **1854, when** they **were divided between the** Whig **nominee and Anson** P. Morrill, the **candidate of the Maine Law and** Know Nothing parties, giving **him the** largest number, but not a majority ; and his election, also, **came** from the Legislature. In 1855 the Democrats had their turn again, electing Samuel Wells, of Portland, to the gubernatorial chair.

21. At this period new questions were claiming the attention of citizens, and, naturally, new parties were **formed upon the** new issues. **The** Temperance, the **Abolition and the Know** Nothing parties **each had aims peculiar to** itself: that of the **Abolitionists or Liberty party being the abolition of slavery in the United States; and that of the Know** Nothing or American party, opposition to foreign influence (especially the Roman Catholic) in our public affairs. The Free Soil party, which the Abolitionists joined, had merely a more practical plan than they, but this

also, a little later, became absorbed in **the new Republican party.** The **latter arose in** consequence **of** the effort of the **slave** power to gain possession of Kansas, **where the** resulting "Border Ruffian" outrages were arousing the indignation and exciting the **alarm of the most** conservative people.

22. The principles of the new Republican party, **formed in** Maine early in 1856, were found to be consistent with the views of many **of all other** parties; **while its** leading principle of opposition to the extension of slavery rapidly gained for it an immense **following.** John C. Fremont, the Pathfinder of the **Rocky Mountains, was** its candidate for the presidency **of the United** States, while the pro-slavery **candidate was** James Buchanan, **a Democrat,** and who gained **the election.** In Maine, however, the Republican candidate, **Hannibal Hamlin, was elected** by a very large majority. **Governor** Hamlin having been chosen United States Senator, Lot M. Morrill, one of the noblest characters in American politics, **was** elected as his successor.

23. No other parties than the Republican and the Democratic appeared again in elections **in Maine until 1860, when** there was a small Whig **vote; but there was none the next year.** There was, however, **in this and the following year,** a new organization **called the War Democrats, who were simply Democrats who desired to** support **the** government in the **suppression of** the rebellion by military force. Colonel **Charles D.** Jameson, of Bangor, was its candi**date in both years.** After its second campaign its members joined the Republican ranks, or went back to their old party. Again it was Republicans and Democrats until 1873, when Joseph H. Williams, of Augusta, who **had** twice been acting-governor, was **the** candidate **of the** Liberal Republicans. The leading principle **of this new party** was leniency to**ward** the States which **had been in** rebellion. In

1876 appeared the Greenback party, whose platform of principles varied in different States, but agreed always in advocating an exclusively paper currency of national treasury notes, similar to the greenbacks issued during the war of the rebellion.*

24. The governor was elected by popular vote every year from 1856 to 1878, when the Greenback party threw a larger vote than the Democrats. The Republican candidate had not obtained a majority, and the Legislature elected, choosing Dr. Alonzo Garcelon, of Lewiston, the Democratic nominee.

25. In 1879 the three parties had each a candidate, but in members of legislature and in county officers there was much fusion on the tickets of Democrats and Greenbackers, and some certificates of election to the Legislature were granted to persons not entitled to them by the vote, these persons belonging in most cases, to one of the two fusion parties. When the day of the legislative session arrived, some of the Republicans, who supposed themselves elected, appeared to claim their places, but found them occupied by persons holding illegal certificates, so that for a time there were two legislatures. There not having been an election of governor by the people, the fusion Legislature chose Joseph L. Smith, national Greenbacker. The contention between the rival bodies was severe, and threatened civil disorder, but Major Gen. Chamberlain, commander of the State militia, held possession of the state house and kept the peace until the question at issue had been decided by the Supreme Court of Maine. The decision of the court gave several of the contested seats to the Republican claimants. It also made the doings of the fusion body invalid; therefore the Legislature, as now constituted, proceeded, according to the provisions of the constitution, to select a governor from the four who had received the largest popular vote. The two receiving the largest number of votes in the House

*See note on page 271.

of Representatives were **Joseph L. Smith of Bangor, and Daniel F. Davis of Corinth; and these names being sent to the Senate, the latter gentleman was chosen. Governor Davis** was a young lawyer who had **been a corporal in** the war of the rebellion, **and was Republican in politics.**

26. **An amendment to the** constitution adopted **this year,** directed the election **for** governor, State **senators** and representatives **to be** held biennially after 1880, the official term **also** being made two years, while the regular session of the Legislature was fixed to occur once in two years, instead **of** annually.

In 1880 another amendment **to** the constitution was adopted, by **which a** plurality **of** votes only, instead of **a majority, was** made sufficient for the election of **a** gubernatorial candidate.

27. **At the same time** Governor Davis was a candidate for re-election, and there were also a Temperance and a Prohibition candidate; while between the Democrats and Greenbackers there was such cordial and extensive union of forces, that in the published summary of votes, they appeared not at all under their names, but as Fusionists. Their candidate was Harris M. Plaisted, of Bangor, who was **elected the first governor under the new plurality rule, and the first for a term of two years. In ten counties the** Republican **candidates were elected with two or** three **exceptions, but in the** other six nearly all the officers **were** divided between the Democrats and Greenbackers, who in a few cases were voted for on distinct tickets. Fusionists also were elected to Congress in what were at **that** time the fourth and fifth Congressional districts, one being a Greenbacker, with free liquor tendencies, the other a Democrat and Greenbacker.

There were still more numerous differences **of sentiment in** 1882, candidates being nominated by **the Republicans,** Fusionists, Greenbackers, Independent

Republicans and Prohibitionists; **but the** Republican candidate, Col. Frederick Robie, **of Gorham, was** elected **over all by a handsome** majority.

GREENBACKER. — Members of the Greenback party, which proposed the abolition of national banks, and the issue by the national treasury of a sufficient volume of currency to cover and pay the whole national debt. The name "greenback" arose from the color in which the back of the treasury note is printed. This note is a promise to pay coin, gold or silver, United States minted, and of a fixed standard of fineness, and is *money* in virtue of being made by law *legal tender*. The **Greenback** party proposed to convert **the greenbacks into an** irredeemable currency by **leaving out the words "on demand,"** thus making all payments **of coin (which alone is the current** money of the world), to depend **on the will of the Government.** This would constitute "fiat money," **which does** not rest on a specie basis, but derives its purchasing power from the declaratory fiat of the person or government issuing it. The Greenbackers were necessarily "Inflationists,"—who favor increased issues of paper money or other means of increasing the volume of currency.

What beneficial movement began in Maine **in** 1841 ? At what date was the first **law** enacted in Maine, making the sale of inintoxicating liquors **as** beverages unlawful? Who was **the** framer of the law of 1851, known as the "Maine Law"? **In** what year was prohibition incorporated in the Constitution **of** Maine? Does the credit of the establishment of prohibition belong to any one political party? What parties have existed in Maine? **Was the Republican party of 1820 the same as that** of the present **time? What two parties have had the longest** existence?

CHAPTER XXXIV.

1. THE antagonism between free society and a civilization based upon human slavery was marked in our country by the rise of the Abolition party, and of the Free Soil party, into which the former was merged, and by the formation later of the grand body of the Republican party, which embraced the other two. The members of these parties saw that slavery was debasing to the master as well as to the slave, and that it was unfavorable to the highest national prosperity; they also found the system to be aggressive and grasping in respect to both government and territory. It was for these reasons that the northern people arose in their might and said to the overbearing slaveholder: "Thus far mayest thou go, but no farther"; and with the principle, *No more slave territory*, Abraham Lincoln was elected President of the United States.

2. Maine had first suffered from the slave power at the very outset of her career as a State; again, in 1837, her commerce with Georgia had been injured by restrictions imposed only upon Maine vessels by that State, contrary to the Constitution of the United States; again in several years following 1854, hundreds of her families who had removed to Kansas, were subjected to unnumbered outrages, even pillage, arson and murder, by "Border Ruffians" from slave States, who, incited by the slave power, were determined to change free Kansas into slave territory. With the triumph of the Republican party in Lincoln's election in 1860, the slaveholders found that the control of the government had passed from their hands; and they determined to secede from the

Union and set up a nation of their own, with human slavery for its corner-stone.

3. Then came the attack of the Secessionists upon the United States fort, Sumter, in Charleston Harbor, South Carolina, April 12th, 1861; and the consequent call of President Lincoln for 75,000 volunteers, for three months, to assist the navy and the regular army in the defense of the national property in all parts of the country, and in the capital itself.

Immediately the hills and valleys of Maine resounded with martial music. In several towns volunteer companies were formed within twenty-four hours after the President's call reached them. The Lewiston Light Infantry was the first company to fill its ranks and be accepted and ordered into service by the Governor. In four hours after the enlistment roll was opened in Cherryfield, fifty volunteers had entered their names. Other towns did as nobly, if not so quickly. Many individuals did much beyond what could have been required of them, to save the nation.

Henry Humphreys, of Thomaston, offered to arm and equip a company of artillery himself, at an expense of fifteen thousand dollars.

4. The President's call was issued on April 15th, and on the 16th Governor Israel Washburn sent out a proclamation calling members of the Legislature to a session on the 22d, for the purpose of considering and determining necessary measures. On the assembling of the Legislature, an act was passed providing for the raising of ten regiments of volunteers, and authorizing a loan of a million dollars. On May 3d the President issued another call for troops, this time for volunteers to serve three years.

From the long prevalence of peace the militia of Maine was in a disorganized condition. There was an enrolled but unarmed militia of sixty thousand men, but not more than twelve hundred of these were in a condition to respond to calls for ordinary duty within the State; yet within two weeks of the President's call, the First Maine Regiment of infantry was organized, and before a month had passed the Second Regiment had left for Washington, armed and equipped so well that it was expressly commended by the Secretary of War.

5. After sending forward the first six regiments Governor Washburn discontinued enlistments, having received notice that the government at Washington would not accept additional troops from Maine. All other organized companies were now required to disband, or, at their option, be placed upon such a footing as to drill and compensation as would in a degree relieve them, yet secure their services when required. But after Brigadier-General Sherman visited the State and concerted measures with Governor Washburn in regard to his naval expedition, it was made certain that additional regiments would be required, and the work of organizing recommenced with vigor; four other regiments were speedily filled, the last being mustered into the United States service on the 4th of October, 1861. At the close of this year there had been fourteen regiments mustered into the national service, and twelve of them had gone forward to the seat of war, while several companies of Home Guards were placed as garrisons in forts on the Maine coast. Fort McClary, at Kittery, was garrisoned on the 30th of April; Fort Scammel, in Portland Harbor, on July 22d; and Fort Sullivan, at Eastport, on the 4th of December.

6. The act of the Legislature had caused the First and Second regiments to be enlisted for two years unless sooner discharged; the former being mustered into the United States service for three months, the latter for two years. The Third, Fourth, Fifth and Sixth regiments were also thus enlisted; but later

orders from the **War** Department required all State **volunteers to be mustered into the** national service **for three years, making a** change necessary in the terms **of enlistment.** The First and Second regiments had already left for the seat of war, but all **others** who refused to sign a contract to serve an additional year were discharged.

7. On the 21st of July, 1861, twelve Maine regiments were in the field; two being stationed for the defense of Washington, while **several were that day** engaged with the enemy in the **battle of Bull Run.** The Second Regiment, after **a long march in the early morning, rested on the Warrenton turnpike. About ten** o'clock they **were ordered** to the front, **and** marched three miles under a burning sun at double-quick, many falling out of the ranks exhausted. As they came up where Sherman's battery was engaging the rebels, the men threw aside their coats and **packs, and again** advanced at double-quick through **the woods, over streams** and ditches, **until they came upon a rebel battery. Twice they charged almost to the muzzles of the guns, and twice they were driven** back. **Several officers fell in these assaults. Color-Sergeant Deane was mortally wounded** while carrying the flag presented to the regiment on the previous day. He beckoned to the chaplain, who knelt and put his ear close to the mouth of the dying **soldier.** "Is it safe?" whispered the hero. "What?" asked the chaplain. "The flag." Being assured of **its safety, he nodded** his head, smiled, and closed his eyes. He never spoke again.

8. The flag, stained with his blood, had been seized, as he fell, by Corporal Moore, **and, he, too, was almost instantly shot** dead; **and the** flag **was left on the** ground, which the rebels immediately occupied. When its loss **was** noticed by the regiment, **all** shouted, "We must have that flag!" and up the hill they went, Colonel Jameson leading. The enemy

almost had it in their grasp, **when** our men rushed upon them, and the sacred emblem was recovered unpolluted by touch of rebel hands. The regiment continued the conflict with great bravery and effect. Other **portions of our** force had done as well. The **rebels were** driven back at almost every point, and **at two o'clock** victory appeared to perch upon our **banners.**

9. Soon after this hour a dust cloud appeared over the trees at the west. **It came nearer** and **nearer.** That cloud marked the approach of a body of troops, who, at first, were thought to **be of** the Union army, and were permitted to take a flanking position within musket shot of Rickett's **and** Griffin's batteries. They proved **to be** 1,700 men of rebel General Johnston's division, **from** Winchester. Their **first volley** caused great **slaughter, and the** batteries **were abandoned** by the **few men** who had not fallen.

10. Colonel Howard's brigade, consisting of **the** Third, Fourth and Fifth Maine regiments and the Second Vermont, had rested barely fifteen minutes, after a long and hurried march, when they were ordered to advance upon the enemy. But the batteries **they were** to support were already retreating, and a **rebel battery** and a large **body** of infantry in **protected positions opened upon them with deadly effect.** They were forced to **retire to the protection** of a wood, but formed again and **returned to** the conflict. The panic from the flying **men and horses** of the beaten **batteries** now extended far **and** wide. Entirely unsupported, this brigade also **was** forced to join in the retreat, which at four o'clock **had** become a rout. Though the army of McDowell numbered about 40,000 men, nearly one-fourth **of** the troops actually engaged in this battle were from Maine.

11. This disaster **to** our forces led Governor Washburn to issue another **order directing the** enlistment of additional regiments **as volunteers.** In this docu-

ment he said: "While observing with most grateful pride and admiration the brave conduct of our regiments in the field, the Governor and Commander-in-Chief calls upon the loyal sons of the State to emulate the patriotic zeal and courage of their brothers who have gone before them. The issue involved is one on which there can be no divided opinion in Maine. It affects not only the integrity of our Union, but the very life of Republican government. For the preservation of these, Maine will pour out her best blood, and expend her richest treasure. Having already contributed generously of the flower of her youth and manhood, Maine must send yet more of her stalwart sons, to do battle for the preservation of the Union, and for the supremacy of law."

12. The Government found that more troops were necessary for the suppression of the rebellion; and as other States were still rapidly forming new military organizations, authority was given Maine by the War Department to organize five more regiments of infantry (with power to increase the number to eight) a regiment of cavalry, six batteries of light artillery, and a company of rifle sharp-shooters. These were promptly raised, together with four additional companies of coast guards.

13. In the meantime the regiments already sent forward were having experience of the vicissitudes of war. Sometimes it was but the easy service of guarding a road, military stores, or public property; oftener it was the long march through deep mud, or in heat and dust; or it was exposure for hours to rain, or snow and sleet; again it was hunger not wholly satisfied for days; then it was severe toil upon intrenchments with spade and pick; or, again, it was hurried marching to battle, miles away. Here were the rattle of musketry, the screaming of shells, the mowing of the ranks by grape and canister, or the fearful charge of the glittering bayonets,

and the trampling of **horses and the swift stroke of** sabres in the terrible cavalry **charge.**

14. In February, 1862, **Fort Henry, on the** Tennessee **river, had** been taken **from the** rebels by **Commodore Foote;** Roanoke Island, by General Burnside; **while the** battle of Millsprings had **cleared Kentucky of** the **rebels.** General Grant **had taken** Fort **Donelson, on** the Cumberland; **in March,** General Pope **and** Commodore **Foote had** captured Island **Number Ten,** near **the mouth** of the Ohio; in **April, the** rebels had **suffered a** defeat at Pittsburg Landing, by **General** Grant; while General Gilmore had taken **Fort** Pulaski, at the mouth of the Savannah; and **Commodore** Farragut, with General Porter, had **taken** forts Jackson **and St. Philip,** commanding the **entrance of the Mississippi river.**

15. After Bull Run **the army of the Potomac was** distrustful, **and many** months passed before any general advance was made. This battle had shown the liability of new troops to panic, and made the necessity of discipline apparent. The remainder of **the** summer and the autumn and winter were chiefly **spent by** our forces in **the** East in drill, **strategic movements** and **many** intrenchments, instead of **persistent fighting. The first important** conflict after **Bull Run in which the** Maine regiments of the army **of the** Potomac were engaged **was** at Williamsburgh, **immediately** following the seige **of** Yorktown. At the latter place the Second, Third, Fourth and Sixth regiments distinguished themselves in reconnoissances and skirmishes, and made themselves exceedingly useful in less **exciting** labors; so that they were mentioned as "those marvellous New England soldiers who built batteries by night and in the rain with the same energy and skill with which they repair locomotives, construct railroad bridges, run **gristmills and** reconstruct abandoned saw-mills."

16. The retreat of the confederated rebels from Yorktown took place on the 3d of May. Our forces promptly pursued; and on the 5th was fought the battle of Williamsburgh, on the way to the rebel capital. During the battle the confederates were suddenly reinforced by a large body of troops, and our lines were in consequence slowly forced back. General Hancock, who commanded the left wing, ordered his first line to fall back to the second—about half a mile. Here they re-formed, the new line including the Fifth and Sixth regiments of Maine infantry.

17. The enemy came rapidly on, confident of victory. They poured a terrible fire upon our center, but the men never wavered, giving volley for volley with much effect. The Third and Fourth Maine regiments were stationed on the plain at the left of the battlefield, to prevent the enemy from moving upon our flank. The Eleventh Maine was with General Casey's brigade, three miles away. At about half past three o'clock Casey was ordered up to support General Hancock. The brigade moved at double-quick, through mud to the ankles, arriving in view of the battle field in less than an hour.

18. The Seventh Maine in the earlier part of the day were on the left flank of the second line, but had been ordered, with three companies of a New York regiment, to move behind the hill. Here they remained for several hours, impatiently listening to the varying sounds of the battle. As the advance of Casey's brigade appeared in the distance, the Seventh were ordered to charge. They dashed up over the hill, shouting from their long restrained excitement, General Hancock cheering them on. The enemy heard the shout, and saw the long line of sabre bayonets coming over the hill, and, without firing another gun, they broke and fled. Our whole line pursued, capturing about five hundred prisoners,

including the wounded. Darkness ended the hostilities, and our men bivouacked on the field. All that night the cries of the wounded confederates were ringing in their ears, and they cared for them as they would for their own; many giving up their blankets to them, and sitting in the rain themselves until morning.

19. As the result of this victory, Norfolk on the farther side of the James River, the great navy-yard of the nation, was evacuated by the rebels, and the ram "Merrimac," which had commanded the river, was blown up to avoid her falling into Union hands.

In the West there had been an almost continuous series of victories. The Confederate cause had gone under a cloud.

What marked the antagonism of a free and a slave system of civilization in America? How had Maine suffered from the slave power? How soon after the President's call for troops was the first regiment organized in Maine? What regiment was the first to leave for the seat of war? At the close of 1861 how many Maine regiments had been mustered into the national service? At what date did the battle of Bull Run occur? What was done in Maine as a result of this battle? What was the next important battle in which Maine troops were engaged? Was a greater degree of heroism shown at Williamsburgh than at Bull Run by Maine troops?

CHAPTER XXXV.

1. SEVERAL of the later battles of the rebellion, if not more decisive than that of Williamsburg, were of so much greater importance from the numbers engaged, that this contest appears a small affair in comparison. There were also a great number of smaller combats unnamed as battles, in which as much valor was shown as in the more celebrated conflicts. In most of the latter the troops of Maine were so mingled with those of other States, and their activities were so complicated and extensive that to intelligibly describe them would require a large volume; so that their many heroic performances can rarely be mentioned except in a general manner.

2. A succession of victories during the last part of 1861 and the earlier months of the following year, in both East and West, led the Northern people to believe that the Confederacy would soon collapse. On the first of January, 1862, the national government relieved the authorities of Maine from all participation in the recruiting service; and on April 3d, the Adjutant-General of the United States ordered the volunteer recruiting service to cease. All enlistments were in consequence suspended; but on May 21st, authority was given for raising the Sixteenth regiment of infantry for three years service. This was after "Stonewall" Jackson's victory over the Union army under General Milroy in Western Virgina. No further call for recruits was intimated.

3. Then came the rout of the army under General Banks, and the escape of Jackson's army from those of Generals Fremont and Shields, followed by the defeat of the latter by the wonderful commander

whom he was pursuing. Scarcely four weeks later came the withdrawal of General McClellan's army from the Peninsula, after six days of terrible fighting before Richmond. From these occurrences it became apparent that the war was far from ending, and that the armies must be greatly increased. Within a few weeks a requisition was made upon Maine for her quota under the call of July 2d, 1862. The Sixteenth Regiment was ready; and this, with the Seventeenth, Eighteenth, Nineteenth and Twentieth, together with numerous recruits furnished by cities, towns and plantations, were accepted in satisfaction of the requisition. Volunteering was prompt, and these regiments were filled very quickly; but before their organization was completed, the President, on the 4th of August, called for three hundred thousand militia, to be raised by draft, and to serve for nine months, unless sooner discharged.

4. Our loss of men in these battles, and by sickness, had been great, and the necessity of more troops for the Eastern battle-ground became more and more apparent. Indeed, it was said that had McClellan been reinforced on the Peninsula by twenty thousand men, he would at once have brought the war to a close; but the government could not furnish them. The quota of our State under the call of August 4th, was 9,609. From this, some reduction was made because of the large number of enrolled militia in the merchant marine and the navy. The privilege was also given of supplying with volunteers, instead of drafted men, the whole or any portion of the quota. On the 9th of August, the War Department issued, in General Orders, regulations for the enrolment and draft of men under this requisition. These directed the selection of rendezvous for the troops, commandants for the encampments, and the enrolment of all able-bodied American citizens between the ages of eighteen and

forty-five years; it also **directed**, provisionally, the appointment of **a commissioner from** each county **to** superintend **the drafting, and to hear** and determine **the excuses of persons claiming** exemption **from military duty. But the** statutes of our State were **deemed** sufficient for **the** emergency, and no commissioners **were at this time** appointed in Maine.

5. The draft was first ordered to be made on the third day of September, then was postponed to the tenth, when proceedings directed by **the Orders were** commenced in **those** towns which, **at this date, were** found **to be** deficient in their quotas. **Thus stimulated, the** towns and cities **made** a further effort to **make up** their deficit with **volunteers.** The places of rendezvous for the **troops** were Portland, Augusta and Bangor. At the **close** of October it was found that a few towns had **not** yet furnished the balance **of their quotas** upon the calls of July and August, **and a** commissioner was appointed for each county, **to make a draft on the** 29th of November **in** such **towns as by that time should not have enlisted** the **required number.** These officers, instead of at once preparing **for a** draft, gave **their** efforts to facilitate enlistments in the delinquent towns, and with such success that in no instance did they resort to **the** measure which they were appointed to enforce; and **new** regiments were still formed and old ones recruited without the aid of a draft.

6. Many towns even exceeded their quota, to the **relief of** other **parts of the** State. The city of Saco **sent no less than** twenty-five men in **excess** of her quota under **both** calls, while **the town of Machias,** having furnished its full quota **with promptness,** expressed a determination to respond **in like manner to all future calls.** A great aid **in** procuring **enlistments** was found in the **town** and State bounties, and in **the assurance of** State aid to such families as were

left without support by the absence of husband, father, or son, in the service of the country.

Meanwhile the conflict raged completely around the Confederacy. After the defeat of McClellan's army in the several battles along the line of the Chickahominy, the rebels prepared for an invasion of Maryland. They worsted General Pope's army at Cedar Mountain, in the battle of Manassas, or Second Bull Run, and at Chantilly; then they crossed the Potomac, near Harper's Ferry, into Maryland.

7. Here, on September 17th, they were met by the consolidated armies of McClellan and Pope, which, advancing from Washington, met the enemy at Antietam Creek. In this battle the Second Maine Infantry was the first regiment under fire; the Fifth was under fire for thirty hours with unabated courage; while the Seventh, by some blunder, was ordered to charge alone a rebel reserve of infantry and a battery well-posted on a hill three-fourths of a mile away. But obedience is the soldier's first duty; and their brave colonel, Hyde, led them on,—crossing, of necessity, an open plain exposed to the artillery of both friend and foe. The rebels were driven back until they found shelter behind a stone wall. The heroic band then retired by a circuitous route to their brigade line, having lost eleven out of fifteen officers, and more than half the privates which the regiment could then muster. Others of our regiments performed well their part in this battle,—which turned the rebel army back from loyal soil.

8. After his victory at Antietam, McClellan's army made no forward movement until late in October, when it began to cross the Potomac to operate against the rebel forces along the Rappahannock. Distrust of his abilities, or of his patriotism, led President Lincoln to remove General McClellan from

his command; which was then given to Burnside. **The army of General Lee was strongly posted at Fredericksburg; but, urged on toward Richmond by the popular demand, General Burnside decided to cross the Rappahannock and attack the enemy in his position.** The roar of four hundred cannon ushered in the dreadful conflict, in which a dozen Maine regiments and batteries took an active part. On the 12th of December, the Union forces crossed the river to make their grand assault upon **the Confederate lines.** Burnside had **nearly 100,000 men, and Lee opposed** him with 80,000; but **the latter were so strongly intrenched on** the crests of **the hills, that after a long day, full of** determined assaults upon **the enemy's lines, the Union** forces were repulsed **with such** heavy **loss** that they soon withdrew to their former position across the river.

The country was shocked to learn that this battle had cost us 13,000 men. The Sixteenth Maine alone **lost two hundred and twenty-six killed and** wounded, —nearly **half of those who went into the** action. "Whatever **honor we can claim in that conflict,**" said Burnside, "**was won by Maine men.**"

9. President Lincoln **was** greatly distressed **by** this disaster, but it did not deter him from fulfilling a religious vow which he made just before the battle **of** Antietam, that if the rebels were driven back **from** Maryland he would free the slaves. Accordingly, on January 1st, 1863, he issued a proclamation **emancipating every slave** within **the** national domain. Thus, at last, **the chief magistrate of the** nation, **by virtue of his war-power, brought him** by the **slaveholders themselves** in making war, struck the **blow which destroyed the** principal cause of **the** rebellion.

The effect of this **act on the** Confederacy was to weaken its armies; since the negroes, wherever the news came, were not to be depended upon for agricultural purposes, while there was increased fear of their insurrection. On the other hand, the Union forces were, in the course of a few months, strengthened by several regiments of the freedmen,—the aggregate number in Union service finally reaching upwards of 80,000. Yet these results were not at once realized, and there was an urgent need of more troops. Accordingly, on the 3d of March, Congress passed the Conscription Act; and thereafter the general government enforced the drafts under this law.

10. Our forces in the West and upon the southern coast had met with both successes and reverses. The army of the Potomac remained at Falmouth, opposite Fredericksburg; the deep mud making army movement so difficult that little was attempted, until General Burnside was superseded by General Hooker. Having re-organized the army to his mind, and received accessions until he had 150,000 men under his command, Hooker moved against Lee, whose army was still about Fredericksburg. The forces met at Chancellorsville, a few miles north of Lee's position and on the southeastern border of the ten miles square, or more, of rough and barren country known as the Wilderness. It was in the battle fought here that our gallant General Berry fell, while stemming the tide of "Stonewall" Jackson's corps. It was here, too, that the latter received his death wound. The number of Maine troops under fire was about the same as at Fredericksburg, and the loss was almost equal. With every reason to expect an effective victory, Hooker's army had suffered a very damaging defeat; and, under cover of a storm on the night of the 3d of May, he withdrew his whole force to its old position on the other side of the Rappahannock.

11. During these years of the war the Confederates had made increasing efforts to acquire a navy,

and already several powerful vessels under the rebel flag were preying upon our commerce. In the spring of 1863 some attacks had been made upon vessels off the Maine coast by rebel privateers. Among these was the Tacony, a small bark commanded by a Lieutenant Reade. On the 24th of June, 1863, he captured a fishing schooner; and transferring to her his crew and effects, he burned the Tacony. In the disguise of a fisherman, the rebels, on the 26th, entered Portland Harbor. In the following night they succeeded in capturing the United States revenue cutter, Caleb Cushing, an armed vessel, while she lay unsuspectingly at anchor. Early the next morning the cutter was missed; and, after some inquiry, the method of her disappearance became known. The collector of the port, Jedediah Jewett, together with Captain Jacob McLellan, Mayor of the city of Portland, at once prepared for pursuit. Thirty men from the garrison at Fort Preble were placed on board the steamer Forest City, with such officers, guns and ammunition as could be quickly procured. Meanwhile the New York steamer Chesapeake, another small steamer and a tug boat were pressed into service, and manned with experienced pilots, gunners and naval officers, and about one hundred volunteer privates. Having been supplied with ammunition, the little squadron, about eleven o'clock, steamed down the harbor. The cutter was soon sighted in the outer harbor. Being a sailing vessel she made little headway in the light breeze, and the rescuing fleet was soon within range of the small cannon carried by each of the hostile parties.

12. The rebels were not found to be in such force as had been expected; and after a short resistance, they set the cutter on fire and took to their boats, attempting to reach the fishing schooner. The fire soon communicated with the magazine, containing about four hundred pounds of powder, which, at

two o'clock, exploded with a terrific concussion. Thousands of citizens watched the proceedings from elevated points in the city, and witnessed the impressive closing of the career of their familiar vessel.

In the meantime, the steamers pressed on and captured the flying boats, with the twenty-three rebels engaged in this bold but ill-judged exploit. It appeared that they were an offshoot from the Confederate man-of-war, Florida, and that their leader held a commission from the Confederate government; wherefore they could not be hung as pirates. They were placed in confinement at Fort Preble for a while, and some months later were exchanged.

13. By the urgent solicitation of our State authorities, the general government was this year induced to strengthen the permanent fortifications in the harbor of Portland, at the mouth of the Kennebec river, and at the Narrows of the Penobscot, and to construct earthworks at Rockland, Belfast and Eastport. At the latter places two batteries of five guns each were mounted, while single batteries of five guns were placed at Castine and Machiasport. On the part of the State, some additional companies of Home, or Coast, Guards were authorized and placed at such points as appeared to be in danger.

Were the Maine troops massed by themselves in the battles? What occasioned the suspension of enlistments? When did another call for militia occur, and what cause was there for it? What was the quota of our State under this call? Was it raised by draft or by volunteering? When and where was the battle of Antietam fought? What was the result? When and where was the battle of Fredericksburg? What vow did President Lincoln carry into effect on the first of January, 1863? At what date was the Conscription Act passed by Congress? What occurred at the battle of Chancellorsville? What surprising event took place in Portland harbor in June? What action was taken, and what was the result?

CHAPTER XXXVI.

1. Their success at Chancellorsville encouraged the rebels to attempt another invasion of the North. Accordingly, early in June there were concentrated near Culpepper, in Virginia, nearly 100,000 rebels, of whom 15,000 were cavalry. It was nearly the largest and by far the best organized and equipped army which the Confederacy ever placed in the field. The three corps into which it was divided were under the command of Generals Longstreet, Ewell and A. P. Hill,—the cavalry being under Stuart. As it moved slowly down the Shenandoah Valley, Hooker broke up his camp opposite Fredericksburg and moved northward on a line parallel with that of Lee. Having routed General Milroy and his ten thousand at Winchester, Lee crossed the Potomac, and pressed on until his advanced corps under Ewell entered Pennsylvania.

2. General Hooker was disposed to fall upon the enemy's communications rather than to attack his army, and asked of General Halleck, commander-in-chief, that the ten thousand men who were holding Harper's Ferry, be added to his own command. When this was refused, he resigned; and General Meade was immediately appointed to his place.

The Union forces were now advanced northward and thrown upon the Confederate rear. Lee at once turned to meet them. Meade perceived that the enemy's divisions were directed southward so as to join at Gettysburg, and hurried his army forward to secure the choice of position. After General Reynold's fierce fight on the first day of the battle (in which he fell), General Howard came up and took a strong position on Cemetery Hill. Here his artillery covered a wide range of the field, and great efforts were made to dislodge him, but in vain. On the extreme left, on the second day, General Sickles made his grand fight against Longstreet. It was here that some of our Maine regiments displayed a valor not surpassed by any troops upon the field, and maintained the left, where the rebel attacks fell the fiercest and longest, unbroken to the end of the battle. It was not until the night of the 3d of July, and the third day of fighting, that the enemy retired from the field, and then retreated without delay to his old position on the north of Richmond.

3. The presence of this great army of rebels on their north, had greatly alarmed the Washington authorities, and on June 29th a draft of 100,000 men was ordered by the War Department. For the first time in Maine, there was a slight opposition, which, in the towns of Kingfield, Freeman and Salem, in Franklin county, assumed the form of a forcible resistance.

In the minds of some uninstructed persons there is apt to be a confusion of ideas as to what constitutes Liberty and Freedom. These erring citizens forgot that the measure against which they rebelled was the proper act of a government whose members their towns had helped to elect, and who were therefore their legitimate representatives; who, in framing this law, were doing what, in their superior judgment and more comprehensive view, they believed to be best for their constituents. When the American colonies rebelled against Great Britain, they did so on the ground that they were taxed unjustly by a government in which they were not represented, which was located 3,000 miles away, and did not understand the needs of the colonies, but disregarded their rights, refused their just claims, and imposed unjust and oppressive restrictions upon their commerce and manufactures.

4. In 1860, and the earlier months of the following year, there had been actively disseminated in Maine suggestions that there would be great advantages to its citizens in the secession of our State from the United States, and its union with Canada. Added to the influence of these suggestions was the belief on the part of many that the Southern rebels were about to succeed in their purpose,—and the snare of disloyalty was fully set. The malcontents in Maine found their rallying place in Kingfield; where an old piece of cannon, manned by men who had played with it on Independence days, and these supported by a dozen or two unwise persons, armed with old muskets and a few guilty-looking bayonets, constituted the only abettors the Confederates found north of the drunken rioters of New York city.

Against this handful of conceited fellows, marched, in July, Company G, of the 3d division of State Militia (made up mostly of returned veterans), together with a detail of regulars; the whole under the command of Post-Adjutant Webber, of the staff of the Assistant Provost-Marshal. When this force arrived at the rebellious vicinity, the cannon was not to be found, and the figures which had hovered about it had vanished away, as the unfledged brood of a partridge disappears before a farmer's boy. Thus ended the rebellion in Maine; and the draft was made without further trouble.

5. Following this draft, another call was made by the President on the 17th day of October, for 300,000 volunteers to serve for three years. In response to this call Governor Coburn issued a stirring proclamation, of which the following is the leading paragraph: "Of this additional force Maine is expected to furnish her quota, and she will not disappoint that expectation. Now, as heretofore, her patriotic men will respond to the call, and promptly furnish her full share of the force necessary to vindicate the

integrity of our government, **and maintain** the supremacy of the laws **of the** Union."

In the autumn, Lee again advanced northward, but fell back when Meade set his forces in motion to meet him, and no general engagement resulted. In October, General Meade also thought that the time had come for another advance upon Richmond; but at Mine Run he found the enemy in his way in full force, and prudently drew back to avoid a battle.

6. West of the Alleghanies during this autumn were fought the battle of Chickamauga, in which General Rosecrans was defeated by the rebel General Bragg, and the battle of Chattanooga, in which Bragg was defeated by General Grant. In the spring of 1864 the expedition up Red River under Generals Banks and Steele proved a disastrous failure; while in February a strong movement upon Atlanta by General Sherman also failed. The rebels at this period were greatly elated.

On the 12th of March, General Grant was appointed Commander-in-Chief of the armies of the United States, and the grade of Lieutenant-General was conferred upon him by Congress. Meade's veteran army of 90,000 men now lay on the northern bank of the Rapidan. On the southern bank of the river, a little to the west, was Lee's disciplined army of 70,000 Confederates, sheltered by the shrubby trees and rough ground of the Wilderness.

7. On the 5th of May, at the command of General Grant, Meade crossed the Rapidan, as the commencement of another movement upon Richmond. The right wing of the army moved westward on the south bank of the river upon Lee's left; but that commander, anticipating such action, massed his forces there and firmly repelled the attack, even gaining some advantage at first. The next day Burnside's division arrived, and an attack was ordered upon the whole line. This day's line of battle

extended seven miles. The **rough ground and scrubby woods admitted of but slight use of artillery; and regiment faced regiment and blazed away, thinning each other's ranks** with fearful rapidity. **Wave after wave of the Union** host moved over the open **ground** of the forest, rushing upon the sheltered line **of the** Confederates. Before the repeated volleys of the enemy the first brigades gradually fell unflinchingly, and succeeding ones moved over their bodies, delivered their fire, as did their **comrades,—then like** them fell upon the blood-soaked **sod. The loss this day** on either side, in killed, **wounded and prisoners, could scarcely have** been less than **15,000.**

8. **Unable** to gain **any advan**tage because of the sheltered position of **the** rebels, **Grant changed his plan;** and moving his divisions one after another **from the right to** the left southward in the rear of his **front lines,** he sought to **flank Lee's** right wing, **and cut him** off from Richmond.

The **rebel commander was** also **moving his force in the same direction, strengthening his right.** This movement **bore the appearance of a retreat; but** Grant found **him** again **at S**pottsylvania, **and too** strong in his intrenchments to be wholly driven from them, though many prisoners were captured in his advanced lines. In the battle of the 9th fell General Sedgwick, one of our ablest division leaders. The 10th **and 11th were** spent in unavailing assaults upon the **rebel lines; a**nd **again Grant attempted to turn** Lee's **right flank in order to cut him off on the south. Near Po River at daylight on the 12th, was made the famous** charge **by the Second Corps, in which it took 8,000** prisoners and **eighteen guns. In this action** several Maine regiments bore an honorable part.

9. The army **continued moving by the** left flank, while frequently fighting Lee's army on the front. The Second Corps reached Milford on the 21st, and on the 23d moved southward and joined the Fifth

Corps at the South Anna river. Here was another attack upon the enemy in position; the army again moving away on the left flank. On the night of the 26th our forces moved rapidly southward, and across the Pamunky river, where they again encountered the enemy. On the 2d of June the advance moved by the left flank to Cold Harbor, where another severe contest occurred between divisions. On the 13th the army crossed the Chickahominy, and on the 15th, the James; marching thence to the vicinity of Petersburg.

Assaults were quickly begun upon the strong fortifications about the city, and attempts were made to destroy the southern communications of Richmond; but the success in either purpose was only partial. The attempts having failed for the present, Lee decided to threaten Washington, thinking this would induce Grant to release his hold upon Petersburg, which still held out against him. Accordingly Ewell was sent on a raid up the Shenandoah Valley; when, moving with marvelous rapidity, he entered Maryland, plundered Hagerstown, sacked Frederick, and cut off the communications of Washington with the North, even appearing before the forts of the capital itself.

10. Astonished at the presence of a rebel army about Washington, and ignorant of the conditions in that city, our Governor Cony, on July 13th, issued a proclamation declaring the national capital in danger, and calling for volunteers for one hundred days service for its defense. Throughout the State an earnest response was made to the Governor's call.

Greatly to the relief of the country, the rebel army of invasion proved to be small. Being forced to move rapidly from point to point lest the scattered bodies of Union troops should be concentrated against him, Ewell in a few days retreated into Virginia, with much plunder, but without having drawn Grant in the least from his position south of Richmond.

On the 18th of July the President called for 500,000 men to serve one, two and three years; and the preparations under the Governor's call were dropped, and all efforts given to fill the quota,— for a stronger advance upon the rebels rather than for the defense of the national capital.

All through the autumn and winter following, our forces were gaining one after another the important points on the borders of the Confederacy, though not without several reverses. Sheridan, in whose army were many of our Maine soldiers, swept the valley of the Shenandoah clear of rebel squadrons, rendering Washington nearly as safe as New York.

11. Meanwhile General Sherman had been making his splendid march from Atlanta to the Atlantic, crossing Georgia and the Carolinas, fairly cutting the Confederacy in two in the middle. With him were General Slocum and our own Howard, as his two chiefs of division. With the Union successes there became so much territory to occupy that a great number of troops were required merely as garrisons. Hoping with larger armies to speedily crush the rebellion and end the destruction of life which had now been going on for three and a half years, President Lincoln had, on December 19th, called for 300,000 more men. Again the loyal people of the North nobly met the demand, and by draft and bounty, during the winter, brought all the armies up to the necessary strength.

12. On February 16th, Sherman took Columbia, the capital of South Carolina; on the 18th, General Gilmore occupied Charleston, where the first overt act of rebellion was committed. On April 1st and 2d, Grant carried the first and second lines of rebel intrenchments at Petersburg; and, in consequence, the rebel government fled from Richmond, the capital

of their Confederacy. On the 4th of April, Sheridan cut Lee's line of retreat at the west side of Petersburg; and on the 8th, General Weitzel entered Richmond.

These successes were immediately fatal to the rebellion. General Lee found it impossible to escape the encompassing armies, and to engage in battles with the forces gathered against him was certain to be the utter destruction of his army. Therefore, on the 9th of April, he met Grant at Appomattox Court House, and surrendered what remained, and with it all hopes of establishing the Confederacy.

13. In the action of the 29th of March, our General Chamberlain with his brigade and a battery of artillery, after one of the most sanguinary and determined conflicts of the war, put to rout a rebel force much greater than his own. His loss in officers and men was very large, and he was himself twice painfully wounded. General Grant promoted him on the field to the rank of Major-General, and this action was shortly after confirmed by President Lincoln. At the capitulation, General Chamberlain's brigade was designated to receive the surrender of Lee's army. He placed his troops in a straight line, extending the distance of a mile. Not a drum beat nor bugle sounded, neither was a voice heard, as the rebels marched up in parallel line before them, only a few feet away, to lay down their arms. As the ranks of the vanquished army came up, General Chamberlain ordered his men to present arms. This honor in the hour of their humiliation brought tears to many southern eyes. One officer was heard to say, "This is a magnanimity we had not expected."

14. Our troops soon began to return home to their families and friends. Regiment by regiment they appeared in our cities, with countenances sunbrowned and storm-beaten, their uniforms stained and worn, but with their banners waving proudly

over them. Not a flag had been lost by Maine troops during the war, but they had captured many.

During the war the State had furnished to the national armies thirty-one regiments of infantry, three regiments of cavalry, one regiment of heavy artillery, seven companies of sharpshooters, and thirty companies of unassigned infantry. Besides these there were seven companies of coast guards and six companies for coast fortifications. These make a total of 72,945; to which should be added 6,750 men, with whom the State was credited in the navy and marine corps.

The total number who were killed or died of wounds, as shown by the army list, is 2,801; of disease, 4,521. To mention the battles in which Maine soldiers were engaged would be to recite almost the entire list of the war. The blood of our boys has mingled with the soil of every State south of the Ohio river, sealing it for the Union forever.

15. The amount of State bounty paid volunteers up to December 31st, 1865, was $4,584,636. Fifteen regiments of infantry, one regiment of cavalry, and six batteries of mounted artillery entered service with no State bounty whatever. In addition to the State bounties there were paid by towns, bounties amounting to $9,695,320. The generosity of our people who did not go to the war is one of the pleasantest features of our history. The better portion of our citizens of both sexes were almost untiring in their contributions of money, labor and needed articles in aid of sick and wounded soldiers. Nearly every household had its martyr; and their memory will be cherished in the hearts of all who know their noble deeds.

What is said of the rebel army that entered Maryland, at the last of June, 1863? What change was made at this time in the command of the army of the Potomac? What Maine commander held a prominent position at the battle of Gettysburg? What Union General fell in this battle? How many days did the battle continue? What opposition was there in Maine to the draft ordered at this time? When was the next great battle in the East? Who had then been made commander of the Union armies? After the battle of the Wilderness, toward what place did Grant's army move? What startling movement was made by the rebels in July, 1864? What of Sherman's march early in the following year? What caused the flight of the rebel government from Richmond? How was the surrender of Lee's army brought about? What number of men did Maine send into this war? How many were lost by battle and by disease? What amount of money was paid in bounties by this State?

CHAPTER XXXVII.

1. It is more than a matter of curiosity to observe what were the effects of the civil war upon the industries of our State. The production and price of cloths, made from the medium and coarser grades of wool, increased immediately; great quantities being required for soldiers' garments and military blankets. Large quantities of cotton beyond the previous needs were used in the manufacture of canvas for tents. The cotton and woolen mills, therefore, were generally kept busy through the war, and with large profits; for the prices of cloth continually became higher, because of the limited supply of wool and of the reduction in the supply of cotton from the loss of the southern product. Prices of nearly all kinds of merchandise increased because of the scarcity, and, consequently, the high cost of labor,— the male laborers being largely in the armies; while paper money, which soon became the chief currency, depreciated more and more, as the ability to redeem it in coin — the only universal currency — became less. The cause of this was that we were sending large amounts of the latter to other countries in payment for purchases, having proportionately less of our own products to sell than formerly.

2. When the Confederate government succeeded in setting armed vessels afloat, our ocean carrying trade became precarious, and, in consequence, greatly diminished. The result was that many of our merchant vessels were sold to foreigners, fewer vessels were built, and the carrying trade passed to other nations, principally the English.

With the close of the war there came a change. The supply of wool was greater than ever, and the number of factories was no less. Male laborers were more numerous, and the cost of labor decreased; but the profits from the wool manufacture were greatly reduced. The cotton factories did better, for while the supply of raw material became plentiful, there was, as the price decreased, a greater sale of cotton cloth for domestic purposes. The exports of hay and grain were not so large; but our lumber, granite and ice industries took a fresh start.

3. The increase in farm products has been very large during the last thirty years; but in the leading articles there have been great fluctuations, owing to unfavorable seasons, pests, or a temporary falling off in the demand. In 1880, the wheat crop was 665,714 bushels,— more than double that of 1850. The oat crop, also, was considerably augmented, being 2,265,575 bushels, while Indian corn fell off more than one-third. Pease and beans show an increase of about fifteen per cent, and the potato crop has more than doubled — amounting, in 1880, to 7,999,625 bushels. The production of butter, also, nearly doubled, bringing it up to 14,103,026 pounds, while cheese has fallen off in equal proportion. The hay product was also one of those that almost doubled in quantity,— the figures, in 1880, showing 1,107,778 tons; while the yield of orchards has quadrupled in value, being set down at $1,112,026. The lesser crops show similar variations, but larger quantity and value in the aggregate.

The great enlargement in the wheat and potato crops is owing to the development of Aroostook county, comparatively few of whose farms were cultivated prior to 1850. The greater part of the latter crop in that county goes to supply its starch factories, which have all sprung up since 1875. There are now thirty-two in the county, with an annual product of 7,400 tons.

4. In close connection with the farms are the starch

factories, just mentioned, the cheese and butter factories, and the canning factories. These are new forms of old manufactures, from their enlargement becoming almost new industries. By adapting the articles to reach a larger market they have greatly increased their production without augmenting the labors of farmers' households.

In the thirty years we have chosen for examination, our live stock has nearly doubled in value, if not in numbers, and our annual wool clip has more than doubled in quantity,— being, in 1880, 2,776,407 pounds.

While, with the exception of wheat and potatoes, our crops in recent years have scarcely kept their proportion to our growing population, there are now other products of large value, which forty years ago were not reckoned as articles of profit at all. These are granite, slate and ice. The last may be called a crop, since it is gathered annually, being all the more profitable because its season is that in which farm labor is least in demand. There is scarcely another crop so secure to Maine as this, from the peculiar adaptation of her climate and the purity of her waters. For its market, she is almost equally sure of the patronage of most of the Atlantic cities south of New York, and of those on the Gulf of Mexico. The number of hands employed during the ice-harvest is about 6,500, and the annual storage rarely falls short of 1,000,000 tons.

5. The supply of granite in our State is practically unlimited, but those quarries only which are near railroads or navigable waters have yet been operated to much extent. The granite islands of Penobscot Bay have unusually easy opportunities for shipping their product, and the industry has been carried on to a much greater extent than elsewhere. Gray is the principal color of our stone, but black granite is found at Addison and St. George, red and

variegated at Jonesport and Calais; and the noted white granite of Hallowell has long been used for monumental work. The number of men employed in this business is estimated at three thousand, to whom is paid, on an average, the sum of $1,500,000 annually. The product of our granite quarries has been used in the construction of public buildings, for monuments or for paving, as far west as the Mississippi, and as far south as New Orleans.

6. It was in 1828 that the first slate quarry was opened in Maine, and in 1884 there were eight companies operating quarries in Monson and Brownville alone, employing some four hundred men. The value of our annual product from these, and other quarries operated irregularly, is about $200,000. At the national centennial at Philadelphia in 1876, Maine roofing slate won the first prize for "strength, durability and permanence of color."

Though lime rock of various qualities exists in several parts of the State, it has not been found convenient and suitable for quarrying and burning, except in Knox county, on the west side of Penobscot Bay. The amount annually produced here, in the three towns of Rockland, Thomaston and Camden, is about 1,500,000 barrels.

While there is no sufficient cause for such expectations of wealth from deposits in Maine of valuable metals as were entertained a few years ago, the State really furnishes a large number of ores, of which several are found in such quantities as might yield a good profit for mining. Graphite, lead, iron, copper, silver and gold were mined in the State, in 1880, to the value of about $40,000; and there are deposits of other valuable metals still unworked.

7. According to the most reliable surveys, Maine contains 19,132,800 acres, — an area almost equal to all the rest of New England In 1880, 6,552,578 acres were embraced in farms, leaving upwards of

12,000,000 in water surface and wild land. A large portion of the last is in forest, from which were cut the six or seven million feet of logs reported in the census of 1880. This product, when sawed into lumber in its various forms, sold at the usual rate to the amount of $7,923,868. This amount probably required something more than the annual growth of our forests; and, fortunately for them, our lumber product is less on the average by fifteen to twenty per cent. The amount of lumber sawed in 1860 was about sixteen per cent less; yet we had then nine hundred and twenty-six saw-mills, against eight hundred and forty-eight, in 1880,—showing a reduction in number compensated by an increase in capacity. Observation shows, also, that the producing mills were those nearest railroads or navigable waters.

There are certain of our woods, which, within a few years, have acquired a new value by reason of their beauty as material for furniture and for the interior finish of buildings, a value which is certain to increase largely in the future. The value of our softer woods has also been increased by their use in the manufacture of pulp, for paper stock and other articles. There are five mills in various parts of the State which are devoted exclusively to the manufacture of wood pulp, while some of the paper mills also produce it in limited quantity. The total capacity of our pulp and paper board mills is given, in the annual directory of the paper mills of the country for 1887–88, as forty tons of pulp daily. Four mills manufacture leather board, reporting a capacity of ten tons every twenty-four hours. The possible paper product is given as 101 tons daily, employing eleven mills,—of which two are devoted to manilla paper, the others to book and newspaper. The actual production is probably twenty-five per cent less than these figures indicate. The paper factory at Mechanic Falls (the largest but one in the

State) includes six mills, each devoted to its own special process in the manufacture. The Cumberland Mills, at Westbrook, are said to form the largest paper factory in the world.

8. From the forest proceeds directly one of the earliest industries of enterprising races. This is ship-building, and it is the earliest recorded manufacture of Maine. If the readers of this statement will turn to the third chapter of this history, they will find that Captain John Smith, afterward of Virginia, while exploring our coast, in 1614, built here "seven boats." But Popham's colony had been before him in a larger undertaking, having, in 1607, built a vessel. Theirs was the first ship-yard on the Kennebec, which, in the modern period, has been a greater producer of wooden vessels than any other river in the world.

Not this river alone, but almost all our numerous streams emptying into the ocean have been the scene of this industry. In the year 1884, the number of sailing vessels and steamers owned in Maine was 2,868, with a carrying capacity of 628,954 tons. The estimated value of these was $19,415,675. This was an increase over 1880 of two hundred vessels, a tonnage of 120,614, and a value of $5,995,275. Were it not for the extensive use of iron ships in recent years, the ship-yards of Maine would doubtless now be sending out shipping in largely increased quantities.

9. In the year 1880 there were engaged in the fisheries six hundred and six Maine vessels, having a tonnage of 17,632 tons; and above eleven thousand persons were engaged in catching, canning and shipping the fish. The value of the products of the fisheries in that year was estimated at $3,614,178. There is a large fluctuation in this industry, some years exceeding, others falling short of these figures. In this business Maine ranks fourth among the

States in the **number** of persons, and third **in capital** invested, value **of** products and tonnage of **vessels.**

A necessity of manufactories is **the iron** machinery **for the** various **processes in** forming **the** product, **whether this be stately** ships or cotton sheeting. **Though** producing **but** small quantities of iron, Maine sends out **from** her machine shops great numbers of implements, varying in size from a nail **to a** ton anchor, and machinery, from apple-parers to cloth-looms and steam engines. The **value of the** farming tools, made chiefly **in the** factories **of Oakland,** would reach **nearly a million dollars annually.**

10. **Workmen having been found in** America **who could construct the** machinery to manufacture **cloth by the** vast and untiring **power of** our waterfalls, **the hand-looms, which** had **so** long furnished **the clothes of** the **world,** rapidly went out of use **here.** Naturally, the first cloth mills in Maine were **woolen** factories; **though, in** the early days, farmers raised flax **rather than wool,** since wild animals were **too numerous for sheep-raising to be profitable.** At first, **the good housewife only carried her wool to** the factory **to be** carded **into** " rolls," **which she had** before done with her own hands; but she still, **for** a long time, wove the family flannels and full cloth, carrying the latter to the mills to be "dressed."

There was a census taken in 1810, by which **we learn** there were then in operation in Maine **seventy-five carding machines,** carding into rolls 450,255 **pounds of wool per annum, and** fifty-nine fulling **mills, dressing 357,386 yards of cloth annually,** while the household **looms turned out, in the same** period, 453,410 yards of woolen **cloth. This** census **also** gave Maine the credit of making 811,912 yards of cotton cloth annually. Compared with the total manufactures of the country, Maine exceeded its proportion in **the** quantity of cloth produced. In 1850 **the number** of woolen mills was only thirty-six, while in 1880 they numbered ninety-three, employing 3,095 persons; and **the value of their annual product at** wholesale prices was stated as $6,686,073. **They are** now very generally located in **small villages; while** cotton mills, **employing a larger number of** operatives, usually **cause a large municipal growth.**

11. Cotton factories, almost from the first had a capacity **for** producing **a much greater number of** yards of cloth than the **woolen factories, and soon** became the more numerous. **The** earliest **of the present** cotton manufacturers **of the State** appears to **be the** Cabot Company **of Brunswick,** which **was the** successor **of** the **" Maine Cotton and Woolen** Factory," which **was incorporated in 1812. In 1831** the York Manufac**turing Company, of Saco, and the** Portsmouth **Company, of South Berwick, were** started, **and in 1844 the Hallowell** Company **was** organized. **Biddeford followed in 1845;** and **in 1846** was built **the first cotton** mill **in** Lewiston, **which** has now become **the chief** cotton manufacturing city **in** Maine. In the **same** year cotton manufacturing was commenced in Augusta, and Saccarap**pa entered the list in** 1858. **Waterville** followed **in 1874, Lisbon in the next year, Sanford in 1877, and Richmond in 1881.**

By the census of 1880 it appears **that** the annual **production of cotton cloths in** Maine, at that period, **was 144,368,675** yards, weighing 44,352,698 pounds, **and having** a value of $13,319,363. The number of persons employed was **11,864**

12. No large industry, **in** recent **years,** has shown such a marked **change as** the manufacture of boots and shoes. **Still carried on to a** very limited extent as formerly, **when all the shoes** worn in a village were made in **the village, it has** also **passed** nearly **out of** the intermediate **stage, when a large** central **establishment sent out its leather and** linings to binders and bottomers, who, in many instances, lived in the midst of farming communities hundreds of miles away. By the invention of machinery for lasting, sewing, pegging and other operations, the work of making a shoe, which was formerly done by three persons (the cutter, the binder and the bottomer), is now divided among a large number. By this method there is a great reduction in the cost of making, so that the manufacture has been almost wholly brought into great factories, generally in cities or large villages. In accordance with this movement, we find that in 1870 there were in Maine eighty-five shoe-making establishments, while ten years later, there were but fifty-two. Yet, in the former year, the number of persons employed was but 2,105 against 3,919 in 1880. At the first date, the capital invested was $667,300, with a product valued at $3,155,221, which, at the last, had increased to a capital of $1,369,000, and a product of $5,823,541.

13. Several other industries have undergone similar changes, while the kinds have multiplied; the number mentioned as now established in the State being nearly one hundred and fifty. There is a difficulty in fixing the date of the beginning of nearly all the industries, from the lack of public record; but by going back to the year 1810, when some partial statistics were compiled, we may make a radical start; but in the census of 1850 we have a much nearer approach to completeness. From the report of the latter date it appears that our manufactories then numbered 3,974, employing 28,020 persons, and had a yearly production valued at $24,661,057. By the still more satisfactory statistical work of 1880 it is shown that our manufactories had increased to 4,481, employing 52,954 persons, and yielding an annual product of $79,829,793. The individual industries had, in the intervening years, suffered many

fluctuations, the leading industries being sometimes affected to an extent very perceptible in the general finances.

14. The total amount of power used by the manufactories of this State in 1880 was 100,476 horsepowers, of which 79,717 was from water, and 20,759 from steam. The latter is more costly than water power, and is used chiefly because economy of transportation of the material and the product, or the supply of labor, has induced location of the factory at a point where water power is insufficient.

An immense amount of power is running to waste in Maine, because it is not yet sufficiently accessible. Our solid land holds more than 1,600 lakes, at a mean elevation of 600 feet above the sea, kept full and flowing by rains and mists and winter snows. These lakes cover more than 2,300 square miles of surface; their streams, in their course toward the sea, supplying a power greater than that of 6,000,000 horses. Properly utilized, this is equivalent to great wealth. The chief means to make these powers practically useful to our citizens are our railroads. The opening of one at once gives an additional value to property along its line. Maine has now twenty-four railroads, varying in length from one mile up to 645 miles, — the last being the length of the Maine Central Railroad system.

15. The first railroad for steam cars operated in New England was the Boston and Lowell, in Massachusetts, completed in 1835; the second one was put in operation in Maine in 1836, and connected Bangor and Oldtown. It was equipped with cars brought from England, and these were drawn by locomotives made by the earliest engine builder, George Stephenson. The track was made of flat iron bars, three-fourths of an inch thick, laid on wooden stringers. Yet this was not the road from which our present railroad system grew, nor about which the new roads

clustered. In 1869 it was purchased by the European and North American Railway, to escape the competition of a line parallel to its own, and has finally been discontinued.

The Maine Central Railroad Company, whose roads constitute the great trunk line of the State, was organized in 1862, and commenced business by consolidating two railroads,— the Androscoggin and Kennebec and the Penobscot and Kennebec,— both chartered in 1845, but the first not completed until 1848, nor the last until 1855. In 1871 the consolidated line was extended from Danville Junction, its former southern terminus, to Cumberland, where it formed a junction with the Portland and Kennebec Railroad, which it had leased. The latter, having previously built a branch to Bath, completed its line to Augusta in 1852. With this road was also added, by virtue of its lease, the Somerset and Kennebec Railroad, extending from Augusta to Skowhegan. In 1871 the new trunk line leased the Androscoggin Railroad — extending from Brunswick to Leeds Junction and Lewiston,— also the section of road from Leeds to Farmington, since extended to Phillips.

16. All these roads in 1873 became consolidated into one piece of property bearing the name of the corporation which had united them. A further extension of the Maine Central system was made by the acquisition of the Belfast and Moosehead road, extending from Burnham Junction to Belfast; of that from Dexter to Newport; of the Eastern Maine Railroad, connecting Bangor and Bucksport; of the European and North American Railway, from Bangor to Vanceboro, on our eastern border; by the building of the Mount Desert branch from Bangor, through Ellsworth, to Mount Desert Ferry, completed in 1884; and by a perpetual lease of the Portland & Ogdensburg road, in the present year.

These form a powerful corporation; but so far from being oppressive or injurious to the people, the consolidation has been of general advantage; for it has placed the control of these several roads in the hands of a single company, with a harmony of management that has afforded greater convenience to patrons than formerly, has kept the roads in better condition, and by avoiding the expense of so many sets of officers, has been able to earn dividends for its stockholders without exorbitant transportation rates.

17. Connected with this road, by means of a ferry, is the Knox and Lincoln Railroad — opened in 1871,— extending to Rockland on Penobscot Bay. Another connection is the Somerset Railroad, opened in 1875, and extending from the junction at Oakland to Anson on the Kennebec. Another important road is the Boston and Maine Railroad, which connects with the Maine system at Portland, and by means of numerous lines between that city and Boston and in southern New Hampshire, affords easy communication in all those directions. This great road has grown from two and one-half miles of road, built from Salmon Falls in New Hampshire to South Berwick in Maine, under a charter granted in 1836. After two acts of legislature, each authorizing some change of location or of name, and a new charter in 1871, the line was completed to Portland in 1873. The Portland, Saco & Portsmouth Railroad (next to the oldest of our roads), was chartered in 1837, and on its completion in 1842, became part of a through line from Portland to Boston. In 1871 it was leased to the Eastern Railroad for nine hundred and ninety-nine years, but in 1884 came under the management of the Boston & Maine Railroad, by the consolidation of the two latter.

18. Another road of the Portland system is the Portland and Ogdensburg Railroad, which was

opened to Conway, N. H., in 1871, and to Lunenburg in 1875; when, by means of its connections, it became one of the trunk lines to the West. It was leased to the Maine Central Railroad in 1888. There is probably no railroad that excels it in the beauty and grandeur of the views afforded along its line.

The Portland and Rochester Railroad was opened to the Saco river in 1851, and then, by a perpetual lease, became a part of the Boston and Maine Railroad system.

A great event for Portland transpired in 1853, when that city was connected with Montreal by means of the completion of the Atlantic and St. Lawrence Railroad. This road purchased wharf property in Portland, upon which has been fitted up as good terminal facilities for a line of ocean steamers as can be found on the Atlantic coast. In the year of this road's completion it was leased to the Grand Trunk Railway of Canada for nine hundred and ninety-nine years. Connected with the Grand Trunk road is the Rumford Falls and Buckfield road, extending from its junction with the Grand Trunk at Mechanic Falls to Canton Point on the Androscoggin.

19. One of the most important roads of the Bangor system is the European and North American Railway, extending from that city to our eastern border, where it connects with the New Brunswick system of railroads. In aid of its construction through an unsettled region, the State gave the timber on ten of its townships, and claims on the national government from which were realized $824,956. The line was completed in 1871, and eleven years later became the property of the Maine Central Railroad by a perpetual lease.

The valuable slate quarries and the noble lakes, no less than the lumber tracts and the rich farms of Piscataquis county, demanded communication with more populous regions, and this was found in 1869, when the Bangor and Piscataquis Railroad was completed to Dover, extended to Blanchard in 1877, and to the foot of Moosehead Lake in 1884.

20. Eastern Maine also had a local road as early as 1856, now extended so as to connect the Schoodic River towns with Calais. In 1873 the nucleus of an Aroostook system of railroads was begun by a line connecting at the State boundary with the New Brunswick Railway, and extended to Caribou in 1875, and to Presque Isle in 1882.

The total number of miles of railroad for steam-cars in Maine in the year 1886 was 1,167, while the entire length of lines, a part or all of which are within the State, is 6,316.

In Portland, Auburn, and Lewiston, street railroads have for some years been in operation; the cars being drawn by horses.

With these conveniences of transportation, the telegraph and telephone seem more than ever a necessity. Many short lines of the latter are in use in the State; while no less than seven telegraph companies operate lines in Maine. At every station along our numerous railroads, and at half a hundred villages beside, the potent little instruments are heard ticking out their messages from all parts of the world.

CHAPTER XXXVIII.

1. **Following** the War of the Rebellion, the spirit of enterprise, with sanguine expectation, **and a** certain recklessness attending **the** prevalence **of the** "greenback" fallacy, **led** to pledges of town **and city** credit in aid of railroads and other public **improvements.** Most **towns were already burdened by soldiers'** bounties **and other indebtedness, and the further** straining **of their credit was in many instances damaging to their prosperity. Therefore, to restrain their action in some degree and thus to prevent the ruin of municipal credit, an amendment to the Constitution of the State was adopted in 1877, prohibiting cities and towns from creating any debt or liability which, in the aggregate with any** preceding **debt, should exceed five per cent of** the **last** regular valuation. **The good effects of this amendment** have been increasingly manifest.

With the building of the first railroads in Maine began the influx of laborers; and the peasant from Erin wielded the pick and shovel, and built his **cabin of slabs and turf along the line of the growing roadbeds,— so** that the elderly Irishmen of to-day are warranted **in the boast** that **they were the** builders of **our railroads. Later they might well** assert that **their children ran our factories and our kitchens. There has also been a considerable influx of English and Scotch, confined chiefly to our cloth factory towns; while in our slate regions, and among our iron workers, the Welsh people are found in fair proportion.**

2. In the later years of the **civil war, there came a** change in the immigration. **The French Canadians from** the Madawaska region **and from Lower Canada**

began quietly, one by one, to come in — to till our farms and run our mills; and they now form a numerous portion of the inhabitants of our manufacturing towns, and are rapidly becoming good citizens.

Widely different was the coming of our latest immigrants, the Swedes. The first of these came as a colony, and their arrival was an interesting event to the whole State. In 1869 a commission was appointed by the State to promote the settlement of the public lands, of which those remaining were in Aroostook county. From various sources several of our public men had received favorable impressions of the qualities of the Swedish peasantry; therefore, early in 1870, Hon. William W. Thomas, jr., of Portland, was sent to Sweden to recruit a colony. He was successful; and they sailed from Sweden in June, 1870, reaching Halifax on the 13th of July. On Friday, the 22d, they drove across the border into Maine.

3. The colony numbered twenty-two men, eleven women and eighteen children,—in all, fifty-one persons. They presented an excellent appearance; and among them, after paying the expenses of their passage, they brought into the State $3,000. On Saturday, July 23d, they reached their new home, to which they promptly gave the name of New Sweden. The colony was well pleased with the country, and their messages to friends were so favorable that large numbers of their countrymen have followed them, and have also prospered; so that now no less than three towns are chiefly populated by Swedes. They have brought into Maine more than one hundred thousand dollars in coin, beside the vastly greater value of their character, skill and strength.

In 1880 we had, out of a total population of 648,936, a foreign element numbering 58,883, while there were in other States of the Union 182,257 natives of Maine.

In the first period the inhabitants of Maine were almost wholly Protestant, and in general there was unanimity in matters of religion so far as concerned the public schools. With the present conditions, the educational question has become more difficult, not only on account of religious differences, but from the ignorance of the new element, and the difficulties caused by our large factories, which too readily receive children as operatives when they should be in school.

4. Previous to 1846 no special means existed for obtaining information about our schools, nor for qualifying their instructors. Teachers were isolated from each other; schoolhouses were neglected and frequently unfit for their purpose, and furnished with seats that were utterly uncomfortable. Neither wall maps nor blackboards were found, and the discipline was generally defective, often brutal. In the year mentioned the Legislature established a State board of education and provided for holding a teachers' institute annually in every county. The effect of this was very great, and rapid improvement was made in our schools until 1852, when this whole valuable system was swept away by another legislature, and county school commissioners appointed by the Governor were substituted. This system proved a failure; and two years later it was followed by a State superintendency, formed by a single officer appointed by the Governor for a term of three years. Yet the retrogression in the schools still continued, until 1857, when the institutes were re-established. Not being properly sustained, these did not succeed as formerly; and in a few years they were discontinued. The only real progress was the introduction of graded schools, and the establishment of a normal school at Farmington for training teachers.

5. In 1869 Hon. Warren Johnson, then superintendent of schools, secured a law for the appoint-

ment of county supervisors, **who** also constituted a State Board of Education. Institutes were re-established, and again popular interest was awakened; and schools improved until 1873, when **the law** establishing co**unty** supervisors was repealed. How**ever, there** was a permanent gain **at** this time in the **establishment at** Castine of a second normal school, **which was** opened for pupils in **1873.**

The institutes were continued **by various means a few years** longer, and were **succeeded by** State and **county** educational associations, **and the** State Pedagogical Society. These unofficial organizations, formed by the more public-spirited of **our educators,** have done **what they** could, and **have succeeded with** the aid of the normal schools in **keeping our public** schools from retrogression.

6. **In 1878 Gorham** Academy, **established in** 1803, **was changed to a normal school; and in the** same year a training school for teachers was established in the Madawaska region at the northeast extremity of the State, for the benefit, chiefly, of our youth of French parentage in that region. Provision had also been made by the **State** for **normal classes in the** Maine Central **Institute at Pittsfield, and at the** O**ak Grove Seminary at** Vassalboro, **the** latter **under the direction of the Society of Friends.** Many, **also, of our private schools of higher** grade give **special attention to** pedagogical **training.**

To our collegiate institutions there **have** been added **W**estbrook Seminary, incorporated in 1831, —being the first school of this kind in New England under the patronage of the Universalists; **the** State College of Agriculture and Mechanic Arts, at Orono, established in 1868; **and** Maine **State** Seminary at Lewiston, incorporated **and** endowed by the State in 1855, further endowed **by** its friends, **and changed into "Bates College"** in 1863; **to which a Free Baptist Theological** Seminary **was added in 1870.**

With these various means of improvement have come better city and town high schools, and incorporated schools with normal classes; and among all these there has been a friendly rivalry, with reciprocal influences, tending to sustain public interest, and to develop individual and local methods. The most marked feature in education in the recent period is the increased attention given to physics and the industrial arts. A further aid in the improvement of our rural schools has been found in the gradual substitution of the town for the district system of management, by which the length of the school terms is equalized and increased, and better qualified teachers are provided.

7. One of our most effective educational forces for youth as well as for mature persons, is the newspaper press, whose influence is direct and universal. On the 31st day of December, 1784, no newspaper had ever been issued in Maine; from the first day of 1785 we have never been without one. From the *Falmouth Gazette* and *Weekly Advertiser*, of Portland, which had its birth on that date, have sprung others, and from its office have come several persons of eminence in this and other callings. The *Portland Transcript*, our first and still our chief literary paper, was founded in 1837. The *Christian Mirror* and *Zion's Advocate*, our two leading religious papers have both been published for more than half a century, while the *Eastern Argus* follows close after them. The *Kennebec Journal* was first published in the autumn of 1823, and the *Whig and Courier*, of Bangor, was formed from papers etablished in 1833 and 1834 respectively. A newspaper now for many years of large influence is the *Lewiston Journal*, founded in 1847. Our newspapers, since Maine became a State, have increased faster in proportion than the population, in circulation, if not in numbers. From inquiry made in

1886, it is learned that the number of weekly papers published in that year was one hundred and eight, with eleven dailies; and there were semi-monthlies, monthlies and quarterlies to the number of twenty-six.

8. It was, no doubt, the influence of the higher education, as well as of his noble war record, that in 1866 induced the election of General Joshua L. Chamberlain as governor of the State; and both the schools and the military organizations received a beneficial impulse from his official action. He was succeeded in 1871 by Hon Sidney Perham, a worthy citizen of Oxford County, an earnest advocate of the temperance cause, and an active public man. His successor in 1874 was Hon. Nelson Dingley, jr., of Lewiston, a wise economist and an effective forwarder of the interests of Maine. The next chief magistrate was General Selden Connor, a valiant soldier and courtly gentleman, who served the State from 1876 to 1879, when Dr. Alonzo Garcelon, of Lewiston, was chosen to succeed him. The latter had done the country valuable service during the war as Surgeon-General of the State, but he was unfortunate in being associated as chief magistrate with the most disgraceful political year that Maine has known; and he served but a single term. His successor was Daniel F. Davis, of Corinth, a promising young lawyer, who had made a good record during the war without reaching a rank higher than corporal.

9. Colonel Harris M. Plaisted, another worthy soldier, succeeded Governor Davis in 1881. He was the first governor elected after the gubernatorial term had been made two years, and the only one of our governors who was a "greenbacker" in politics. His successor in 1883 was Colonel Frederick Robie, of Gorham, — worthy physician and farmer as well as soldier. Governor Robie was one of our most popular chief magistrates. He was re-elected in

1885, and in 1887 gave way to **Governor Bodwell. Mr. Bodwell** began life as a farmer's boy, **and became successively shoemaker,** a driver **of quarry** teams, **quarry owner and laborer,** and finally one of the **chief** developers **of the** large granite interests **of Maine.** He died much lamented, before the expiration of his first term, **being the** second of our governors to die in office.

In the years following the **war,** when the attention of our people turned more entirely to industrial affairs, there **sprang up a** great interest **in agricultural and manufacturing exhibits, and the State, county and town fairs increased in number and magnitude, much to** the advantage of **most of the interests represented.** Among those who contributed **largely to the** stock entries of the fairs was the **family of** which Edwin **C.** Burleigh, of Bangor, **is a** member. Mr. Burleigh served several years as **land agent,** and later, as State treasurer,—and has become well acquainted **with the** interests of **the** northern part of the State. **In the present year he** received **the Republican nomination for governor,** and on September **10th** was **elected by a handsome majority over** all competitors.

10. Maine has now reached an age when many of **her** towns can celebrate their centennials; and with **the** events of three generations of men, many of **which are now** perceived **to have** had a far-reaching **influence, the rehearsal of their** history possesses a **growing interest. As one of our** chief **towns, Portland has in its annals** many **incidents of importance to the State as a whole.** In common **with most of** our larger villages, she has known large fires **in both** her earlier and later periods, but none in the State has ever reached the magnitude of the conflagration which swept through this city in 1866, starting on the 4th of July, from a carelessly thrown fire-cracker. After raging above fifteen hours, a change of wind

enabled the numerous firemen and engines of its own and other cities, to overcome the insatiate enemy. In those hours it had destroyed fifteen hundred buildings, laid in ashes fifty-eight streets and courts—eight miles of closely-built thoroughfares—thrown ten thousand of its thirty thousand inhabitants, houseless and penniless, upon the charity of others, and destroyed, it is believed, upward of ten millions of dollars worth of property.

11. After this calamity there was much improvement in the fire departments of most of the cities and larger villages in the State, and steam fire-engines began to take the places of those operated by hand, so that now the use of one of the latter is a rarity. The steam fire-engine being much more effective, and greater care being taken with respect to fires, no disaster of proportional magnitude from this cause again occurred in Maine for twenty years. Portland had been rebuilt with nobler edifices, better streets, and had "beauty for ashes," enlarged railroad accommodations, larger commerce and augmented wealth. In 1886 she celebrated her centennial as a town in a manner worthy of her history and her prosperity.

In the autumn of this very year the fire-demon again fell upon the State, and, first, the village of Farmington, early in October, suffered the destruction of nearly one half of its principal business street. The ashes of Farmington were scarcely cold when the flames enwrapped the greater portion of the village of Eastport, consuming nearly all its numerous fish establishments, stores, and many dwellings. Generously aided, however, its hardy and enterprising citizens soon rebuilt their houses and regained their business, and traces of the great fire are being rapidly hidden away.

12. The last fifty years have been marked by social as well as industrial and commercial changes.

Formerly, no Maine community, as a whole, observed more than the two religious days, appointed for fasting and for thanksgiving, and the civic festival of Independence Day. With larger intelligence and better acquaintance of the religious sects with each other, there has come a larger tolerance of differing forms of belief and worship, a dismissal of prejudices, and an observance by the Protestant sects generally, of Christmas, while many congregations beside those of the Episcopalians, observe Easter Sunday, and do not wholly disregard Good Friday and Ascension Day. Of secular holidays we have gained Washington's Birthday; the civil war gave us Memorial Day; the village improvement societies, perhaps, as much as any influence, have given us Arbor Day; while the physical toilers, claiming a date for themselves, have given us Labor Day.

13. Camp-meetings have become a uniform feature of our summer life, and camp-grounds have been established at many points in the State. Livermore, Fryeburg, Northport, Old Orchard Beach, and Maranocook have come to be familiar names to the ears of many people beyond the limits of the State. The last two places have a wider use than that of religious meetings only. While the Old Orchard grounds are opened for temperance associations, Maranocook, on the shores of a lovely lake, is annually the scene also of musical festivals and aquatic sports.

All these things are indicative of more courteous relations and of general economic ease. An observer among the people would find that the wage-workers dwell in better houses, and have more of the comforts, and even of the luxuries of life, than did many of the princes of Europe when this country was first discovered by their rude mariners. The increase of individual wealth is not without its benefits to others than its possessors. A wealthy class creates **a demand for articles of personal apparel, furniture, and ornament of** more elaborate **workmanship than would exist without them, and which require large** numbers of extra workmen. Thus **the money** of the rich flows out to the skilful **artisan and** needlewoman, providing multitudes with **an abundant support, who,** without this employment, **would of necessity overcrowd the ranks in less skilful** occupations.

That those whose **hands must earn** their daily **bread** are sharing the general prosperity of the period **is** shown by the large deposits in our savings banks, **made** chiefly by farmers **and the** industrious and prudent wage-workers. **The official report for** 1887 **showed there** were then fifty-six **of these institutions in Maine, with** 119,229 depositors, which **during the year had increased by** 4,538. The deposits **at the close of year were $38,**819,643; having **increased during the year to the extent** of $1,604,571.

14. In **the** period since the civil war Maine has been discovered anew. People of wealth, who could spend at least a large portion of each year in any part of the world which might **prove most pleasant to them,** have found **in our good State a summer climate tempered** to their liking. **The purity of** its **air, the degree and uniformity of** its temperature, **and the mildness of its breezes, whether** coming **from the mountains or the ocean,** impregnated with salty **vapors, or** bearing the **balsam of** piny forests, —form a combination uncommonly fitted to personal comfort, and the restoration of diminished energies.

The scenery is not **less** satisfactory. The sea-line of the State **is about two hundred** miles direct; but following **the sinuosities of the shore it** is nearly twenty-five hundred. **All this** space is interspersed with beaches of pebbles **or** sand, frequently **firm** enough for carriages. **Between these project** picturesque ledges, often **precipitous, sometimes** rising inland to mountains. Around them are woods, often of the unstunted growth of the interior uplands.

15. The extreme length of Maine, from northeast to southwest, is three hundred and three miles, and the greatest breadth is two hundred and eighty-eight miles. The settlements extend on an average only about eighty miles inland. North of this limit, rarely broken by a clearing, except on the east, is a vast forest, extending beyond the Canada line. This extensive tract affords a noble hunting ground, stocked with deer, caribou, moose, and bear.

A ride after horses through the older parts of Maine brings before the eyes of the traveler wider vistas and more charming views than are afforded by the railroads, for he descends lower into the valleys and rises higher upon the hills. The roads are uniformly good, without interruption by turnpike gate, or toll, even at the longest and finest bridges. The houses are generally neat and commodious, and the people orderly and courteous.

16. These features in our State are not to be despised, even by the most sordid; for owing to their attraction, millions of dollars are annually expended within our borders by tourists and summer residents. It thus becomes a matter of pecuniary interest, as well as of local and State pride, that we continue to improve all those features that make Maine desirable. As our State becomes known to the wealthy and enterprising, their capital will be increasingly invested here, to develop her abundant resources, and thus further enhance her prosperity.

SUPPLEMENTARY NOTES.

ACTING GOVERNORS.— In order not to interrupt the movement of the narrative, and the connection of events in the body of this history, mention was omitted of two of our acting governors.

The gubernatorial office being vacated by the death of Governor Lincoln, in 1829, the President of the Senate, Nathan Cutler of Farmington, by provision of the Constitution for such an emergency, acted as governor during the remainder of the term.

In like manner, Edward Kavanagh, of Newcastle, took the seat of Governor Fairfield, when the latter was, in March, 1843, elected United States Senator.

CLIMATE.— In comparing Maine with the interior districts of the continent in substantially the same latitude, it appears that its summer temperature is lower by over twenty per cent of their temperature, reckoning from the freezing point of water. The mean winter temperature of the northern third of Maine is 14°.01; of the southern two-thirds, 22°.90; the annual mean for the State, 40°.88. The mean winter temperature of districts west of Maine in the same latitude of observation, at many points ranging from Burlington, Vt., to Fort Ripley, Minn., is 18°.53. The winter in Maine, therefore, is not so severe as in the corresponding latitudes in the interior. [*Varney's Gazeteer of Maine.*]

MOUNT DESERT (page 27).— There is a diversity of pronunciation of this name, some placing the accent on the last syllable, as though it were a French word. In the year 1604, the voyager Champlain named this island "Mons Deserts." Some English narratives of voyages in years following, speak of the island as Mount Desert, though others called

it Mount Mansel. Whichever language has the
priority of the application, it is only those who use
the English pronunciation of the name as now spelled
who are consistent philologists; for those who affect
the French speak half the name in English. It is
not the last, but both words, which constitute the
name of the island in either language.

RAILROADS (pages 257, 308).— In the statement
that our "first railroad charter" was granted in
1836, *steam* railroad was meant,— that being the new
power for locomotion. Our first *rail* road charters,
however, were granted in 1832, — both being for
horse-railroads for the conveyance of freight. These
were only tramways, a sort of modification of the
ancient turnpike, of which the plank road was
another form.

The first railroad in America was built in Quincy,
Mass., in 1825–26, to connect the noted granite quarries in that town with tide-water, which was found on
the Neponset River. Its main line was about three
miles in length, and it was operated only by horse-power. Its first use was to convey the stone for
Bunker Hill monument.

One of the roads chartered in Maine in 1832 connected Calais and Milltown, and was two miles long;
the other road was to connect Bangor and Oldtown,
but was not built the whole distance for several
years. In the meantime it passed to another ownership, with a later charter. When completed in 1836,
as has been stated, it was operated by steam power.

PIGWACKET.— In the early accounts of the Indian
wars, this was the name applied to the chief village
or group of villages of Indians on the head-waters
of the Saco River, while the aborigines themselves
were called Pigwackets. Later, the name came to
be spelled *Pequaket*, which is more euphonious, if not
more correct. The general name for the Indians
who inhabited the region about this river is *Sokokis*,

and from this term, it is believed, the designation of the river Saco, has come.

RALLE (page 126).— The proper orthography of the name of the noted priest of the Norridgewocks, is, no doubt, *Rasle*. The spelling "Ralle" is found in some of the earlier accounts of him, and is used in this book because it gives to English readers the true pronunciation of his name.

ROYAL "R" (page 146).— This is the term used by Williamson (in his annals of the period between the close of the Indian wars and the opening of the Revolution) in describing the mark placed upon the choice pine-trees in the accessible forests of Maine, by the King's surveyor. The token long in use by the British admiralty is in the form of an arrow, (the "broad arrow" is the usual term), and it seems that should have been the mark cut upon the pines, had the claim been national rather than personal. Mr. Williamson was born at a date early enough to have known lumbermen to whom these marks were familiar, and we must believe him to be correct in stating that the token of the King's ownership affixed to the trees was the capital R, this being the initial letter of the word *Rex*, king.

SENATORS AND REPRESENTATIVES OF THE U. S. — Owing to the plan of this work, it was not practicable to mention even the most eminent of our national representatives, except where their election affected the incumbency of the State offices. The following is a complete list of senators from the formation of the State to the present time: —

*(Abbreviations — rs., resigned; f. v., filled vacancy; **d., died.**)

Choice.	Name.	Politics.	Residence.	Term of Office.
1st	John Holmes,	Rep.	Alfred,	1820-1827
	John Chandler,	Rep.	Monmouth,	1820-1823
2d	Albion K. Parris,	Rep.	Portland (rs.),	1827-1828
	Appointed Judge of S. J. Court.			
	John Holmes,	N. Rep.	Alfred (f. v.),	1829-1833
	John Chandler,	D. Rep.	Monmouth,	1823-1829

SUPPLEMENTARY NOTES. 327

3d.	Ether Shepley,	D. Rep.	Saco (rs.),	1833-1836
	Appointed Judge of S. J. Court.			
	Judah Dana,	Dem.	Fryeburg (f. v.),	1836-1837
	Ruel Williams,	Dem.	Augusta (f. v.),	1837-1839
	Peleg Sprague,	N. Rep.	Hallowell,	1829-1835
4th.	Ruel Williams,	Dem.	Augusta,	1839-1843
	Resigned Feb., 1843.			
	John Fairfield,	Dem.	**Saco (f. v.),**	1843-1845
	John Ruggles,	Dem.	**Thomaston,**	1835-1841
5th.	John Fairfield,	**Dem.**	Saco (d.),	1845-1847
	Wyman B. S. Moor,	**Dem.**	**Waterville (f. v.),**	1848-1849
	Appointed by Governor.			
	Hannibal Hamlin,	Dem.	**Hampden (f. v.),**	1848-1851
	George Evans,	Whig,	**Gardiner,**	1841-1847
6th.	Hannibal Hamlin,	Dem.	Hampden (rs.),	1851-1857
	Elected Governor of State.			
	Amos Nourse,	Rep.	Bath (f. v.),	1857
	Appointed by Governor.			
	James W. Bradbury,	Dem.	Augusta,	1847-1853
7th.	Hannibal Hamlin,	Rep.	Hampden,	1857-1861
	Elected Vice-president of United States.			
	Lot M. Morrill,	Rep.	Augusta (f. v.),	1861-1863
	Wm. Pitt Fessenden,	Rep.	Portland,	1854-1859
	*Elected, 1854, for term commencing 1855, on **account** of failure of Legislature to elect.*			
8th.	Lot M. Morrill,	Rep.	Augusta,	1863-1869
	Wm. Pitt Fessenden,	Rep.	Portland (rs.),	1859-1864
	Appointed Secretary of Treasury.			
	Nathan A. Farwell,	Rep.	Rockland (f. v.),	1864-1865
	*Appointed **by** Governor.*			
9th.	Hannibal Hamlin,	Rep.	Bangor,	1869-1875
	Wm. Pitt Fessenden,	Rep.	P'ortland,	1865-1869
	*Died Sept. **8**, 1869.*			
	Lot M. Morrill,	Rep.	Augusta (f. v.),	1869-1871
10th.	Lot M. Morrill,	**Rep.**	Augusta,	1871-1876
	*Appointed **Secretary of** the Treasury.*			
	James G. Blaine,	**Rep.**	Augusta (f. v.),	1876-1877
	Hannibal Hamlin,	**Rep.**	Bangor,	1875-1881
11th.	James G. Blaine,	Rep.	Augusta (rs.),	1877-1881
	Appointed Secretary of State (U. S.).			
	William P. Frye,	Rep.	Lewiston (f. v.),	1881-1883
	Eugene Hale,	Rep.	Ellsworth,	1881-1887
12th.	William P. Frye,	**Rep.**	Lewiston,	1883-1889
	Eugene Hale,	**Rep.**	Ellsworth,	1887-1893

SUPREME JUDICIAL COURT OF MAINE: CHIEF JUSTICES.

Prentiss Mellen, Portland, July 1, 1820, to Oct. **22**, 1834.
Nathan Weston, Augusta, Oct. 22, 1834, to Oct. 21, 1841.
Ezekiel Whitman, Portland, Dec. 10, 1841. Resigned Oct. **23, 1848.**
Ether Shepley, Portland, Oct. 23, 1848, **to** Oct. 22, 1855.
John Searle Tenney, Norridgewock, Oct. 23, 1855, to Oct. 23, 1862.
John Appleton, Bangor, Oct. 24, 1862, to Sept. 19, 1876.
John A. Peters, Bangor, Sept. 20, 1883.

* From **the Maine Register.**

SCHOOL FLAGS. — In the year 1889, a movement towards purchasing "A Flag for Every School-house," was originated in Michigan by Mrs. E. S. Moffatt, Assistant Superintendent of the National Woman's Christian Temperance Union, Department of Soldiers and Sailors. This movement spread rapidly, and soon penetrated the towns and cities of our own state, Maine. The idea was received with the eagerness that every new idea receives, and before many months, flags were floating over a number of school-houses in Portland, Bangor, Biddeford, Lewiston, Cape Elizabeth, and other places. At the present time, January, 1890, Portland has a flag for every public school-house within its limits.

INDEX.

	PAGE
Abandoned, Maine, east of Wells,	97
Abnaki language,	126
Abolition Party, The	267
Aborigines of Maine (see Indians),	
Acadia,	52, 120
Acadians, French, transported,	171
Acadie,	37
Acts of Trade,	179
Adams, John	199, 260
Alden, John	46
Alexander, Sir William	
proprietor of New Scotland,	33
sells New Scotland,	37
Allan Col. John	
a refugee from N. S.,	196
controls the east'n Indians,	196,197
Amendment to the Constitution,	269
Anasagunticooks, (Androscoggins),	
	57, 71, 72, 112
Andros, Sir Edmund	
Governor of New England,	88
sent a prisoner to England,	93
Annapolis founded,	19
Antietam, Battle of	284
Area of Maine,	302
Argal, Capt. Samuel, at Mt. Desert,	27
Arnold, Benedict, expedition of,	
through Maine,	191-194
Aroostook, conflict in	252
Aroostook county formed,	255
Arrowsic Island,	79, 86, 127
Assacombuit,	115
Augusta (formerly Cushnoc),	
	35, 169, 191, 219, 248, 253
Bangor,	234, 254, 270, 283, 308, 309
Bang's Island,	79
Baptists find refuge in Maine,	44
Baron Castine's war,	110
Barrie, Capt. Robert	232
Bashaba, The	23, 29, 57
Bath,	185, 309
Belcher, Gov. of Massachusetts,	147
Belfast taken by the British,	232
Bellamont, Earl of, Gov. of Maine,	111
Bells tolled for oppressed Boston,	183
Bernard, Governor	181
Berry, General, killed,	286
Bethel, raided by Canada Indians,	205
Berwick,	74, 75, 76, 96, 117, 118, 310
Betterment Act,	218
Biard, French priest, at Mt. Desert,	27
Biddeford (see Saco),	306
Biennial sessions of Legislature,	269
Bigelow, Mt., Arnold's camp near	192

	PAGE
Bills of credit,	100
Bingham, Bingham's land,	214, 215
Black Point attacked,	82, 86, 87
Blake, General, at Hampden,	232
Boats built at Monhegan,	27
Bomazeen on Jesuit teaching,	124
Bonython, John	48
Bonython, Richard	40
Border Ruffians,	272
Boston Massacre,	182
Boundaries,	35, 248, 255, 256, 257
Bounties, state and town	283
Bowdoin College founded,	216
Bowdoin, Gov. James	216
Brackett, Anthony	78
Braddock's defeat,	170
Bristol bought of Samoset,	32
British Proclamation to East'n Me.,	228
Brock, Rev. John	51
Brown, John, buys land of Samoset,	32
Brunswick (Pejepscot),	40, 47, 71, 72, 100, 102, 110, 123, 127
Bull Run, Battle of	275, 276
Bunker Hill, Battle of	186
Buonaparte, Napoleon	223
Burnside in command,	284
superseded by Hooker,	286
Burton, Major	
captured by the British,	204
escapes from captivity	207
Cabot, John and Sebastian	13
Calais,	312
Caleb Cushing, The, destroyed	287
Call of Pres. Lincoln for men,	273
for volunteers,	291
for men by draft,	291
for 500,000 men,	295
for 300,000 men,	295
Canmock, Thomas	40
Camp-meetings,	321
Canada, fall of French power in	176
union with, incited	291
Canal, Sebago, opened,	247
Canibas or Kennebeeks,	57, 112
Cannibals in the northeast,	58
Cargill, kills friendly Indians,	171
Carriages,	244
Casco Bay,	18, 23, 36, 96
Casco Neck (see Portland),	
Casey, General	279
Castine, Baron	90
driven away by the Dutch,	90
attacked by Andros,	90
peaceful messages to	93

HISTORY OF MAINE.

	PAGE
Castine, the younger, outrage on	113
wife of, captured,	118
guides Livingston to Quebec,	120
carried prisoner to Boston,	126
Castine captured by the British,	201, 202
brilliant military action at	202
British garrison re-inforced,	204
escape of Wadsworth and Burton from	206
again captured by the British,	231
the importance of	237
Centennials,	319
Census of Maine,	215, 314
Chadwick, Paul, shot by Malta "Indians,"	219
Chadwick's murderers tried,	221
Chamberlain, General	269
Chancellorsville, Battle of	286
Charleston retaken for the Union,	295
Chattanooga, Battle of	292
Chaudiere, The march to, in 1775,	192
Cherryfield Volunteers,	273
Chickamauga, Battle of	292
Chignecto, Col. Eddy at	196
Chubb, Capt.	108
Church, Benjamin, Major, in command in Maine,	95
Church, Major, 2d exp. to Maine,	100
goes up the Penobscot,	100
ascends the river to Oldtown,	109
takes spoil in Bay of Fundy,	109
again goes East,	118
Church, customs of	149, 150
Cilley, Jona., killed in a duel,	250, 251
Civil outbreaks in Lower Canada,	250
Clark and Lake, fort of, attacked,	79
Climate,	325
Cocheco (Dover) a second time destroyed,	108
Cold winter, A, and late spring,	239
Colnmbus, Christopher, voyages	13
Collier, Sir George, defeats Saltonstall,	203
Colonization, Father of American	45
Conquest of Maine,	54
Congress, Maine represented in Provincial	215
Provincial	183
Continental	194
Constitution, State, adopted,	241
amended,	269
Continental Congress,	194
Converse, Capt, at Wells,	104
put in command in Maine,	107
Cony, Gov., calls for volunteers,	294
Cornwall, county of	53
made a part of Massachusetts,	55
Cornwallis surrenders at Yorktown,	207
County of Canada,	40
Court in Maine,	42
Courts in Maine,	53
in Yorkshire,	48
Cromwell prevails in England,	44, 50
Cruelty to family of Squando,	70
Cumberland County formed,	178
Currency, Continental	190

	PAGE
Cushnoc, Pilgrim trading-house there,	35
fort at	169
Customs of the people in 1820,	244, 245
Damariscotta,	82, 100
Danforth, President, at Wells,	102
D'Aulney, dep.-gov. of Penobscot,	39
Davis, Captain	79, 86
Dead River, Arnold on	192
Dearborn, Henry	191
Am. commander-in-chief,	224
Deerfield attacked by Indians,	117
Democrats,	265, 266
Democratic Republicans.	266
DeMonts explores the Maine coast,	18
Dermer, Capt. Thomas	30
D'Estaing, Count, in America,	201
Devonshire, first Cornwall,	55
Disasters in Maine.	179, 239, 319, 320
Discoverers of America,	13
Districts, Commercial, of Maine,	215
Dixy Bull, piracies on Me. coast,	38
captured and hung,	39
Dogs,	25, 31, 163
Dover, N. H., burned by Indians,	94
Dow, Neal, author of "Maine Law,"	261
Draft, call for troops by commissioners appointed,	282
commissioners appointed,	283
Dresden, a fort built in	169
Dress of Puritan ministers,	149
of the people,	153
after the Revolution,	210
of Indians after Revolution,	212
Duchambon, Gov. of Louisburg,	156
Dudley, Joseph, Gov. of Maine,	112
Dummer, Gov., and the Indians,	143
Du Quesne, Fort, captured,	174
Dunbar, Col. David surveyor of the royal woods,	146
settles towns with Protestants,	147
conflict with squatters,	147
Dutch, The, in N. Y.,	19, 52
in New York subdued,	55
regain New York,	55
at Castine,	90
Eastport taken by the British,	227
burned,	312
Eddy, Col Jonathan, raid of, on Nova Scotia,	195
Education,	123, 150, 151, 216, 243, 313, 314, 315
Elizabeth, captivity of	72
Elizabeth, Cape, Church skirmishes with Indians at	101
Emancipation proclaimed,	285
Embargo, The	204
Embargo of 1812,	224
Emigrants from Maine,	239
Enlistments, term of,	274, 275
Enterprise and Boxer, Battle of	225
Etechemins,	57
Exportation of goods prohibited,	204
Ewell's raid north of Washington,	294

INDEX. 331

	PAGE
Falmouth (Portland), treaty at	88
battle of Maj. Church with the Indians at	95
treacherously assailed,	116
Indian depredations in	166
bombarded,	181
Gazette,	214
Farmington,	320
Farm produce 1850 to 1880,	299, 300
Federalists and Anti-Federalists,	265
Fire in Portland,	319
First English colony for Maine,	20
First fruits of culture in Maine,	15
Fisheries,	304
Flag, American	214
defence of our	275
Forest area of Maine,	303
Fort Frederick assailed,	159
Fortifications in Maine,	288
Forts of Maine garrisoned,	274
Fox Islands discovered,	14
France takes New Scotland,	37
resumes control of East'n Me.,	55
and Spain at war with Eng.,	155
Frankfort taken by the British,	232
a party of British captured at	236
Franklin county formed,	251
Fredericksburg, Battle of	285
Freedmen in Union army,	285, 286
Free Soil Party, The	267
French, The, on the Maine coast,	18
withdraw from Maine,	98
at Wells,	104
and Indian war, Old	110
fail to retake Louisburg,	164, 165
Neutrals removed from Acadia,	171
power in the North broken,	176
Friendship (Meduncook),	174
Frost, Maj., sent against Indians,	81
Frye, Chaplain, killed in Lovewell's fight.	139
Fryeburg, scene of Lovewell's fight,	137
Fryer's, Capt., mishap,	83
Fundy, Bay of, Col. Church in	109, 118
Fusionists,	268, 269, 270
Gage, General, in Boston,	181
appointed governor,	182
Gardiner, Dr. Sylvester	218
Gendell, Captain Walter	91
George, Fort, attacked by Indians,	127
Georgia places restrictions on Maine vessels,	250
German colonists,	147, 215
Gettysburg, battle of	289
Gilbert, Capt. Raleigh, admiral of Popham's expedition,	23
Gilead raided by Canada Indians,	207
Godfrey, Edward	40, 47
Goods, British, oppress our manufacturers,	239
Gorgeana, city of	43
Gorges, Sir Ferdinando	29, 30, 33, 34, 35, 40, 41, 44, 55
Gorges, Robert	35

	PAGE
Gorges, William	40
Gorham suffers by Indians,	162, 168
Gosnold, Bartholomew	14
Gosselin, Gen. Gerard, takes possession of Belfast,	232, 236
Government of State removed,	248
Governments, Six, in Maine,	45
Governors of Maine,	
King,	241, 242
Williamson (acting),	242
Parris,	247
Lincoln,	247
Hunton,	247, 266
Smith,	247, 266
Dunlap,	249, 266
Kent,	250, 257, 266
Fairfield,	252, 257, 266
Anderson,	266
Dana,	266
Hubbard,	261, 266
Crosby,	262
Morrill, A. P.,	266, 267
Wells,	263, 267
Hamlin,	268
Williams (acting),	268
Morrill, Lot M.,	268
Washburn,	273, 274, 276
Coburn,	291
Cony,	294
Chamberlain,	318
Perham,	318
Dingley,	318
Connor,	318
Garcelon,	269, 318
Davis,	269, 318
Plaisted,	270, 318
Robie,	270, 318
Rodwell,	319
Burleigh,	319
Grandfathers and grandmothers,	299
Granite,	300, 301
Grant, General	292, 294
Greenback Party, The	268, 271
Gyles, Judge, and party, Indian victims,	91, 92
Halifax, Fort	123, 163, 169
Hammond, Richard, a settler at Woolwich,	79
Hampden, conflict at	232
pillaged,	235
Hancock, John	183, 218
General	279
Hard times in Maine,	239
Harmon, Captain	127, 131
Hardy, Sir Thomas	227
Harvard College,	150
Hawthorn, Capt.	81, 82
Holidays,	320, 321
Holmes, Dr. Ezekiel	251
Hopehood,	96
Horse, troop of, at Portsmouth and Wells,	116
Houses, construction of	152, 153
Howard, General	276, 289, 295

	PAGE		PAGE
Hubbard, Governor John	261	Kennebecks, or Canibas,	57
Hull, Gen., surrenders Detroit	224	Kidd, Captain, the pirate,	111
Hunniwell, bravado of	116, 117	Killed in first season of first Indian war,	76
Hunt, Thomas, kidnaps Indians,	28		
Hutchinson, Gov. Thomas	181, 182	King Charles, persecutes emigrants,	41
		overcome,	44
Iberville at **Pemaquid**,	107, 108	King, Major-General, orders out	
Ice,	301	the militia,	236
Immigration to Maine,	212, 313, 314	King Philip's war begins,	71
Impressment of Am. seamen,	223	Kingfield, opposition to draft in	290
Independence declared,	195	King's Dock in Bath, The	185
Independence of Am. conceded,	208	Know Nothing Party The	267
Independent Republicans,	268	Knox, Gen. Henry, early life of	216, 217
Indian Old Point, site of Ralle's		bravery at Bunker Hill,	217
village,	134	brigadier-general of artillery,	218
Indian wars in prospect,	56	Secretary of War,	218
Indian view of the white people,	69	removes to Thomaston,	218
Indians of Maine,			
appearance of	15, 17, 59	Laconia,	31, 36
tribes of	57	**Land and water** area of Maine,	
dress of	58		302, 303, 308
remains of	58, 59	Land grants,	213
domestic customs of	59	Lane's Island, savage carousal on	91
dwellings of	60	La Tour buys New Scotland,	37
hunting of	61	La Tour's contest with D'Aulney,	39
implements of	61	Legislature, patriotism of the Me.	273
social customs of	62	Legislatures, Two	269
sports of	63	Leverett, Captain John	53
hygiene and medicine of	64	Levett, Captain, meets Samoset,	31
religious system of	64	Lewiston,	100, 306, 309, 312
state-craft of	64, 65	Lewiston Light Infantry,	273
language of,	65	Lexington, Battle of	184
names of	65	Lightfoot, Captain, feat of	96
education of	65, 66, 123	Lincoln county formed,	178
inscriptions of, on rocks,	65, 66	Lincoln, Pres., election of	272
numbers of	69, 177	Liquor Law in Maine, first	41
Indians' wives and children restored to them,	101	Liquor Law of Maine,	259, 264
		Liquors, intoxicating, sent out of	
rights,	124	the State,	261
Indians cared for by Mass. gov't,	184	**Liquor riot in Portland**,	262
Indians, raid Androscoggin towns,	208	Liquors, **cost of**	264
Insane asylum established,	257	Little **Belt fires** on **the President**,	224
		Livingston, Major, bears a message to Canada,	120
Jameson, Charles D.	268, 275		
James II, abdicates,	93	London Company, The, **sends ships**	
Jackson, Dr. **Chas.** T , survey by	251	to Virginia,	20
Gen , victory over the British,	237	Lottery townships,	214
" Stonewall," mort'y wounded,	286	Louisburg, expedition against	155-158
Jamestown, destroyed,	91	captured a second time,	174
Jesuits, French, among the Indians,	68, 107	Lovelace succeeds Nichols,	54
		Lovell, Gen., expedition to Castine,	201
Jewell's Island,	80	Lovewell, Captain, excursions of,	
Jordan, Rev. Robert	50	north,	136
Josselyn, Henry	40, 82	Lovewell's Pond,	137
		Lovewell's fight,	137-142
Kancamagus, wives **and** children of, captured,	101	Lovewell's war ends,	113
		Loyal, Fort, Major Church at	95
Kansas,	272	garrisoned by Maj. Church,	96
Kenduskeag, Indian village at	142	garrisoned by militia,	96
Kennebec, British driven from	184, 204	capitulates to Indians,	97
Kennebec patent sold,	213	again attacked,	116
Kennebec, Popham's colony on	20	Lumber,	302, 303
Kennebec, shipbuilding on	23, 304	Lutherans in Maine,	147, 215
Kennebec steamer,	245	Lygonia, or Plough Patent,	36, 43

INDEX. 333

	PAGE
Machias, Pilgrim colony at	38
men capture British vessels,	186, 187
expedition from	195
fortified,	197
attacked by British,	197, 198
fort abandoned,	236
garrison capture British,	236, 237
Madawaska represented in the Legislature of Maine,	248
hostile act of the British in	249
Madockawando,	83, 85, 104
Mails in 1820,	245
Maine, province of	42
district of	201
admitted to the Union,	240, 241
contribution of, to the war for the Union,	297
men, tribute to	278, 285
Malta war, The	219, 220, 221, 222, 223
Manhattan,	52, 83
Manufactures of	
boots and shoes,	306, 307
butter,	309
canned **foods**,	301
cheese,	300
cotton,	306
iron,	305
leather board,	303
lumber,	303
paper and wood pulp,	303
starch,	300
shoes and boots,	306, 307
wood pulp,	303
woolens,	305, 306
Maquoit,	100, 102
March, Major, expeditions against the Indians,	109, 117, 119
Mare Point,	84, 109
Marechites,	57
Margaretta, The, captured,	186
Martha's Vineyard,	30
Mason, Capt. John	34
Masons, The	244
Massachusetts Bay Colony,	36
revises her boundary,	47
resisted in Maine,	47
rule sought,	52
re-establishes her rule in Yorkshire,	54
government extended to the Kennebec,	55
government extended to the Penobscot,	55
Massé, French priest, at Mt. Desert,	27
Mather, **Cotton**	111
Mavooshen,	58
McClellan superseded by Burnside,	284
Meade supersedes Hooker,	289
movements of, in Virginia,	292
crosses the Rapidan,	292
Medumcook (Friendship) attacked by Indians,	174
Merrymeeting Bay,	85, 126
Micmacs,	57, 127

	PAGE
Military divisions,	194
weapons,	48
Militia organized in **Yorkshire**,	49
of Maine,	273, 274
Mining,	302
Ministers, Early,	
Whitefield, Rev. **George**	147, 155
Brock, Rev. John	51
Jordan, Rev. Robert	50
Moody, Rev. Samuel,	148
Seymour, Rev. Richard	22
Missionaries to Indians,	123
Mohegans,	118
Mohawk Indians,	86, 127, 128
Money in the Revolution,	199
paper, first, in America,	100
Monhegan **Island,**	13, 14
Marks on	13
Capt. **J.** Smith builds boats at	27
a refuge from Indians,	80
Monmouth, Battle of	201
Moody, Rev. Samuel	148
Moosehead Lake,	312
Morality, depressed by war,	238, 239
Morris, Captain Charles	232
Moulton, Capt., at Norridgew'k,	129, 131
Mount Desert settled,	27
Mowatt, Captain	
at Falmouth (Portland),	184
takes guns from Fort Pownal,	184
a prisoner,	185
bombards Falmouth,	188-190
on the Penobscot,	201
Moxus,	92, 104, 115, 122
Munjoy Hill, Indian slaughter on	97
Mugg,	82, 83, 84, 87
Muscongus Patent,	36, 216
Nahanada,	21
Natick Indians,	81
Navy of the Confederacy,	286, 287
Neddock, Cape, suffers by the Indians,	82, 102
Newagen, Cape, settlement of	37
New Brunswick,	120
New Dartmouth,	54
New England Company,	33, 34, 36
territory of, divided,	40
New Hampshire, origin of	36
Newichawannock (Berwick),	74, 75, 96
New Meadows River,	74
Newry raided **by** Canada **Indians,**	207
New Scotland,	34, 37, 120
New Somersetshire,	40
Newspapers in Maine,	214, 240, 317, 318
Nichols, Governor for Duke of York,	53
Nicholson leads **a** force against Acadia,	120
Norridgewock,	118, 126, 131-136
North Yarmouth,	91
Nova Scotia,	120, 170, 195
Norwegians in America,	13
Oakland,	305

	PAGE
Ohio emigration,	239
Openangoes,	57
Ossipee ponds,	116
Pond,	137
River,	83
Oyster beds,	58
Parties, political	265
Passamaquoddy ponds,	56
Bay	57, 118, 227-229, 236
Passamaq **noddies**,	57
Passaconaway,	69
Patriots, American	180, 181
Pangus,	138, 140
Peak's Island,	82
Pitt, William	180
Pejepscot,	47, 100, 104
purchase of	218
Pemaquid,	54, 91, 106, 108
Patent,	37, 18
Pennacooks,	69, 81, 112
Penobscot Bay and River,	13, 14, 18, 39, 40, 53, 90, 106, 109, 129, 174, 201-207, 214, 231-237, 243
Indians.	29, 172
Penhallow, Captain	126
Pequods,	118
Pepperell, Sir William	155
Perry, Commodore	227
Persecution,	50
Pestilence,	29, 69
Philip, King	71, 78
Phillips, Major William	73
Phipps, Sir William	96, 98, 99, 100, 106, 111
Pigwacket (Pequaket),	116
Pine trees,	213
Pilgrims, The	31, 34, 35, 38
Piscataqua,	44
Piscataquis County,	251
Plaisted, Lient. Roger	75
Plymouth (Eng.) Company,	20, 33, 218
Patent,	218
Political parties,	265
Popham, Capt. George	20, 23, 25, 34
colony,	34
Population of Maine,	215, 314
Porpoise, Cape	115,
Portland (Casco Neck),	72, 88, 95, 97, 112, 115 116, 129, 166, 185, 188-190 '262, 263, 287, 313, 320
Portsmouth,	76, 121
Pownal, Gov. **Thomas**	174, 178, 179
Port Royal,	19, 120
Portneuf (Burneff),	104
Potomac, Army of	278
Preble, Commodore	225
Presumpscot River,	47, 72
Prices in the Revolution,	199
and production in the Rebellion period,	299
Pring, Martin, voyage of, to Maine,	14
Proctor, Lieutenant	161
Prohibitory Law against liquors,	259
first effective,	261

	PAGE
Prohibitory Law annulled,	263
re-established,	264
in the State Constitution,	264
Prohibitionists,	270
Prospect, a fort built in	174
Provincial Congress,	183
Punishments in Yorkshire.	50
Purchas, Thomas	40, 47, 71, 72
Puritans secure a grant,	36
oppose Gorges,	41
preaching and laws,	148
customs,	150
Purpooduck, massacre at,	115
Putnam, Major Perley	227
Quakers, or **Friends**,	44, 53
Quarrying **of granite**,	301
slate,	302
Quebec,	175, 194
Queen Anne's **war**,	115, 122
Quoddy Indians,	57
Quota of Maine,	282
Raid, rebel, above Washington	294
Railroads,	257, 308, 309, 310, 311, 312
Ralle, the Jesuit missionary,	126, 129, 132
Razilla, General	39
Rebel gove't flies from Richmond,	295
Recruiting, cessation of, ordered,	281
Red River, Banks' expedition up	292
Regiment, First Maine	274
Second Maine	274
others authorized,	277
Regiments in the field,	275
in the war,	297
Religious freedom in Maine,	50
Republican Party of 1820,	265
of 1880,	265, 267, 272
Republicans, Liberal,	268
Reverses to the Union arms,	281, 282
Revolution, first **act** of, in Maine,	182
Revolutionary **War**,	184-203
Richmond,	35, 128
Va., rebel government fly from	295
entered by Union troops,	296
Richmond's Island,	83
Rigby, Sir Alexander	43
Riot, liquor, in Portland,	262
Road, military, to Madawaska,	230
Robin Hood sells Woolwich,	37
Robbinston visited by the British,	223
Rockland,	302, 310
Rocroft, Captain Edward	30
Rogers, Col., destroys St. Francis,	175
Roman Catholics, Indians become	68
Rowles' prophecy,	70
Ryswick, treaty of	109
Sabino,	22
Saco,	72, 73, 101, 107
Sagadahoc,	101
Saint Francis Indians,	127, 165, 175
Saint George's River,	123, 126, 129, 159, 16
Saint Sauveur (see Mount Desert),	20

7

INDEX. 335

	PAGE
Saltoustall, Commodore	203
Samoset,	31, 32
Scalps, bounty for Indian	108
Scammon, Colonel	184
Scarborough,	82, 117, 129
Scenery,	28, 322, 323
Schools and Colleges,	150, 151, 216, 243, 315-317
School usages,	150, 151
Schools for Indians,	123
Scouting in Southern Maine,	171
Scotch-Irish in Maine,	215
Scott, General Winfield	254, 255
Sea line of Maine,	322
Seal of the State of Maine,	242
Sebago Pond,	247
Secession,	272
Sedgwick, Major Robert	53
Seguin,	22
Separation from Massachusetts,	240
Settlements in Maine,	
condition of	101, 102
east of Penobscot,	179
Settlers at Arrowsic warned,	126
come into Maine,	145
Seymour, Richard, preaches to Popham's colony,	22
Sheepscot Plantation,	37, 53, 99
Sherbrook, Sir John	232
Sheridan, General	295, 296
Sherman, General	274, 295
Shipbuilding,	23, 27, 304
Shirley, Fort	169
Shirley Governor	174
Shurte, Abraham	78
Sickles, General	290
Simmo, Captain	112
Simon, the Yankee Killer,	78, 85
Sixth Indian War,	172
Slate.	302
Slavery,	241, 263
Slave Power, The	250
Slaves, Indians sold for	78
Snow-shoeing for Indians,	117
Smith, Captain John	27, 28
Smuggling,	237
Social life after the Revolution,	211
usages in Maine,	150, 154
Sokokis,	29, 57, 112, 137
Soldiering,	277
Soldiers, British, arrive in Boston,	181
Soldiers of Maine, qualities of	278
return of	296
Southwick, Captain	116
Squando, the Sokokis.	70, 85
Squanto, one of Hunt's captives,	30
Squatters,	218
Stage-coaches,	244, 245
Stamp Act,	180
State House of Maine built.	249
Statistics of Me. in 1810, 1820,	240, 244
1850, 1880, 1886,	298-316
Steamboats in Maine,	245, 246, 304
Stinson's Point attacked by Indians,	79

	PAGE
Subercase yields Acadia,	120
Sullivan, Fort, surrendered to the British,	227
Surrender of the Rebel army,	296
Swaine, Major, attacks the Indians,	95
Swan Island, Major Church meets the Indians at	107
Swedish Colony, The	314
Swett, Captain Benjamin	87
Tarratines,	57, 82, 112
Taxes, Import	179
Tea-chests emptied in Boston Harbor,	182
Teaching of Jesuits,	124
Teconnet,	78, 107, 112
Telegraph,	312
Temperance movement begins,	257
societies,	258-261
reform in Maine,	259
Sons of	260
parties,	207
Temple, Sir Thos., Gov. of Acadia,	53
Thomaston,	302
Thrift of settlers,	42
Topsham,	127, 164
Torture of captives by Indians,	91, 94, 106, 127
Towns and Plantations,	56, 177
laid out,	145, 213
Township, lottery	214
Tozier, house of, defended by a young lady,	74
Traveling in Maine in 1820,	244, 245
Treaties with Indians,	88, 107, 109, 110, 112, 113, 121, 122, 143, 166
Treaty of Breda,	55
Ryswick,	109
Utrecht,	121
Paris,	208
Ghent,	237
Webster-Ashburton,	255
Trees of Maine,	213
Tribute to Maine men,	278, 285
Troops, Maine, in the Revolution,	184, 185
Tucker, Commodore Sam'l	199-201, 229
Tyng, Colonel Edward	155
Vaughn, Lieut.-Col. William	155
Vessels building	23, 27, 30
captured by Indians,	88
saved by a breeze,	105
burned by British,	235
Vines, Richard	29
Virginia Company, north and south,	20
Volunteers called for,	273
Voting allowed to non-Puritans,	50
Wadsworth, Gen. Peleg	202, 205, 206, 207
Waldo patent,	36, 175, 216
Samuel, Brig.-Gen.	147, 155, 175
Waldoborough,	147, 163

Waldron, Major	77, 78, **81, 84,** 85, 93
Waldron's Ruse,	81, 93
Wakely, Elizabeth	72, 76
Walton, Colonel,	120
Wampum	38
War, First Indian	68
King Philip's	71
First Indian, ends,	89
First French and Indian	90
Queen Anne's	115
Lovewell's	136-143
King George's	155
Last Indian (sixth)	169-177
of Independence (the Revolution),	184-208
of 1812-14,	223
Aroostook, The	252-255
of Slaveholder's Rebellion,	273,297
effect of, on morals,	238
Warren, Commodore	156
Washington burnt by the British,	227
George	167
Washingtonians, The	259
Waterpower of Maine,	308
Waterville,	243
Wawennock Tribe, The	23,29,57, 69, 136
Wells,	76, 83, 102, 104, 115, 121
Westbrook, Colonel	126, 128
Western, Fort	169, 191
Weymouth, Captain George	14, 16
Wharton, Richard	218
Whig, A, chosen Governor,	262
Party, The	266
Whitefield, Rev. George	**147,** 148, 156
Wilderness, Battle of the	292, 293
William and Mary,	93
William and Mary's War,	110
Williamsburgh, Battle of	278, 279, 280
Williams, Joseph H.	268
Williamson, William **D.**	242
Windham,	166, 172, 173
Winnepesauke Lake,	47
Winslow, Captain Josiah	129, 130
Winter Harbor,	115, 119
Wiscasset,	165, 236
Witchcraft,	111
Woolwich,	37, 79
Worumbee,	101, 104
Woods, The King's	146
Yarmouth,	**160**
York, Duke of	**40, 53**
York, town of	**43, 86, 103**
Yorktown,	**207, 278**

www.ingramcontent.com/pod-product-compliance
Lightning Source LLC
Chambersburg PA
CBHW021153230426
43667CB00006B/383